DUCATI *50 GOLDEN YEARS*

DUCATI

Luigi Bianchi & Marco Masetti

Haynes Publishing

DUCATI *50 GOLDEN YEARS*
Through the pages of 'Motociclismo' magazine

First published in 1997 by Motociclismo, Edisport Editoriale, Via Grandisca 11, 20151 Milan, Italy, as *Motociclismo tells the story of Ducati*. This English-language edition, re-titled *Ducati: 50 golden years, through the pages of Motociclismo magazine*, was published in 1999 by Haynes Publishing, with minor amendments.

First published in February 1999

A catalogue record for this book is available from the British Library

ISBN 1 85960 618 0

Library of Congress catalog card no 98-74170

Haynes North America Inc., 861 Lawrence Drive, Newbury Park, California 91320, USA.

Published by Haynes Publishing, Sparkford, Nr Yeovil, Somerset BA22 7JJ, UK.
Tel: 01963 440635 Fax: 01963 440001
Int. tel: +44 1963 440635 Int. fax: +44 1963 440001
E-mail: sales@haynes-manuals.co.uk
Web site: http://www.haynes.com

Printed and bound in Britain by J. H. Haynes & Co. Ltd, Sparkford

Foreword

by co-founder *Bruno Ducati*

Ducati was started on 4th July 1926 by Antonio Cavalieri Ducati and his three sons, Adriano, Bruno and Marcello. At the time the Ducati brothers were very young, so young that together their ages just reached fifty. Adriano, just twenty, was an enthusiastic wireless engineer. As a young boy he had invented a minuscule short-wave wireless set which won the world transmission distance record for low power apparatus. Just 60 watts (the same power as a light bulb), the radio set established the first two-way radio contact between Italy and the USA. This was in 1924. The Italian Naval Ministry then adopted Adriano's set for ship-to-shore communications and for the first time a seagoing vessel could be linked by wireless to five continents at once. In 1926 Guglielmo Marconi, inventor of the radio telegraph, came to Bologna to receive an honorary degree at the university. In the same year the Ducati family founded their "Società Scientifica Radio Brevetti Ducati" – Ducati Patented Wireless Company, at the time the only Company of its kind in Italy to manufacture wireless apparatus.

In this period Ducati produced an electrical capacitor under the name Manens, Latin for "fixed", and a basic feature of radio circuitry. Samples were sent to leading radio engineers in Europe and America and received an enthusiastic response. This was the start of a small factory in Bologna at no. 51 Via Guidotti next door to the Ducati house. The Company grew rapidly and ten years later had 100 employees and a factory covering 200 square metres. In 1935 Ducati decided to start manufacturing variable condensers for wireless applications. This new product also led the Company to branch out into mechanical engineering, starting with the production of aluminium alloy for the condenser plates. Ducati became the first Italian Company to purchase the Genevois, the famous Swiss spot welder/boring machine. The machine was so precise that the variable condensers it produced required no further machining. This was the beginning of precision engineering. In 1935 Ducati moved to a modern, purpose-built factory at Borgo Panigale on the outskirts of Bologna. Italy entered the Second World War in 1940 and in 1945 the factory was completely destroyed by Allied bombing. At the beginning of the war Ducati already had 7,000 employees. Worried about the future the Ducati family set up a series of research laboratories called POST in Bologna, Florence and Rome to research and design products which would go into production at the end of the war. It should not be forgotten that during this period Ducati works manufactured a wide range of products. The famous "Raselet" electric razor. A futuristic intercom, the "Dufono". The "Duconta" calculating machine. Cameras, juke-boxes and movie cameras. Fridges and refrigeration compressors followed and later Ducati began to look at ways of powering bicycles. At the end of WWII, a lawyer and motoring enthusiast Aldo Farinelli set up the SIATA factory in Turin to produce a patented light engine known as the Cucciolo. SIATA did not have the capacity to meet the demand for its engines so the Ducati family purchased the production machinery and started to produce the Cucciolo 48 cc at its Cameri foundry. The Cucciolo was an overwhelming success and over 100,000 were sold world-wide. The Cucciolo story is studded with success. Someone even composed a hit song in its honour which goes something like this: "The engine might be small but it beats like my heart …"

Contents

Introduction

from the 1997 edition

Writing is an activity which involves a lot of introspection and inevitably something personal always shines through, even when you are writing about motorcycles. When I went looking through the new Ducati museum archive with curator Marco Montemaggi I came across a piece of my family history. And much more besides. I found a rather ungrammatical article (it must run in the family) written fifty years ago by Armando Governatori, a lathe operator at Ducati in 1941, brother of my grandfather Arturo, a great motorcycle mechanic, inventor, socialist and bon viveur. This set me off on a fascinating trip down memory lane which ran parallel with my journey though the history of Ducati.

Most of my family and relations come from a district covering an area of about fifteen kilometres centred around Borgo Panigale. I have always lived around here. Writing this book awakened a strong sense of identity in me. This, I thought, is my place, my home. A strip of land between the Po plain and the hills, stretching towards the sea along the ancient Via Emilia. A place of strange people who go mad about the strangest of things. A place where people go wild about a prancing horse and a motorcycle valve gear system which must be, just has to be, perfect. People who tend their gardens with scrupulous care. The Japanese are famous for their bonsai. We are perhaps less severe but we tend our fruit trees with the same passionate attention. You'll find fruit trees even in the smallest of town house gardens. We have the same absorbing passion for engines and for us "engine" means "motorcycle" (not a bad idea when you think about it). Obsession might be more apt a term for this passion. A total commitment to precision mechanical engineering with something approaching the same dedication as a Zen monk. The only difference is that the ascetic monk does not eat, drink and love with the same intensity and passion as we do. As Pirsig wrote in *Zen and the Art of Motorcycle Maintenance*, "Buddha is in a gear wheel", to which I would add "and also in a tortellino" (a local pasta speciality). Travelling back in time through the old copies of *Motociclismo* I encountered champions and also-rans, thoroughbreds and nags, triumphs and flops, and colleagues (dare I call them my teachers) who taught me the little I know and to whom I owe much. This book owes a lot to them. In a way, I wrote like someone composing electronic music, sampling the facts, processing them, making them resound once again.

Last, but certainly not least, a special mention for Ducati enthusiasts — the Ducatisti. I am sure you will wheedle out the thousands of inaccuracies in what I have written — and quite rightly so too. I beg a thousand pardons in advance but at the same time enter a plea for clemency on my own behalf. This book recounts the enthralling story of Ducati as told through the pages of *Motociclismo*. As a history of a world famous marque it must recount the bad times with the good. Making and writing history has never been easy and the road is littered with mistakes, but hopefully we learn from our mistakes.

Marco Masetti

Over the last fifty years Ducati has changed ownership several times and this combined with the fact that for a long time the company did not keep systematic records meant that the only complete archive on the Ducati Marque was the *Motociclismo* magazine archive. The archive covers everything about Ducati from its inception to the present day. Unpublished photos of the Cucciolo at the Company's start in the Fifties, through the first desmodromic machines designed by Fabio Taglioni, the helical gear singles and twins that dominated the Sixties and Seventies, right through to the present day and the latest models by Massimo Bordi and his design team.

This book is mainly a photographic history intended to give the reader a complete overview of the Company from its beginnings through to the present day and provides a background to the Company's current triumphs.

Luigi Bianchi

(KEL EDGE)

Introduction
to this 1999
English-language edition

Only Italians could produce a Ducati. Only in Italy, where style matters in all things, but especially in things powered by an internal combustion engine, could form and function come together so perfectly. So here is the story of Ducati as told by Italians. Specifically, this is the history of Ducati as seen through the pages of the Italian monthly magazine *Motociclismo* which has been reporting the motorcycle industry and motorcycle sport since 1949. Ducati's changes of ownership, and lack of early systematic records, meant that the only complete archive was in the *Motociclismo* library.

A quick flick through the pages of this book will show you that Luigi Bianchi and Marco Masetti, the *Motociclismo* editors who put this compilation together, have just as good an eye for style as the men who conceived the Pantah or the Supermono. The clever use of contemporary sales leaflets as well as the photos *Motociclismo* took for its road tests provide an interesting sub-text, illustrating the change in fashions and styles through the decades, as well as a parade of famous names who have been involved at some time with the Bologna factory. Carl Fogarty we all know about, and the immortal Mike Hailwood's 1978 TT comeback, but Mike the Bike's in there in 1960 as well. And then there are Ducati engineers and designers who are almost as well known as their bikes; it's amazing how early men like Fabio Taglioni and Franco Farné turn up in these pages. Their continuing presence reinforces the family feeling that all Ducati riders and enthusiasts enjoy the world over.

The history of Ducati is — more than any other factory, even Norton — the history of its racing, and what comes through loud and clear from these pages is that when Ducatis win on the race track then Ducati sells all the motorcycles it can make. That is something that would no doubt gladden the hearts of all the people you will see on these pages, and of every Italian.

Julian Ryder

DUCATI MANAGEMENT AND EMPLOYEES IN AN HISTORIC COMPANY PHOTO FROM 1939. IN THE THIRTIES DUCATI EMPLOYED NEARLY 11,000 PEOPLE IN ITS VARIOUS FACTORIES PRODUCING CAPACITORS, RADIOS AND PRECISION MECHANICAL ENGINEERING PARTS.

6

1925/1940 Electrical engineering

In 1922 Adriano Cavalieri Ducati, a nineteen-year old Physics student, started to experiment with radio transmitters, which, at the time, were a novelty. These were boom years for radio, especially at Bologna, home town of Guglielmo Marconi inventor of the radio telegraph. In 1925, Marcello, Adriano and Bruno Cavalieri Ducati together with Carlo Crespi started their Company Società Scientifica Radio. A few years later their Manens capacitors were being exported world-wide.

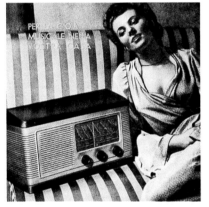

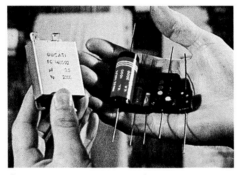

ABOVE, A RADIO CAPACITOR. IT WAS THANKS TO PATENTS FOR THIS COMPONENT THAT BETWEEN 1925 AND THE START OF THE SECOND WORLD WAR DUCATI BECAME A LARGE INDUSTRIAL COMPANY.

HOUSEWIVES, ALL DAY AT HOME WITH THE WIRELESS FOR COMPANY. REALITY WAS A DIFFERENT MATTER. MANY WOMEN WERE ALREADY WORKING IN INDUSTRY AND AT DUCATI MADE UP A HIGH PROPORTION OF THE WORK FORCE. BELOW, THE THREE DUCATI BROTHERS: ADRIANO, BRUNO AND MARCELLO IN A PHOTO TAKEN IN THE EARLY EIGHTIES.

ABOVE, A HISTORIC PHOTOGRAPH OF 1942. KING VITTORIO EMANUELE III OPENS THE TECHNICAL TRAINING COLLEGE DEDICATED TO ALBERTO CAVALIERI DUCATI.

GOVERNATORI ARMANDO *Tornitore*

Da diverso tempo desideravo di vedere il Duce da vicino come lo vidi il giorno sette del corrente mese.

Fino dalle prime ore del mattino ero impaziente di vederlo apparire all'entrata del reparto, ma solo verso le ore dodici e trenta circa, la mia curiosità fu appagata. Così l'immaginavo, passo marziale, sorriso sulle labbra, energia e sicurezza e più lo guardavo e più mi convincevo che la vittoria finale è nostra.

Con lo stesso slancio che lo vidi entrare lo vidi partire in piedi sulla sua automobile salutando cordialmente, mentre da tutte le parti si sentiva gridare: « Evviva il Duce ».

WHEN I WAS RESEARCHING THIS BOOK I CAME ACROSS AN INTERESTING PIECE OF MY FAMILY HISTORY. THE INGENUOUS AND RATHER UNGRAMMATICAL TEXT ABOVE WAS WRITTEN BY ARMANDO GOVERNATORI, MY GRANDFATHER'S BROTHER AND A LATHE OPERATOR AT DUCATI IN 1931. THE TEXT IS PART OF A COLLECTION OF INTERVIEWS WITH DUCATI WORKERS ENTITLED: "HOW I SAW IL DUCE", FOLLOWING A VISIT BY THE ITALIAN DICTATOR BENITO MUSSOLINI IN OCTOBER 1941. (M.M.)

A SMALL GIRL NEARLY DWARFED BY THIS LARGE RADIO OF THE EARLY FORTIES. AT THE TIME DUCATI WAS A LEADER IN THIS SECTOR OF INDUSTRY AND ITS PRODUCTS WERE VERY POPULAR.

WORLD WAR
II LEFT ITS
MARK. HERE, THE
REMAINS OF THE
DUCATI WORKS AFTER
ALLIED BOMBING IN 1944.
GERMAN TROOPS ENTERED AND
OCCUPIED THE WORKS WITH 20
TANKS IN 1943. DARING ACTION BY
DUCATI WORKERS SAVED THE PLANT AND
MACHINERY
FROM FURTHER DAMAGE.

8

1925/1945 Destruction and reconstruction

Nearly 10,000 employees, a very modern factory just opened at Borgo Panigale on the outskirts of Bologna, manufacturing the very latest optical and electrical engineering products. This was Ducati in 1940. Five years later, after heavy bombardment, nothing but a pile of rubble remained. Rebuilding seemed an impossible feat but the Ducati family tried just the same. They sold everything and took out a government loan.

RIGHT, OPTICAL SPECIALISTS DUCATI PRODUCED THIS HIGHLY PRIZED "PHOTOGRAPHIC MICROCAMERA". RESEARCH HAD STARTED DURING WARTIME BUT HAD BEEN STOPPED BY A MYSTERIOUS ORDER FROM ON HIGH IN THE FASCIST REGIME. PRODUCTION STARTED AFTER THE WAR.

TO CELEBRATE THE LAUNCH OF ITS CUCCIOLO MOPED, DUCATI COMMISSIONED MAESTRO OLIVERO TO WRITE A SONG WHICH SOON BECAME A HIT. ABOVE, THE ORIGINAL SCORE.

AS A YOUNG GIRL, 50S ITALIAN SINGER NILLA PIZZA WORKED AT DUCATI. RIGHT: JUNE 1ST, 1935 THE LAYING OF THE FOUNDATION-STONE.

RASELET, THE FIRST ELECTRIC RAZOR PRODUCED IN ITALY, MARKETED IN 1940 JUST THREE YEARS AFTER THE FIRST AMERICAN RAZORS. FOR MANY AGED ITALIANS THE NAME RASELET IS STILL SYNONYMOUS WITH ELECTRIC RAZOR.

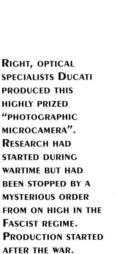

DESIGNED BY TURIN LAWYER
ALDO FARINELLI, THE
CUCCIOLO ("PUPPY") ENGINE
WAS DUCATI'S FIRST
MOTORCYCLE PRODUCT,
ORIGINALLY MANUFACTURED BY
SIATA (IN 1945) AND THEN BY
CANSA AT NOVARA. IN 1946
THE CUCCIOLO ENTERED
PRODUCTION AT DUCATI AND
BECAME THE BASIS FOR THE
COMPANY'S POST-WAR REVIVAL.
COMPARED WITH ITS TWO-
STROKE COMPETITORS, THE
CUCCIOLO WAS MORE POWERFUL
AND CONSUMED LESS. IN IDEAL
CONDITIONS CONSUMPTION WAS
100 KM/LT.

1946/1950 The Cucciolo years

Ducati successfully revived the fortunes of its Borgo Panigale works with the moped engine — the first step in mass motoring for post-war Italy. Initially Ducati produced the original four-stroke Cucciolo moped engine under licence from SIATA in Turin. The engine was a success which relaunched the Marque and provided bike builders with the basis for a wide variety of applications, some of them very interesting.

A TORINO E' NATO UN "CUCCIOLO"

BELOW, A CUCCIOLO-POWERED TANDEM FOR THOSE SPRING-TIME JAUNTS IN THE COUNTRY. THIS UNUSUAL VEHICLE HAD A RECORD WHEELBASE FOR A "POWERED BICYCLE".

TODAY'S MOPEDS ARE CERTAINLY NOTHING NEW. TOP, THE HIGHLY ORIGINAL Z-48 WITH REAR CANTILEVER SUSPENSION. ABOVE, MUCH MORE ELEGANT, THE MUSETTA "LIGHT CYCLE" PRODUCED BY M.U.S.A. OF MILANO FITTED WITH A T2 SERIES ENGINE.

ITALIANS HAVE NEVER BEEN SHORT OF IMAGINATION. IN THE DIFFICULT POST-WAR YEARS MANY SMALL BIKE BUILDERS USED THE CUCCIOLO. ABOVE, THE SPORTY DONDOLINA WITH SPRING SUSPENSION ON BOTH WHEELS AND A STRAIGHT-THROUGH EXHAUST.

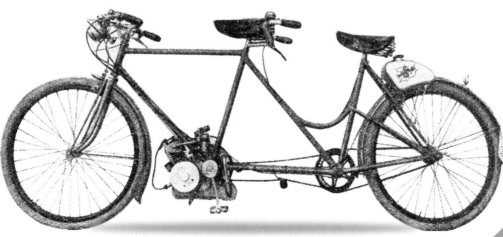

THE GIARDINI MARGHERITA PUBLIC GARDENS IN BOLOGNA ON AN IDYLLIC DAY. A YOUNG COUPLE CAPTIVATED BY A CUCCIOLO. THE SLOGAN "POWER YOUR CYCLE" ACCOMPANIED THIS ADVERT FOR THE FIRST CUCCIOLO PRODUCED BY SIATA IN TURIN.

Cucciolo and its variants

The first Cucciolo ("Puppy"), the T1 manufactured by SIATA, had the cylinder head, block and part of the casing all in one piece. In 1948 Ducati redesigned the engine now christened the T2. The basic design philosophy remained unchanged: to provide a strong, reliable and economical power unit that could be fitted to bicycle or custom-built frames and thus meet the growing demand for private transport. The Ducati redesign bore fruit. Power increased from 1 hp at 4,500 rpm to 1.5 on the 1952 M SS model, a long-running best seller. Maintenance became simpler and separating engine componentry made production easier. Technically, the Cucciolo had some interesting features. Rather than an oil pump, the lubrication system used the much simpler splash lubrication. Valve actuation was by twin rocker arms and pull rods. As an alternative to the two-speed gearbox there was also the T0 automatic. Other versions followed. The 55, 66 and 65, available in various trim from the spartan standard models to sportier racing jobs. Production sports versions were raced in the lightweight bike class. These bikes had T3 series engines with grease-lubricated covered valve gear and three-speed gearboxes.

La motoleggerissima "DUCATI 60"

SPECIFICATIONS

ENGINE: Single cylinder four-stroke, air-cooled. Pull rod and rocker arm valve operation. Bore: 39 mm. Stroke: 40 mm. Capacity: 48 cc. Magneto flywheel ignition. Weber carburettor with 9 mm choke (first models fitted with other carburettors). Oil sump splash lubrication. Gear primary drive, with two-speed gearbox. Power: 1.5 hp at 5,500 rpm.

ABOVE, THE **55R** OF **1954** HAD A TWO-SPEED GEARBOX WITH HANDLEBAR CHANGER AND LINK FRONT FORKS. THERE WAS NO REAR SUSPENSION BUT SUSPENSION WAS AN OPTIONAL EXTRA. THE ENGINE WAS AN **M55**, THE LAST VERSION OF THE FIRST CUCCIOLO TYPE.

THE **65T** OF **1954/55**. THE ENGINE WAS BASED ON THE **T3** BORED OUT TO **65** CC (BORE AND STROKE: **44 x 43** MM). TOP SPEED WAS **65** KPH, OR **70** KPH FOR THE SPORT MODEL USED IN LIGHTWEIGHT RACER COMPETITIONS.

BELOW, THE **60** TURISMO OF **1950** HAD MONOCROSS SUSPENSION WITH TELESCOPIC FORKS AND FRICTION DAMPERS.

OPPOSITE PAGE, THE **65 TS**, TECHNICALLY THE MOST DEVELOPED CUCCIOLO. A MORE FULLY EQUIPPED VERSION OF THE **T** (ON WHICH IT WAS BASED) WITH TRIM INCLUDING A SMALL WINDSCREEN. ABOVE, THE EXPLODED DRAWING BY CAVARA REVEALS THE SECRETS OF THE **T2** VERSION WHICH STILL HAS THE CYLINDER HEAD AND CYLINDER IN A SINGLE BLOCK.

ABOVE, PROBABLY THE FIRST DUCATI SPORTS BIKE, THE **60** SPORT. SPECS FOR THE **T3** ENGINE INCLUDED BORE AND STROKE **42 x 43** MM, **2.25** HP AT **5,000** RPM AND A TOP SPEED OVER **60** KPH. NOTE THE THREE-SPEED PEDAL GEAR CHANGER.

THE ITALIAN LIGHTWEIGHT CHAMPIONSHIP RACE OF 1948, SALINELLI AND BONARDI (RIDING AN ALPINO) LEAD A CUCCIOLO INTO A BEND ON THE MILANO TRADE FAIR CIRCUIT. FIRST ACROSS THE FINISHING LINE WAS ZITELLI (INSET, RECEIVING CONGRATULATIONS) ON THE SMALL DUCATI.

14

1951/1954 Records and race wins

These small lightweight "microbikes" were the only way to go racing cheaply in the hard post-war years. Works teams were already fighting it out on town circuits watched by enthusiastic crowds. Alpino and Cucciolo were the two Marques to beat. In 1950 the small Ducati Cucciolo, with Ugo Tamarozzi riding, set 12 world records. A year later the team went from strength to strength with the arrival of Farné, Miani, Pennati, Caroli and Sozzani, setting one record after another.

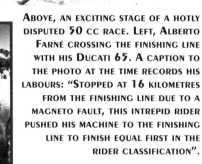

ABOVE, AN EXCITING STAGE OF A HOTLY DISPUTED **50** CC RACE. LEFT, ALBERTO FARNÉ CROSSING THE FINISHING LINE WITH HIS DUCATI **65**. A CAPTION TO THE PHOTO AT THE TIME RECORDS HIS LABOURS: "STOPPED AT **16** KILOMETRES FROM THE FINISHING LINE DUE TO A MAGNETO FAULT, THIS INTREPID RIDER PUSHED HIS MACHINE TO THE FINISHING LINE TO FINISH EQUAL FIRST IN THE RIDER CLASSIFICATION".

IN 1951 THE CUCCIOLO RAN FOR **48** HOURS NON-STOP SETTING **27** WORLD RECORDS, ALSO ESTABLISHING THE **24** HOUR RECORD IN THE **100** CC CLASS.

MAKESHIFT RACE OVERALLS FOR UGO TAMAROZZI. IN 1950, AT THE VENERABLE AGE OF **46**, HE SET **12** WORLD RECORDS IN THE **50** CC. CLASS RIDING HIS CUCCIOLO **48**. TAMAROZZI, A SKILLED TRADESMAN, PREPARED HIS BIKE IN THE CELLAR AT HOME IN MILANO. TUNING WAS LIMITED TO A FEW INEXPENSIVE CHANGES. ENGINES RAN ON A MIXTURE OF PETROL, BENZOL AND ACETONE.

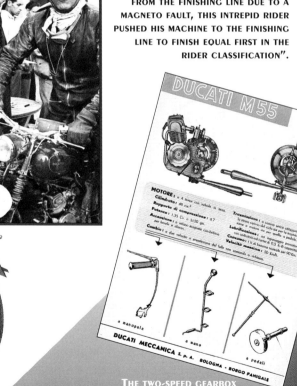

THE TWO-SPEED GEARBOX OF THE M55 ENGINE HAD A CHOICE OF THREE TYPES OF GEAR CHANGER.

The Cruiser scooter

In Ducati history books the chapter dedicated to the Cruiser is probably one of the most agonising; without a doubt this scooter was a commercial fiasco. Technically, however, the Cruiser was a considerable advance on its competitors. Instead of the small, two-stroke engines fitted by competing Marques, the Cruiser mounted a beefy 175 cc four-stroke with electric starter and automatic gear change. Today's bike yesterday. Designed in 1950 the Cruiser entered production two years later. But why this lack of success? There were two reasons. The price tag of 320,000 lire was very high by 1953 standards. And then there were technical problems. Once started using the floor-mounted electric start button, the Cruiser used a hydraulic drive system. When the vehicle touched 40 kph the drive switched over to a direct drive mechanical system. However, in traffic and on uphill sections this Ducati struggled, forcing the engine to operate at maximum revs in order to make up for transmission losses. Despite this the Cruiser remains a notable design and engineering exercise. Two thousand Cruisers were produced and today are much sought after collectors' items.

THE CRUISER 175 SCOOTER, A DECIDEDLY AMERICAN LOOK FROM THE DRAWING BOARD OF THE GREAT TURIN CAR DESIGNER GHIA.

Specifications

ENGINE: Four-stroke, horizontal single-cylinder mounted crossways. Air-cooled. Distribution: rocker arm and pushrod operated twin overhead valve. Bore: 62 mm. Stroke 58 mm. Capacity 175 cc. Compression ratio: 7.5:1. Power: 8 hp at 6,000 rpm. Weber carburettor. Contact breaker ignition with 6 volt 30 Ah battery and 30 W dynamo. Forced lubrication. Automatic gear change with direct drive hydraulic converter. Engine/gearbox linked by flexible coupling. Final drive bevel gear pair with helical teeth. FRAME, FORKS AND RUNNING GEAR: Pressed sheet steel frame. Swinging arm front and rear suspension with rubber inserts. Drum brakes. Tyres 3.50 x 10" (front and rear). WEIGHT (dry): 150 kg.

PRESENTED AT THE MILANO SHOW, THE CRUISER IMMEDIATELY CAUSED A STIR IN THE TRADE PRESS FOR ITS UNCONVENTIONAL TECHNICAL DESIGN - YEARS AHEAD OF ITS TIME.

THE UNUSUAL ENGINE. THE CROSSWAYS CYLINDER HAS THE CARBURETTOR MOUNTED ABOVE THE HEAD - JUST ONE OF THE TECHNICAL "PECULIARITIES" OF THIS SCOOTER.

Cruiser

DUCATI

Le caratteristiche e le prestazioni del « CRUISER » Ducati erano fino a ieri, un privilegio di alcune rare automobili di gran lusso ; oggi tali caratteristiche e prestazioni sono raccolte in un veicolo che interesserà la innumerevole schiera degli appassionati delle due ruote.

Gomme PIRELLI

THE CAR-LIKE STYLING OF THE CRUISER WAS ALSO EMPHASISED IN PUBLICITY MATERIAL. "UNTIL THE DUCATI CRUISER ARRIVED", SAYS THIS BROCHURE, "FEATURES AND PERFORMANCE LIKE THIS WERE THE PRIVILEGE OF A FEW LUXURY CAR OWNERS".

THE CRUISER WAS, WITHOUT A DOUBT, THE MOST TECHNICALLY ADVANCED SCOOTER OF ITS TIME. INNOVATIVE FEATURES SUCH AS AN AUTOMATIC GEARBOX, A FOUR-STROKE ENGINE AND ELECTRIC STARTING MADE LIFE EASIER FOR RIDERS. THE SPARE WHEEL WAS HOUSED INSIDE THE BODYWORK. REAR DIRECTION INDICATORS WERE STANDARD.

ABOVE, THE AUTOMATIC TRANSMISSION UNIT WITH THE HYDRAULIC CONVERTER GEARBOX TO ENGAGE THE DIRECT DRIVE AT SET SPEEDS AND TORQUES. CRUISER TOP SPEED WAS 80 KPH.

1954

The motorcycles that made history

The "98"

The history of this single-cylinder mirrors that of the Ducati Company. Certainly not a sporting bike, the 98 was pressed into competition service by Giuseppe Montano, managing director of the Company since 1953. Tuned up, the bike competed successfully in trials (two silvers at the 1954 Welsh Six Days) and long distance events (third place in the '54 Motogiro with Gandossi riding). The 98 was clearly designed as an economy, low performance model. Rocker arm and pushrod valve gear and a pressed steel frame leave no doubt about this. The 98 appeared in 1952 and was improved year after year. 1956 saw a changeover to a single tube frame. The engine was bored out to 55.2 mm in 1956 for a 125 cc version. Oil coolers were fitted to the S and SS models. The last series produced had the enlarged 125 cc engine. Models were renamed "Bronco" (with American styling) and "Aurea" (with the classic look) and continued in production until the Seventies.

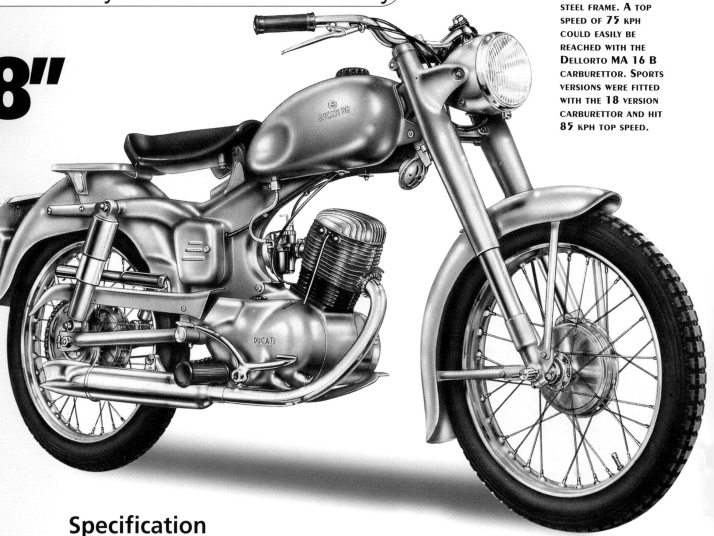

Specification

ENGINE: Four-stroke single-cylinder, with 25° forward angle configuration. Air-cooled. Bore: 49 mm. Stroke: 52 mm. Capacity: 98 cc. Compression ratio: 7:1. Pushrod and rocker arm valve gear with camshaft in the sump. Dellorto MB 16 B carburettor. Maximum power: 4.5 hp at 6,200 rpm. Magneto flywheel ignition. Lubrication: forced wet sump. Gearbox: primary reduction by gears. Chain final drive. Wet, multi-plate clutch. Kick-start (could also be operated with a gear engaged). Fuel tank capacity: 10 litres. FRAME, FORKS AND RUNNING GEAR: Pressed steel frame with overhung engine. Front telescopic forks. Swinging arm rear suspension with twin telescopic shock absorbers. Brakes: front and rear side drums. Tyres: 2.75 x 17" (front and rear). WEIGHT (dry): 72 kg. PERFORMANCE: top speed 82 kph (head down position).

THE TURISMO
LUSSO MODEL OF
1956-58. A
TUBULAR FRAME
REPLACED THE
ORIGINAL PRESSED
STEEL VERSION BUT
THE ENGINE KEPT
THE OVERHUNG
CONFIGURATION.

ABOVE, THE 98 T2 PRESENTED IN 1953 WAS THE MOST
LUXURIOUS VERSION OF THE FIRST TYPE 98. TRIM INCLUDED
LIGHT ALLOY WHEELS, CRASH BARS EITHER SIDE OF THE
ENGINE, A SPRUNG SEAT AND WIDE OPEN HANDLEBARS.
BELOW, A 98 SS WITH THE CHARACTERISTIC SMALL FAIRING
AND OIL COOLER MOUNTED TO THE FRONT OF SUMP. THIS BIKE
REALLY WAS DESIGNED TO GO. EQUIPMENT INCLUDED A
20 MM CARBURETTOR, A 10:1 COMPRESSION RATIO
AND A TOP SPEED OF OVER 90 KPH.

RIGHT, A 98 USED
SUCCESSFULLY IN
ENDURANCE EVENTS
DURING THE 1954
SEASON.

THIS CUTAWAY ENGINE VIEW SHOWS THE ROCKER ARM AND
PUSHROD VALVE GEAR WITH THE STEEPLY ANGLED ROCKER ARMS
TO THE REAR OF THE CYLINDER PRACTICALLY TOUCHING
THE INLET MANIFOLD.

DESIGN ENGINEER FABIO
TAGLIONI AT THE DRAWING
BOARD ENVELOPED IN A
CHARACTERISTIC BLUE HAZE OF
CIGARETTE SMOKE.
TAGLIONI, A NATIVE OF ITALY'S
ROMAGNA REGION, HAD A REAL
PASSION FOR ENGINES AND FOR
MANY YEARS WAS DUCATI'S
"KING OF DESIGNERS".

1954 Taglioni's debut

May 1st, 1954 was a historic day, the day that a young engineer from Lugo di Romagna walked into the offices at No. 3 Via C. Ducati. His name: Fabio Taglioni, for many years the top design engineer at Ducati. Racing triumphs, desmo valve gear, famous engines — all those things which make up the Ducati legend — came from his drawing board. Taglioni "penned" the famous desmo singles and twins.

DEGLI ANTONI RIDING THE DOHC 125 GRAND PRIX ON ITS FIRST OUTING AT THE FAENZA TRACK IN MAY 1956. THE BIKE WAS TAGLIONI'S BEST KNOWN CREATION AND THE PROTOTYPE FOR THE 125 DESMO THAT WENT ON TO CHAMPIONSHIP LAURELS IN THE 1956 SWEDISH GRAND PRIX.

ABOVE, TAGLIONI (RIGHT) WITH BOLOGNA RACING DRIVER CESARE PERDISA. ROARING AWAY ON THE TEST BENCH, SEVERAL HOURS INTO AN ENDURANCE TEST, A 98 SPORT ENGINE. NOTE THE OIL COOLER ON THE FRONT OF THE SUMP.

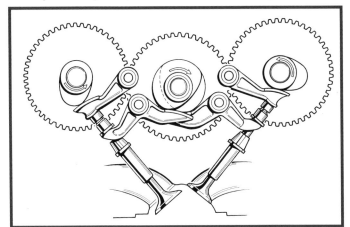

ABOVE, DESMODROMIC VALVE GEAR, THE PRIDE OF ITALIAN MECHANICAL ENGINEERING DESIGN. RIGHT, TAGLIONI'S DEBUT AT DUCATI: THE SINGLE CAMSHAFT GRAN SPORT, SHOWN HERE IN A 1956 VERSION. THE BIKE IMMEDIATELY BECAME A WINNER AND THE STARTING POINT FOR A LONG SERIES OF RACE AND PRODUCTION MACHINES.

TAGLIONI (SUNGLASSES) AND THE MECHANIC FOLESANI (SEATED) PREPARING A MACHINE FOR THE START OF A RACE UNDER THE WATCHFUL EYE OF TAVERI. TAGLIONI WAS A CONFIRMED RACE ENTHUSIAST.

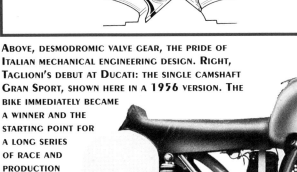

DUCATI 175 S

lightweight motorcycle motolégère

specifications: caractéristiques du bloc:

175 c.c. four stroke — Valves with overhead camshaft
Petrol consumption: 95 m.p.g.
Maximum speed: 84 m.p.h.
175 cm³ - 4 temps - soupapes en tête, arbre à cames en tête
Consommation: 2,3 litres d'essence pour 100 km
Vitesse maximum: 135 Km/h

"FROM THE RACE TRACK TO THE ROAD" RUNS THE DUCATI SLOGAN. HERE A SPORTY 1956 175 S WITH ITS INLET CHOKE TRUMPET, POINTING AGGRESSIVELY UPWARDS.

THE ARRIVAL OF DESIGN ENGINEER TAGLIONI ALSO SAW THE START OF A LONG SERIES OF RACE VICTORIES FOR DUCATI, VICTORIES WHICH ATTRACTED MUCH PUBLIC INTEREST. THE GRAN SPORT 100 AND 125 SHOWN ABOVE WERE STAR ATTRACTIONS AT THE DUCATI STAND OF THE 1955 MILANO MOTORCYCLE SHOW.

1955 From the Marianna to the Pantah

The nickname "Marianna" became widely used to indicate the SOHC Gran Sport 100 and 125. According to Taglioni the single camshaft Gran Sport became known as "Marianna" (literally Marian) in honour of the Holy Marian Year being celebrated in 1955. Other say that the name derives from the day on which the bike made its race debut — the feast day of Saint Anna Maria. Either way, the Gran Sport single soon became the bike to beat. Taglioni was also no slouch when it came to twins...

LEFT, THE STUNNING GRAN PRIX 500 TWIN OF THE EARLY SEVENTIES, A BIKE WHICH PERFECTLY ENCAPSULATED TAGLIONI'S WINNING DESIGN PHILOSOPHY. ABOVE, ONE OF HIS LESS SUCCESSFUL VENTURES, THE 700 CC PARALLEL TWIN OF 1977. ONLY TWO WERE EVER BUILT: A TWIN CAM RACING VERSION DELIVERING A CLAIMED 80 HP AND A ROCKER ARM AND PUSHROD MODEL BUILT FOR AN ITALIAN MINISTRY OF DEFENCE TENDER BID.

DESIGNER FABIO TAGLIONI WITH BRITISH RIDER PAUL SMART AFTER THE VICTORIOUS IMOLA 200 RACE IN 1972.

FABIO TAGLIONI NEVER GOT ON VERY WELL WITH ENGINES WHICH WERE FORCED ON HIM BY COMPANY POLICY. HE WAS MUCH MORE AT HOME WITH MACHINES HE REALLY LIKED... LIKE THIS PANTAH TWIN, OPPOSITE.

TAGLIONI WAS UNBEATABLE AT THE DRAWING BOARD. BUT IN THIS CARICATURE HE WAS FORCED TO SUCCUMB TO THE CARTOONIST'S PEN AND INK.

1955 Motogiro and Milano-Taranto

Motorcycle marathon mania swept Italy. Men and machines raced non-stop from North to South. The Milano-Taranto and Motogiro became the gripping challenges to follow. Ducati participated in 1953 with the Cucciolo and the rocker-pushrod 98 in 1954. At last, in 1955 the single camshaft, helical valve gear bikes designed by Taglioni were ready. This was the start of the Marianna legend.

LEFT, GIOVANNI DEGLI ANTONI AT THE START OF THE RICCIONE SECTION. THIS YOUNG RIDER WON THE 100 CLASS ON A GRAN SPORT ON WHAT WAS VIRTUALLY HIS FIRST TIME OUT. BELOW AND LEFT, WELL-ORGANISED MOBILE WORKS SUPPORT DURING THE MOTOGIRO OF 1957. TOOLS AND SPARE PARTS IN THE BOXES AND, NEVER FAR AWAY, A LUNCH BOX FOR THE RIDERS.

ABOVE, GIULIANO MAOGGI PASSES THROUGH SNOW ON THE PIAN DELLE FUGAZZE DURING THE 1956 MOTOGIRO. LEFT, AN UNUSUAL SCENE, THE DUCATI TEAM IN THE CATHEDRAL OF SAN PETRONIUS AT BOLOGNA TO RECEIVE A BLESSING BEFORE THE START OF THE VICTORIOUS MOTOGIRO. THE BLESSING BROUGHT GOOD LUCK. DUCATI WON THE 100 CLASS WITH GANDOSSI RIDING. OUTRIGHT WINNER MAOGGI ALSO TOOK VICTORY IN THE 125 CLASS.

THIRTY SEVEN MACHINES STARTED, 28 FINISHED. 100 CLASS OUTRIGHT WINNER, DUCATI TRIUMPHED IN 1956 AND CELEBRATED ITS MOTOGIRO WINS IN THIS PUBLICITY.

A CIGARETTE AND A DETERMINED LOOK, READY
TO FACE RACETRACK PERILS: GIULIANO MAOGGI
WINNER OF THE 1956 MOTOGIRO. RIDING A
125 OUT FRONT HE EVEN LEFT BEHIND THE
175S AND WENT ON TO TAKE LAURELS AS
OUTRIGHT WINNER. ABOVE, BOLOGNA RIDERS
LEOPOLDO TARTARINI AND SANDRO ARTUSI
SHARE A JOKE AT THE START OF THE '56
MOTOGIRO. TARTARINI WON TWO SECTIONS BUT
WAS FORCED TO RETIRE AFTER A BAD FALL
DURING THE SALERNO TO PERUGIA SECTION.

1955 More marathons, more successes

The Ducati SOHC machines were now the bikes to beat, the bane of other Marques. The riders with the striped helmets (to make them easy to recognise by pit teams) were unbeatable. Italy went wild with enthusiasm for Maoggi, Degli Antoni and the other Ducati riders. The Marianna dominated endurance events like the Milano-Taranto and the Motogiro.

IL MOTOGIRO NELL'EDIZIONE 1955

ha riaffermato l'eccellenza della produzione motociclistica italiana ed il grande valore agonistico dei nostri giovani guidatori animati da consapevole combattività.

Tutto ciò all'infuori ed al di sopra delle non sempre ortodosse interpretazioni dell'astruso codice sportivo italiano e degli adattamenti di comodo attuati nel regolamento particolare della gara.

FRANCESCO VILLA (213) AND BRUNO SPAGGIARI (215), TWO FAMOUS DUCATI RIDERS AT THE 100 CLASS STARTING LINE OF THE 1956 MOTOGIRO. DUCATI, BACKED BY ITS DEALER NETWORK AND PRIVATE RIDERS, FIELDED REALLY MASSIVE TEAMS WHICH RIVAL TEAMS CAME NOWHERE NEAR TOUCHING.

ABOVE, GIUSEPPE MANDOLINI DURING THE 1957 MOTOGIRO RIDING HIS GRAN SPORT TO VICTORY IN THE 100 CLASS.

PROOF OF THE COMPLETE DOMINANCE OF THE MARIANNA. HERE, FARNÉ WINNING A TRACK TIME TRIAL.

Gran Sport 100

This exceptional single camshaft bike changed Ducati's fortunes. Company management was looking for a bike to win long distance events and designer engineer Taglioni promptly responded with his first masterpiece, the GS. Winning features were the bike's good handling frame and a powerful single cylinder engine, purpose built for the long distance endurance competitions that were very popular at the time. The 100 was soon followed by the 125, practically a twin brother. Some technical features proved a boon during competitions. The valve springs, for example, were exposed to enable rapid changes; this job could even be done by riders who were supplied with a special spring compression tool. The Marianna won the Motogiro and the Milano-Taranto long distance competitions from 1955 to 1957 and became a favourite with an entire generation of competition riders for road and track events. The first Ducati Grand Prix engines and the whole series of engines which made Ducati famous were derived from the Gran Sport 100 power unit. Way back in 1955 this bike was the ideal choice for the private competition rider looking for convincing performance (9 hp at 9,000 rpm), ruggedness and easy servicing.

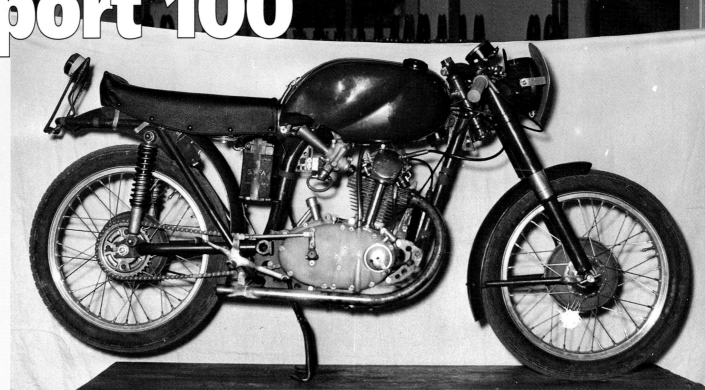

THIS IS THE FIRST OFFICIAL PHOTOGRAPH OF THE GRAN SPORT 100 IN AN UNUSUAL, IMPROVISED PHOTO STUDIO. NOTE THAT THERE IS STILL NO MEGAPHONE ON THE EXHAUST. THE MARIANNA, AS IT SOON BECAME KNOWN BY RIDERS AND FANS ALIKE, WENT ON TO WIN NUMEROUS LONG DISTANCE AND TRACK EVENTS.

Specification

ENGINE: Four-stroke single-cylinder, with 10° forward angle configuration. Air-cooled. Bore: 49.4 mm. Stroke: 52 mm. Capacity: 98 cc. Compression ratio: 8.5:1. Single camshaft, twin valves with shaft/helical valve gear. Dellorto 20 mm carburettor. Maximum power: 9 hp at 9,000 rpm (first type). Battery ignition. Lubrication: forced oil sump. Gearbox: primary reduction by gears. Chain final drive. Wet, multi-plate clutch. Four-speed gearbox. FRAME, FORKS AND RUNNING GEAR: single tube, open cradle frame in tubular steel. Front telescopic forks. Swinging arm rear suspension with twin shock absorbers. Amadori front drum brakes. 17" wheels (first type) with 2.75 tyres. WEIGHT (dry) 80 kg. Top speed 115 kph plus.

A BIKE EQUIPPED FOR A LONG DISTANCE ROAD COMPETITION: PADDING ON THE FUEL TANK THAT ALLOWED THE RIDER TO LIE DOWN ON FAST STRETCHES, SPARE PLUGS, TOOLS STRAPPED DOWN WITH ELASTIC STRAPS AND A LARGE AIR PUMP WITH A BUILT-IN TYRE LEVER.

TWO VIEWS OF THE GRAN SPORT 100 ENGINE DESIGNED BY FABIO TAGLIONI. THE UNIT HAD A SINGLE OVERHEAD CAMSHAFT AND HELICAL VALVE GEAR. EXPOSED SPRINGS ENABLED RAPID CHANGES. THIS DESIGN WAS THE INSPIRATION FOR MANY SUBSEQUENT DUCATI ENGINES.

AN EXPLODED DRAWING OF THE DUCATI 100 AND 125 CC SINGLE-CAMSHAFT ENGINES. APART FROM DIFFERENT BORE AND STROKE AND OTHER SMALL DIFFERENCES, THE TWO ENGINES WERE VIRTUALLY THE SAME.

LEOPOLDO TARTARINI IN ACTION ON A GRAN SPORT 100 DURING THE 1955 MOTOGIRO. THE 100 CLASS WAS WON BY GIANNI DEGLI ANTONI AND TARTARINI HAD TO CONSOLE HIMSELF WITH A WIN ON ONE OF THE SECTIONS. IN LATER YEARS TARTARINI BECAME A MOTORCYCLE MANUFACTURER, MAKER OF ITALJET MACHINES.

MARIO CARINI FLASHES BY ON HIS WAY TO ANOTHER RECORD ON
THE MONZA TRACK. DESPITE THE LONG DISTANCE AND THE
RECORD BREAKING SPEEDS, THIS SPECIAL - PREPARED FOR
RIDERS CARINI AND CICERI - FINISHED THE DAY WITHOUT ANY
TECHNICAL PROBLEMS.

1956

44 records for the SOHC 100

It could only have happened in the heyday of Italian motorcycling. Two private riders, Mario Carini and Santo Ciceri, with a little help from the Company, broke over 40 world speed records using a machine which was virtually identical to those used in road events. Forty-four world speed records fell on Friday 30th November on the Monza test circuit. Thirteeen records were in the 100 class, 13 in the 125 and the remainder in the 175 class. Not content with this, the riders also set five new records for the 250 class.

Sull'Autodromo di Monza
44 primati della "Ducati,,

THE GRAN SPORT 100 HAD A "FLAT FISH" ALUMINIUM FAIRING AND A DELLORTO SS 25 CARBURETTOR IN PLACE OF THE STANDARD 20 MM. THE ELASTIC RAINPROOF COVERING AROUND THE RIDER IMPROVED STREAMLINING.

THE RIDER IN THESE TWO PHOTOGRAPHS IS SANTO CICERI DURING RECORD BREAKING ATTEMPTS ON THE MONZA CIRCUIT. THE DUCATI 100 SET THE RECORD FOR THE FASTEST LAP TIME AT AN AVERAGE OF OVER 170 KPH. OVER A DISTANCE OF 1,000 KM THE BIKE CLOCKED A RECORD BREAKING AVERAGE SPEED OF NEARLY 160 KPH.

ABOVE, MARIO CARINI, FROM MILANO, WAS ALREADY AN ESTABLISHED TRIALS RIDER (ON VESPA) AND SPRINT SPECIALIST (ON MONDIAL 125 AND 175).

RIDER SANTO CICERI FROM LOMBARDY WON THE 1955 TROFEO CADETTI ON A DUCATI 100, PRACTICALLY ON HIS FIRST TIME OUT.

READY FOR ITS RACE DEBUT: THE NEW DUCATI GRAND PRIX
MACHINE. A STYLISH HAND-BEATEN FRONT FAIRING FIXED TO THE
FUEL TANK AND AN EXTENDED TAIL FAIRING. THIS BIKE WAS
RACED BY VETERAN RIDER ALANO MONTANARI.

1956 Arrival of the twin camshaft

This is the story of a scoop in 1956. Ducati managing director Montano, design engineer Taglioni and sales manager Calcagnile all knew that in order to stay up there with the winners they needed a new engine. It was decided to modify the Gran Sport 125 and radically change the engine's valve gear. The result was a DOHC single delivering nearly 16 hp at 11,500 rpm. *Motociclismo* editor Arturo Coerezza and aspiring motorcycling journalist Carlo Perelli braved the elements and travelled down the snow covered Po Plain to the Ducati works where they photographed and described the new engine. The 125 DOHC made sporadic appearances in works livery and then disappeared into the hands of private riders. In the pages which follow you will find out why.

La "bialbero,, DUCATI "Gran Sport,, 125 cc.

ABOVE, JOURNALIST AND FRIENDS SURROUND DEGLI ANTONI AFTER HIS VICTORIOUS ARRIVAL AT TARANTO IN 1956. IN THE FOREGROUND YOU CAN SEE THE MOVIE CAMERA REPORTING THE EVENT FOR "LA SETTIMANA INCOM", A POPULAR CINEMA NEWSREEL AT THE TIME. DEGLI ANTONI MADE HIS TRACK DEBUT AT FAENZA IN MAY 1956 FINISHING SIXTH ON A DOHC.

CLEARLY DERIVED FROM THE GRAN SPORT, MULTIPLE WINNER OF THE MOTOGIRO AND MILANO-TARANTO EVENTS, THE DOHC USED PRACTICALLY THE SAME FRAME AS ITS PREDECESSOR WITH A SINGLE TUBE CRADLE FRAME OPEN AT THE BOTTOM.

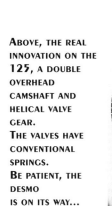

ABOVE, THE REAL INNOVATION ON THE 125, A DOUBLE OVERHEAD CAMSHAFT AND HELICAL VALVE GEAR.
THE VALVES HAVE CONVENTIONAL SPRINGS.
BE PATIENT, THE DESMO IS ON ITS WAY...

DUCATI 200 *il muletto*

DUCATI MECCANICA S.p.A. BOLOGNA

A BROCHURE FOR THE MULETTO THREE-WHEELER TRUCK. THE MULETTO USED MANY COMPONENTS ORIGINALLY DESIGNED FOR THE CRUISER SCOOTER.

ROMOLO FERRI,
SECOND IN THE 1958
TOURIST TROPHY
RIDING A DUCATI 125
DESMO. THE PHOTO
WAS TAKEN AT THE
DIFFICULT SIGNPOST
CORNER.

1957 The 3-camshaft Desmo 125

The technical development of Ducati single-cylinders reached its high point with the desmodromic valve system, a defining moment in motorcycle mechanical engineering. The desmo had already made a victorious debut in Sweden in the previous year. At the time *Motociclismo* interviewed design engineer Fabio Taglioni on the advantages of the desmo distribution system. Here is what he said: "The main purpose of the system is to force the valve to follow the distribution diagram as closely as possible. Energy losses are virtually negligible, performance curves are more uniform and reliability is improved". Success was not long coming...

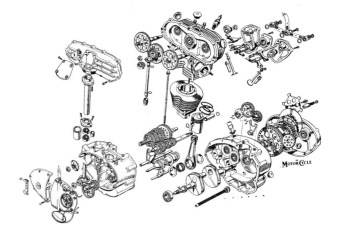

Il motore DUCATI "tre alberi,, con distribuzione desmodromica

Quel che ne dice con esemplare obiettività il suo geniale progettista ing. Fabio Taglioni

LEFT, GANDOSSI (10) FIGHTS IT OUT WITH PROVINI (ON A MONDIAL, NUMBER 8) DURING THE FIRST LAP OF THE SYRACUSE GP IN 1957.

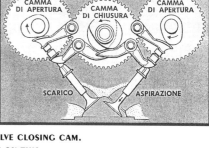

THIS VALVE GEAR LAYOUT DIAGRAM SHOWS THE TWO EXTERNAL GEARS CONTROLLING VALVE OPENING, AND THE CENTRAL GEAR OPERATING THE VALVE CLOSING CAM. BORE AND STROKE ON THIS MODEL WERE **55.3** AND **52** MM RESPECTIVELY. A **31** MM INLET MANIFOLD WAS FED BY A **SS** SERIES CARBURETTOR AVAILABLE WITH **27** OR **29** MM DIAMETERS FOR ROAD OR TRACK TRIM.

THESE TWO CLASSIC SIDE VIEWS CLEARLY SHOW THE **3**-SHAFT'S ANCESTRY AND SIMILARITY WITH THE **SOHC** GRAN SPORT AND THE PREVIOUS **DOHC** VERSION. ONLY THE CHARACTERISTIC LARGE DESMO GEAR DRIVE COVER GIVES THE GAME AWAY; THE COVER HOUSES THE THREE LARGE GEARS, DRILLED TO SAVE WEIGHT. THE DOHC HAD AN ILLUSTRIOUS RACING CAREER. IT WON THE **1956** SWEDISH GRAND PRIX AND WENT ON TO DOMINATE THE FIELD WITH NUMEROUS VICTORIES IN JUNIOR AND FORMULA **2** RACES. SUCCESS IN THE WORLD CHAMPIONSHIPS WAS HAMPERED BY THE BELL-SHAPED FAIRING. IN '58 THIS WAS ELIMINATED, THE DOHC WENT ON TO WIN THE ITALIAN SENIOR TITLE AND NARROWLY MISSED VICTORY IN THE WORLD CHAMPIONSHIPS WITH GANDOSSI IN THE SADDLE. THE BIKE WON RACES AT AVERAGE SPEEDS REACHING **160** KPH (THE ENGINE DEVELOPED **19** HP AT **13,000** RPM) HITTING **15,000** RPM ON THE STRAIGHT. IN '59 COMPETING MARQUES GAINED GROUND AND DESPITE A FEW SUCCESSES THE DOHC WAS NOT ABLE TO REPEAT ITS WINNING PERFORMANCE OF **1958**.

ABOVE, FRANCO FARNÉ ON A **125** GRAN PREMIO OF **1958**. HE STARTED AT DUCATI IN '**51** AND RACED IN TRIALS, TRACK EVENTS AND LONG DISTANCE RACES IN THE **50**s. FARNÉ'S MECHANICAL WIZARDRY WAS BACKED BY YEARS OF EXPERIENCE AS A RIDER. HE WORKED ALONGSIDE DESIGNER TAGLIONI.

The 175 SOHC series

"The bike that heightened my enthusiasm for motorcycling ...", commented Carlo Perelli at the end of a road test in *Motociclismo* No. 43 in 1957. The "bike" in this case was a new 175 T, just reaching the showrooms after a presentation at Milano in 1956. The 175 series was the embodiment of the Ducati philosophy, to produce road machines that won races or, to put it another way, to produce race-bred production bikes. The 175 was the first Ducati production machine to be offered with a SOHC engine. This engine was a direct descendant of the Gran Sport, redesigned to cope with the increased bore. The 175 raced in Formula 3 (production racers). The engine appeared on a wide variety of bikes and became available in a range of different cylinder sizes.

THE 175 TURISMO OF 1957 WAS DESIGNED AS A TOURING BIKE BUT WAS ALSO A FAVOURITE WITH RIDERS LOOKING FOR SOMETHING SPORTY. THE ENGINE AND SUPERIOR ROAD HOLDING MADE THIS A TRULY GREAT MACHINE!

Specification

ENGINE: Four-stroke single-cylinder, with 10° forward angle configuration. Air-cooled. Single overhead camshaft, twin valves with gear shaft/helical valve gear. Bore: 62 mm. Stroke: 57.8 mm. Capacity: 174.5 cc. Compression ratio: 7:1. Maximum power: 11 hp at 7,500 rpm. Dellorto MB 22 carburettor. Fuel tank capacity: 17 litres. Coil ignition with automatic advance. Lubrication: forced wet sump with 2 kg oil. Wet, multi-plate clutch. Gearbox: primary reduction by gears. Chain final drive. Four-speed gearbox. FRAME, FORKS AND RUNNING GEAR: single, open cradle frame in steel tubing. Front telescopic forks. Swinging arm rear suspension with twin shocks. Front and rear drum brakes. Tyres: 2.50 x 18" (front), 2.75 x 18" (rear). DIMENSIONS AND WEIGHT: Length: 1,980 mm. Width: 660 mm. Seat height: 750 mm. Wheel base: 1,320 mm. Weight (dry): 102 kg. Performance: top speed 115 kph (head down position); 44 kph in 1st, 69 kph in 2nd, 90 kph in 3rd.

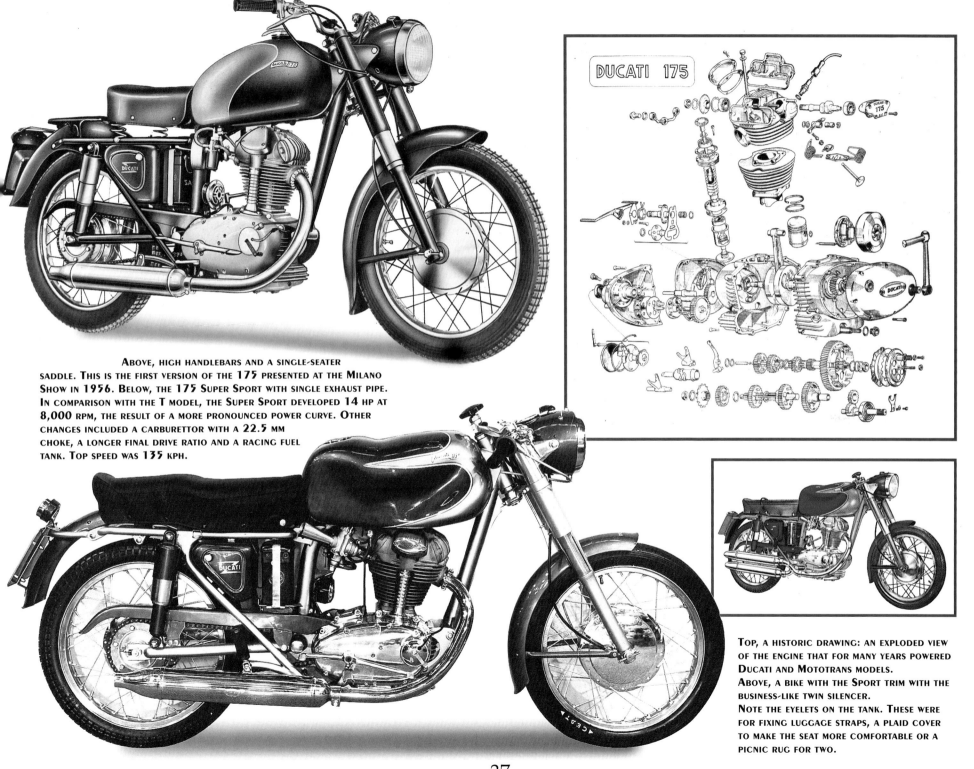

ABOVE, HIGH HANDLEBARS AND A SINGLE-SEATER SADDLE. THIS IS THE FIRST VERSION OF THE **175** PRESENTED AT THE MILANO SHOW IN **1956**. BELOW, THE **175** SUPER SPORT WITH SINGLE EXHAUST PIPE. IN COMPARISON WITH THE T MODEL, THE SUPER SPORT DEVELOPED **14** HP AT **8,000** RPM, THE RESULT OF A MORE PRONOUNCED POWER CURVE. OTHER CHANGES INCLUDED A CARBURETTOR WITH A **22.5** MM CHOKE, A LONGER FINAL DRIVE RATIO AND A RACING FUEL TANK. TOP SPEED WAS **135** KPH.

TOP, A HISTORIC DRAWING: AN EXPLODED VIEW OF THE ENGINE THAT FOR MANY YEARS POWERED DUCATI AND MOTOTRANS MODELS.
ABOVE, A BIKE WITH THE SPORT TRIM WITH THE BUSINESS-LIKE TWIN SILENCER.
NOTE THE EYELETS ON THE TANK. THESE WERE FOR FIXING LUGGAGE STRAPS, A PLAID COVER TO MAKE THE SEAT MORE COMFORTABLE OR A PICNIC RUG FOR TWO.

38

1957 From the race track to the USA

The highly successful standard 175 became the basis for a large number of developments: racing models, production racers, off-road bikes and even a custom-bike forty years before its time. By the end of the Fifties the 175 had become Ducati's fame and fortune.

LEFT, THE SHOWY AMERICANO VERSION ALSO KNOWN AS THE AMERICA OR TURISMO. THIS BIKE WAS DUCATI'S ATTEMPT TO BREAK INTO THE NORTH AMERICAN MARKET. NOTE THE STUDDED BIKER SADDLE, COW HORN HANDLEBARS, TWO-TONE HORNS AND TWIN EXHAUSTS.

BELOW RIGHT, THE TS 175 PRODUCED BETWEEN 1958 AND 1960 REPLACING THE PREVIOUS T VERSION.

PREVIOUS PAGE, FRANCESCO VILLA AND HIS 175 FORMULA 3 SERIES RACER, WINNERS IN THE F3 EVENT ACCOMPANYING THE VICTORIOUS NATIONS CUP GP AT MONZA IN 1958. IN THE 125 WORLD CHAMPIONSHIP HE FINISHED THIRD ON THE TWIN-CYLINDER DESMO MAKING ITS DEBUT RUN.

ABOVE, THE 1958 SPORT: IN COMPARISON WITH THE MODEL SHOWN IN THE TWO-PAGE ADVERT ON THE PREVIOUS PAGE, THIS SPORT HAS A BLACK PAINTED CARBURETTOR BODY (JUST LIKE THE AMERICANO) MOUNTED IN A NEARLY HORIZONTAL POSITION AND WITH A SHORTER CHOKE. SUCH DIFFERENCES WERE VERY OFTEN THE RESULT OF HURRIED STYLING AND TRIM CHANGES MADE BEFORE A BIKE SHOW DEBUT. OTHER DIFFERENCES REFLECT THE MANIA OF MANUFACTURERS OF THE TIME TO HEAVILY RETOUCH THE PHOTOS OF THEIR MACHINES. LEFT, THE 175 FORMULA 3, DESIGNED AS A SERIES PRODUCTION RACER. THE STANDARD ENGINE WAS PEPPED-UP AND RACE-TRIM FEATURES INCLUDED A STRAIGHT-THROUGH MEGAPHONE EXHAUST, SET-BACK RACING FOOTRESTS, A REV COUNTER AND AN AIR INTAKE FOR THE FRONT DRUM BRAKE. ROAD-GOING LIGHTS, NUMBER PLATE, HORN AND STAND MADE THE BIKE STREET LEGAL.

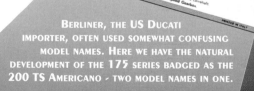

BERLINER, THE US DUCATI IMPORTER, OFTEN USED SOMEWHAT CONFUSING MODEL NAMES. HERE WE HAVE THE NATURAL DEVELOPMENT OF THE 175 SERIES BADGED AS THE 200 TS AMERICANO - TWO MODEL NAMES IN ONE.

40

1958 Round-the-world tour

Departure, Bologna, 30th September 1957. Arrival, Bologna, 5th September 1958 nearly a year later, after 60,000 kilometres, 42 Countries and five Continents. These were the statistics of an adventure at the limits of the foolhardy, a round-the-world trip travelled by Leopoldo Tartarini and Giorgio Monetti. Tartarini, nicknamed Poldino, was a Ducati works rider just recovering from an accident. Monetti a boyhood friend, had just graduated in law. They chose two Ducati 175s for the trip. The engines withstood the punishment but riders and tyres went through hell.

BELOW, A BLESSING FROM CARDINAL LERCARO BEFORE THE START. LEFT, TARTARINI WRAPPED UP AGAINST THE RIGOURS OF THE IRAQ DESERT.

Iniziato il viaggio attorno al mondo
delle "DUCATI 175 cc.,, di Tartarini e Monetti

TARTARINI IS JOKINGLY ATTACKED BY TWO INDIANS IN THE MATO GROSSO. THE TWO RIDERS HAD FIELD BACK-UP FROM LOCAL DUCATI DEALERS WHO PROVIDED MONEY AND MATERIAL.

THERE WERE MANY DIFFICULT MOMENTS. JUST THINK, THEY HAD TO CHANGE OVER 30 TYRES. THERE WERE NICER MOMENTS TOO. DURING THE TRIP MONETTI MET HIS FUTURE WIFE, THE DAUGHTER OF THE ITALIAN AMBASSADOR IN AUSTRALIA. RIGHT, LEOPOLDO TARTARINI VISITS A TEMPLE IN THAILAND.

THE ALUMINIUM SUITCASES SPECIALLY PREPARED FOR THE TRIP WERE REPLACED BY LIGHTER, CARDBOARD CASES - "IMPOVERISHED IMMIGRANT STYLE" AS THEY WERE DESCRIBED BY THE RIDERS. PASSING THROUGH IRAQ, TARTARINI AND MONETTI BRUSHED WITH THE REVOLUTION WHICH LED TO THE DOWNFALL OF KING FEISAL.

PREVIOUS PAGE, SEPTEMBER 1958, TARTARINI AND MONETTI ESCORTED BY DUCATI FANS TAKE A LAP OF HONOUR ALONG BOLOGNA'S MAIN VIA RIZZOLI ROAD AFTER THEIR ROUND-THE-WORLD TOUR. TODAY TARTARINI IS PRESIDENT OF ITALJET MOTORCYCLE MANUFACTURER AND MONETTI HAS A CAR DEALERSHIP.

A MAP SHOWING THE INTREPID JOURNEY UNDERTAKEN BY POLDINO TARTARINI AND GIORGIO MONETTI ON TWO DUCATI 175s. IN A YEAR THEY COVERED 60,000 KILOMETRES, 42 COUNTRIES AND FIVE CONTINENTS.

HISTORIC DAY AT MONZA: THE BATTLE OF THE
125S BETWEEN SPAGGIARI (12) AND
GANDOSSI (8), JUST AHEAD OF THE MVS
RIDDEN BY PROVINI (4) AND UBBIALI (2);
FOLLOWED BY TAVERI (18) AND CHADWICK
(20) ON THE OTHER DESMOS. THE RACE WAS
WON BY SPAGGIARI, WITH GANDOSSI IN
SECOND PLACE, FOLLOWED BY FRANCESCO
VILLA ON HIS TWIN-CYLINDER, CHADWICK
AND TAVERI, ALL ON DUCATIS.
DURING THIS SEASON, THE ITALIAN MARQUE
USED DIFFERENT FRAMES: CHANGING
FROM THE CLASSIC SIMPLEX OPEN CRADLE
TO THE CLOSED DUPLEX CRADLE FRAME.

1958 Triumph at the "Nations Cup"

Nineteen fifty eight was a year of triumph, but at the same time bitter-sweet for Ducati, which dominated the 125 class with the "three-shaft" single-cylinder desmo, but just missed out on the title, won by Ubbiali on the MV. Yet it still had the satisfaction of taking the top five places in the final race, the Nations Cup Grand Prix at Monza. The following year, Hailwood, again on the 125 desmo, was third in the World Championships.

RIGHT, ALBERTO GANDOSSI IN ACTION ON THE FRANCORCHAMPS TRACK IN BELGIUM; THE DUCATI RIDER - WHO DOMINATED THE SEASON - LOST THE WORLD CHAMPIONSHIPS DUE TO A FALL IN IRELAND WHEN HE WAS IN THE LEAD. DESPITE THE INCIDENT, HE GOT STRAIGHT BACK IN THE SADDLE AND CAME IN FOURTH: BUT THIS WASN'T GOOD ENOUGH. BELOW, THE START OF THE 1957

SIRACUSA RACE: NOTICE THE ALL-ENVELOPING "DUSTBIN" FAIRINGS, ALLOWED FOR THE LAST YEAR BY INTERNATIONAL RULES, AND THE PRANCING

HORSE SYMBOL ON THE SIDE - A SIGN OF TAGLIONI'S RESPECT FOR HIS FELLOW CITIZEN FRANCESCO BARACCA, ACE AVIATOR.

TRIONFO DI TECNICA E SPORT

NEL 36° GRAN PREMIO DELLE NAZIONI

Chiusi quanti dei molti spettatori giunti all'autodromo di Monza solamente nel tardo pomeriggio di domenica 14 settembre, si saranno mossi in tanti del dispetto per aver perso le emozioni offerte dalla corsa delle 125 svoltasi invece al mattino come « prima numero » del programma del 36° Gran Premio delle Nazioni, e quando le tribune ed il prato stato ancora semivuoti.

I gusti rielaborati che si sono distorti solamente al richiamo delle le gruppo cilindrate, oltre a perdere lo spettacolo di una corsa momentaneite, han fatto un grosso torto alle 125 ed considerandole immeritevoli del piccolo sacrificio di qualche ora del sonno domenicale, quando invece si deve loro riconoscere, assieme alle 250 ed al grande merito di aver salvato le sorti di questo Gran Premio delle Nazioni dandogli quell'interesse, quella passionalità, quel rumoreggio tecnico che, grazie la previsione, solo in parte si sono avuti dalle cerca delle due maggiori cilindrate.

Perchè con tutto il rispetto e la considerazione dovuta alle preponderati ma pressochè incontrastata vittorie delle M.V. Agusta 350 e 500 che tutto si attacchirano, bisogna riconoscere che il Gran Premio delle Nazioni 1950 è volentio quasi per intero dalle vicende e sui risultati delle corse delle 125 e 250, ed essa remma alce anche su quelli dell stesso Trofeo internazionale della F.M.I. per marchine di formula tre, se non fosse che questa gara, guasto in interludio che ha tenuto ben desiderevolmente il posto di centro del programma, essda dalle finalità e dalle prerogative del Gran Premio, e va considerata una competizione del tutto a se stante.

Le M.V. Agusta e quattro cilindri hanno vinto, anzi straviti ancora e sempre con l'imbattuto John Surtees; e le loro prestazioni, specie quella della 350 di Surtees, sono di grande rilievo tecnico in quanto per senza impegnarsi a fondo stante la assenza di avversari in grado di

star loro alle costole, hanno realizzato nal giro e sulla distanza velocità media orarie molto più prossime a quel le dei records locali di non quanto sia biamo saputo fare le marchine di minor cilindrata. Ma, ripetiamo, le vittorie delle M.V. e quattro - erano larganmente scontate a priori, per cui nessuno nutriva dubbi sulla loro vittoria con questo e con quest'altro dei loro numerosi e valentissimi piloti; e per di più, hanno avuto a che fare con marchine avversarie molto meno in gamba di quanto le loro precedenti prestazioni in gare « mondiali » facciavano supporre.

Le maggiori emozioni ed i Piloti tecnici più indicativi di essa venuti invece dalle corse delle 125 e 250 in cui vicende hanno fatto vibrare le corde della passionalità facenda riaffiorare al bolettismo di Monza i migliori momenti dei più combattuti Gran Premi di recente e lontana memoria.

Il Gran Premio delle Nazioni ha dunque mantenuto appieno le sue

TOP, A PHOTO FROM THE '59 GERMAN GP, WITH HAILWOOD (147) AND SPAGGIARI (149). AT THE END OF THE SEASON, THE ENGLISH RIDER RANKED THIRD AT WORLD LEVEL, BEHIND UBBIALI AND PROVINI'S MVS, WINNING THE ULSTER GRAND PRIX.

FRANCESCO VILLA WITH THE BEAUTIFUL DESMODROMIC TWIN GIVEN TO HIM FOR THE '58 NATIONS CUP GRAND PRIX. THE BIKE WAS PROMISING, ALTHOUGH ITS PERFORMANCE DID NOT GREATLY DIFFER FROM THAT OF THE "3-SHAFT" SINGLE-CYLINDER ENGINE VERSION. VILLA WAS THIRD.

Élite 200

"The most recent SOHC bike to come out of Borgo Panigale has a power ratio of 90 HP/litre." This was how *Motociclismo* summed up the sports model derived from the single-camshaft 175 series, accurately evoking the performance and pleasure promised by this example of a late '50s Italian motorbike. The Élite was designed for the domestic market, but captured the imagination of bikers world-wide, attracted by the fame of the Marque, deservedly earned during many races. The engine was clearly a bored-out version of the known 175 (the bore passed from 62 to 67 mm, whilst the stroke remained 57.8 mm) and was said to be "simple and strong", yet developed 18 hp at 7,500 rpm: it was a fun bike, confirmed by the top speed of 140 km/h, which was interesting for the period. But it was not designed to be a racing bike, rather a vehicle well suited to all occasions. Many people appreciate the two stacked silencers, a solution which later became much more common.

LA NUOVA DUCATI "ÉLITE", 203 cc.

THE ESCALATION IN THE CYLINDER CAPACITY OF DUCATI MOTORBIKES NEARS ITS CONCLUSION. HAVING STARTED AT **98** CC, WITH THE ÉLITE THE **200** MARK IS PASSED; ANOTHER SMALL STEP FORWARD AND OTHER ASPECTS MUST BE REVISED. HOWEVER, THE "WIDE CRANKCASE" PERIOD HAD STILL NOT ARRIVED.

Specification

ENGINE: *Four-stroke single-cylinder, with 10° forward angle configuration. Air-cooled. Single overhead camshaft, twin valves with gear shaft/helical valve gear. Bore: 67 mm. Stroke: 57.8 mm. Capacity: 203.7 cc. Maximum power: 18 hp at 7,500 rpm. Dellorto UB 24 carburettor (the Sport version could be fitted with the optional SS1 27 A and a camshaft with a steeper cam angle). Fuel tank capacity: 17 litres. Magneto flywheel ignition, 6 volt system. Lubrication: forced wet sump with 2 kg oil. Wet, multi-plate clutch. Gearbox: primary reduction by gears. Chain final drive. Four-speed gearbox. FRAME, FORKS AND RUNNING GEAR: single, open cradle frame in steel tubing. Front telescopic forks. Swinging arm rear suspension with twin shocks. Front and rear drum brakes (180 mm front, 160 mm rear). Tyres: 2.75 x 18" (front), 3.25 x 18" (rear). WEIGHT (dry): 106 kg. PERFORMANCE: top speed 140 kph.*

specifications:
125 cc - 4 stroke - Timing with overhead valves arranged in «V» form.
Fuel consumption : 124 miles per gallon
Maximum speed : approx. 53 m.p.h. - Four speed gearbox.

In the large photo, the America (also known as the Americano, depending on the market) with the US trim already seen on the similar 175s, included in the catalogue as an alternative to the "Normal" 200. Almost all of these "Custom" bikes went abroad. Top, Aurea 125 brochure, this bike being the successor to the 98 "rocker arm and pushrod" version. The Aurea was an economical bike with closed duplex cradle frame. The engine is no longer overhung (its mountings have been redesigned). Top speed: 85 kph.

The second version of the Élite, above, differs in few details. For example, the more sporty mudguard and different side markings; the characteristic twin silencer remains, although on the more sporty Super Sport it is replaced with a single silencer to reduce the weight.

.motoleggere DUCATI

Listino prezzi

Modello	Prezzo di vendita Lire
85 T	99.000
85 Sport	115.000
98 TS e bronco	149.000
125 Aurea	167.000
125 TS rossa	179.000
125 TS azzurra	196.000
125 Sport	209.000
175 TS	219.000
175 Sport	229.000
200 élite	239.000
200 America	

MOTOTECNICA ARTIGIANA
CENNA
I prezzi di cui sopra sono franco Fabbrica, al netto delle spese di messa su strada ed Arm.
Via Monticu... Arm.
Tel. 839.186 - MILANO

Left, original price list for the period, with two "special offers", indicated by the blue stamp: the bikes on offer are the 125 TS "Azzurra" and the 175 TS. Ducati fans did not really take to the touring models...

45

On 22 August 1959, Arthur Wheeler (number 2) and Tommy Robb, both on 125 Ducatis, fight it out for third place at Silverstone. The bikes have different fairings: Wheeler's is works produced aluminium, whilst Robb's is a less valuable English fibreglass model.

1959 Racing all over the world

After the many victories at home and in the World Speed Championships, Ducati bikes became very popular among riders all over the world. They were fast, reliable and, above all, available. In fact, after 1959 the Company's commitment slackened and the racing department began working on "commissions" only. Thus, Ducati produced motorcycles and "components" destined to breathe new life into motor sport on all Continents.

THE RIDER WEARING A VEST AS HE APPROACHES THE START LINE IS UMBERTO MASETTI, TWICE WORLD CHAMPION IN THE 500 CC CATEGORY. DURING HIS LONG CAREER, BETWEEN EUROPE AND SOUTH AMERICA, THIS ITALIAN OFTEN RODE DUCATI BIKES. HERE, HE IS SEEN ON A SINGLE-CAMSHAFT 125, VERY POPULAR AMONG PRIVATE RIDERS ALL OVER THE WORLD.

BELOW, JUAN CARLOS MERODIO, SOUTH-EAST ARGENTINA REGIONAL CHAMPION IN 1959 AND "ACTUAL PUNTERO" (AS INDICATED BY THE ORIGINAL CAPTION) DURING THE 1960 SEASON, WITH HIS SINGLE-CAMSHAFT 125, EVIDENTLY DERIVED FROM A ROAD BIKE (THE ENGINE SPRINGS ARE COVERED).

ABOVE, MIKE HAILWOOD IN ACTION AT THE '59 ULSTER GP, WHICH HE WENT ON TO WIN WITH HIS 125 DESMO TWIN. RANKED THIRD IN THE WORLD, MIKE ARRIVED IN BOLOGNA WITH A GREAT DEAL OF CASH AND RETURNED TO GREAT BRITAIN WITH SEVERAL NEW BIKES, ACCOMPANIED BY MECHANIC FOLESANI. RIGHT, SPINNLER WINS THE 125 AT ABBAZIA: NOTICE HOW THE BACK WHEEL IS OFF THE GROUND, DUE TO IMPERFECTIONS ON THE SURFACE OF THE YUGOSLAV TRACK!

UNCOVERED SPRINGS FOR RODA, AT THE MONTJUICH 24 HOUR RACE. THE BIKE HAS REAR-SET RACING FOOTRESTS MOUNTED DIRECTLY ON THE SWINGING ARM. NOTE THE RED AND WHITE STRIPED HELMET CHARACTERISTIC OF DUCATI RIDERS DURING THOSE YEARS.

85 Turismo and Sport

For bikers who, "although seeking something more than the usual sporty bike, cannot afford the 98s or 125s". This was *Motociclismo*'s comment on the new single-cylinder bike in 1959, and they can't be faulted. Ducati created this model with the intention of providing enthusiasts with a valid "entry level bike". In practice, sales of the 85 were more successful abroad, especially in those countries in which bikes with a cylinder capacity below 90 cc had tax remissions. It was a development on the 98 cc engine with rocker arms and pushrods (one of the first engines made at Borgo Panigale) with interesting modifications, such as the four-speed gearbox, used on the Sport model, whilst the Turismo had only three speeds. The other characteristics were the bore reduced to 45.5 mm, modification of the outer right-hand casing and a narrower tappet cover than on the 98 model. But the most interesting aspect is the running gear, with its true duplex cradle frame.

Nuovi modelli della "DUCATI"
Le ultraleggere 85 cc. "Turismo" e "Sport" esaminate nei loro dettagli costruttivi

Specification

ENGINE: Four-stroke single-cylinder, with 25° forward angle configuration. Twin valves with rocker arm and pushrod valve gear. Bore: 45.5 mm. Stroke: 52 mm. Capacity: 84.55 cc. Compression ratio: 7.5:1. Maximum power: 5.5 hp at 7,200 rpm (5 hp on Turismo). Dellorto ME 16 BS 24 carburettor. Fuel tank capacity: 13 litres. Magneto flywheel ignition with external HT coil. Lubrication: forced wet sump with 1 kg oil. Wet, multi-plate clutch. Gearbox: primary reduction by gears. Chain final drive. Four-speed gearbox (three speed on Turismo). FRAME, FORKS AND RUNNING GEAR: twin tube, closed cradle frame in steel tubing. Front telescopic forks. Swinging arm rear suspension with twin shocks. Front and rear drum brakes. Tyres: 2.50 x 17". DIMENSIONS AND WEIGHT: Length: 1,910 mm. Overall height: 900 mm. Seat height: 740 mm. Wheelbase: 1,270 mm. Weight (dry): 80 kg. PERFORMANCE: top speed 76 kph (70 kph for Turismo).

BERLINER, THE US IMPORTER, HAD MANY MODELS SPECIALLY DESIGNED FOR THE US MARKET. BASED ON THE 85, THE BRONCO (NAMED AFTER AN AMERICAN SPECIES OF HORSE), HAD A COMFORTABLE SADDLE, HIGH HANDLEBARS AND ROUNDED FUEL TANK. THE BRONCO WAS MADE IN 85, 98 AND 125 CC VERSIONS.

DUCATI 125 BRONCO

MOTO DUCATI

Specifications: 125 cc. - Four strokes - Timing O.H.V.
Max. speed 53 m.p.h. - Four speed gearbox.

PRINTED IN ITALY

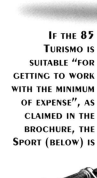

DUCATI 85 Sport

caratteristiche principali — 85 cm³ - 4 tempi - distribuzione con valvole in testa a V
Consumo benzina lt. 2,1 per 100 Km.
Velocità massima circa 75 Km/h. - Cambio

IF THE 85 TURISMO IS SUITABLE "FOR GETTING TO WORK WITH THE MINIMUM OF EXPENSE", AS CLAIMED IN THE BROCHURE, THE SPORT (BELOW) IS A TRUE SMALL SPORTS BIKE. ITS SHAPE IS ENHANCED BY THE WELL-DESIGNED FUEL TANK, WHICH MARKS A RETURN TO THE SHAPE OF THOSE MOUNTED ON THE "MEAN" VERSIONS OF 175 SINGLE-CAMSHAFT BIKES. THE USE OF COMPONENTS WHICH EVOKE THE MOST IMPORTANT MODELS PROMPTED CUSTOMERS TO IDENTIFY WITH THEM, IN WHAT THE MARKETING EXPERTS OF TODAY CALL "FAMILY FEELING" - A CONCEPT WHICH ALREADY EXISTED 40 YEARS AGO...

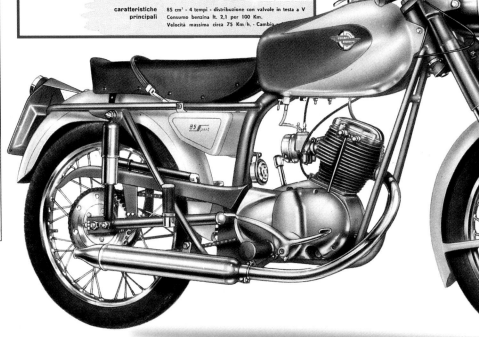

THE "ROCKER ARM AND PUSHROD" ENGINE REPRESENTS A SEPARATE CHAPTER IN THE HISTORY OF DUCATI: DESIGNED BEFORE THE ARRIVAL OF TAGLIONI, IT WAS CHARACTERISED BY HIGHLY RATIONALISED CONSTRUCTION, BUT COULD NOT COMPETE WITH THE TOUGHER SINGLE-CAMSHAFT ENGINES. IT WAS MAINLY USED ON SMALL BIKES, BUT WAS PRODUCED FOR A LONG PERIOD, OF AROUND FIFTEEN YEARS.

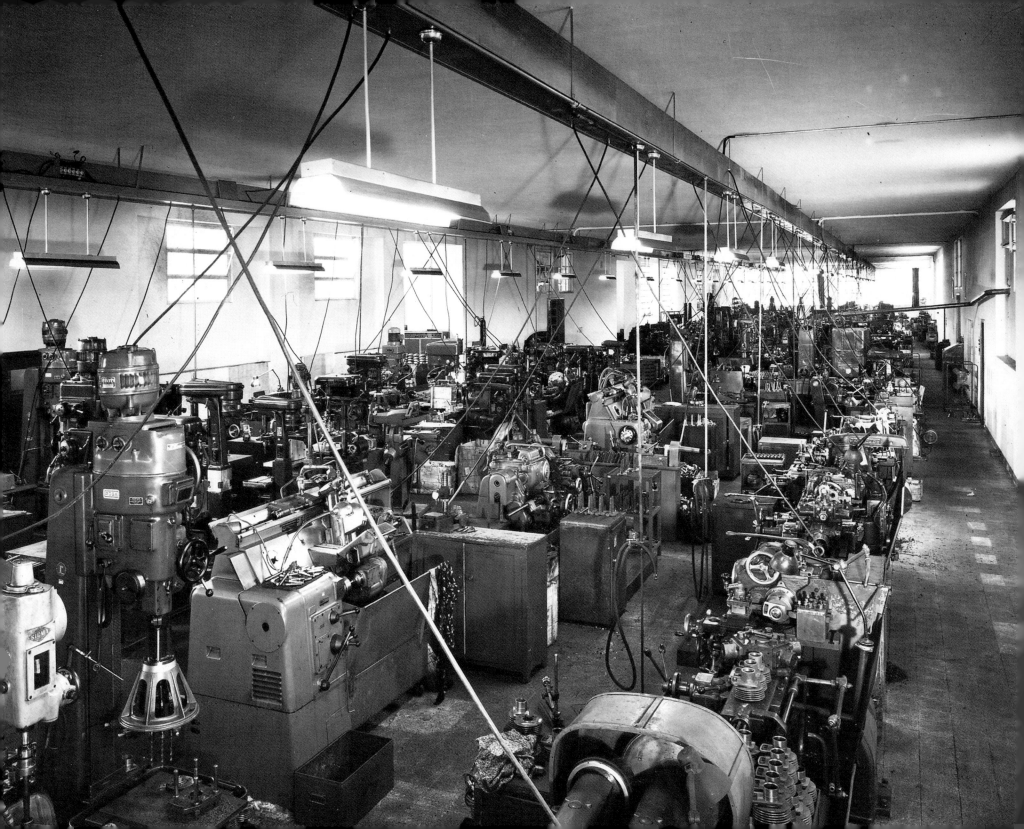

1960 Birthplace of the Ducatis

Ducati has been "based" at Borgo Panigale, on the western outskirts of Bologna since the '30s. The address remains the same today: via Cavalieri Ducati 3. The German occupation in 1943, Allied bombardments in '44-45, the difficult reconstruction, passage under IMI, then IRI (Italian government finance corporations), nationalised industries, the Cucciolo, the Marianna, the desmo, Taglioni, Bordi, Montano, the twins and 4-valve engines... all originated here and, even today, all Ducati bikes are designed here. The works developed along with the Marque, but always remained its inspiration. The racing department was also based here and a museum with the most interesting racing bikes is going to be created soon.

LEFT, A PHOTO THAT WOULD SEND ANY DUCATI FAN OUT OF HIS MIND: DOZENS OF ENGINES (IN-LINE AND V-TWINS) WAITING TO BE FITTED ON THE NEW BIKES. THIS PHOTO DATES BACK TO THE '70S; TWENTY YEARS EARLIER, DUCATI PRODUCED 200 BIKES A DAY. BELOW, AN AERIAL VIEW OF THE FACTORY, STILL IN THE MIDST OF FIELDS AND ISOLATED HOUSES; TODAY THE CITY HAS SURROUNDED THE DUCATI FACILITY.

TOP, DUCATI MANAGING DIRECTOR, DR. MONTANO (AT CENTRE, WITH MOUSTACHE AND HAT) ACCOMPANIES THE IMPORTER BERLINER AND A DELEGATION OF US DEALERS ON A TOUR OF THE FACTORY IN 1959. ABOVE, CONSTRUCTION OF A NEW WING OF THE FACTORY DURING THE SIXTIES.

OPPOSITE PAGE: A BLACK AND WHITE PHOTO OF THE MACHINE SHOP; IF YOU LOOK CAREFULLY, YOU WILL NOTICE A MYRIAD OF CYLINDERS DESTINED FOR SINGLE-CAMSHAFT ENGINES.

FOR MANY PEOPLE, DUCATI BIKES ARE THOROUGHBREDS SYNONYMOUS WITH SPORT, BUT NOT FOR MILAN'S MARCHETTI, WHICH PROPOSED THE STABIL TRAILER, DESIGNED TO TRANSFORM THE 98 INTO A MECHANICAL WORKHORSE.

PRIZE WINNING SMILES AND A NEWLY WON TROPHY. MIKE HAILWOOD SEATED ON HIS DUCATI 250 TWIN WITH TRUSTY MECHANIC OSCAR FOLESANI ALONGSIDE. THE GENTLEMAN IN THE DOUBLE-BREASTED SUIT IS MIKE'S FATHER, STAN HAILWOOD. THE BIKE WAS EQUIPPED WITH BRITISH COMPONENTS. ROADHOLDER FORKS, GIRLING DAMPERS AND SMITHS REV COUNTER. BRAKES WERE THE VERY ITALIAN OLDANI.

1960 Mike's twins

In 1957 Ducati had an in-line twin which raced in the last Motogiro. The design was further developed by Taglioni and the bike raced successfully in the USA. The idea was developed still further and in 1960 Ducati produced a 250 twin which, in effect, consisted of two DOHC 125 cylinder head and block units joined together. Mike Hailwood, a promising young rider backed by a wealthy father, raced the twin. Francesco Villa also developed the design and there was even a 350 with a special frame for John Surtees. This was all happening as the Works Racing Department was about to be closed down.

Pronta per le corse la DUCATI 250 bicilindrica di MIKE HAILWOOD

La Ducati 250 bicilindrica di Hailwood, vista senza carenatura, mostra la sua po001a cilindrica. Si notino le vaschette agglutinate dei carburatori, per ragioni d'ingombro.

ABOVE, A PHOTO TAKEN IN FRANCESCO VILLA'S WORKSHOP IN 1965 SHOWING HIS 250. IN EFFECT THIS WAS A 175 WITH THE SAME BORE AND STROKE AS A 125 GRAN SPORT (55.2 x 52 MM). ALONGSIDE THE 250, A MONDIAL 250 AND A DUCATI 125 DOHC.

RIGHT, A SIGHT TO WARM MANY AN ENTHUSIAST'S HEART: HAILWOOD'S 250 TWIN PHOTOGRAPHED WITHOUT ITS FAIRING AT THE DUCATI WORKS. NOT ALL THE PRIVATE RIDERS OF THE TIME WERE LUCKY ENOUGH (OR RICH ENOUGH) TO OWN SUCH A MACHINE...

ABOVE, THE SPLENDID IN-LINE TWIN CYLINDER CREATED BY JOINING TOGETHER TWO 125 DESMO ENGINES. MAXIMUM CLAIMED POWER OUTPUT AT THE CRANK WAS 37 HP AT 11,600 RPM. THE ENGINE WAS USED BY MOTOTRANS. JOHN SURTEES FITTED ONE INTO A REYNOLDS FRAME. THERE WAS ALSO A 350 VERSION.
RIGHT, THE ORIGIN OF THE RACE TWINS, THE DOHC 175 SINGLE THAT RACED IN THE 1957 MOTOGIRO WITH TARTARINI RIDING.

ANOTHER VIEW OF THE DESMO 250 TWIN. ON THE BACK OF THE PHOTO SOMEONE HAS WRITTEN "APPROX. 35 HP, 11,000 TO 12,000 RPM. I COULDN'T SEE ANYTHING ELSE. YOURS, WALTER". "WALTER" WAS WALTER BERNAGOZZI A WELL-KNOWN BOLOGNA PHOTOGRAPHER WHO TOOK THIS PHOTO DATED 1960.

THE DIANA 250 REMAINS THE EPITOME OF AN ITALIAN SPORTS MOTORCYCLE OF THE SIXTIES. THE PHOTOS WERE TAKEN ON THE GREY OUTSKIRTS OF MILAN, A LONG WAY AWAY FROM TODAY'S EXOTIC ROAD TEST LOCATIONS.

Diana 250

The road test in Motociclismo of March 1962 featured a summary box which reads as follows: "The Ducati Diana is one of the fastest Italian bikes there is. With a stylish line, it is well finished and offers the rider top-range performances. It is therefore ideal for the discerning rider, someone who likes speed and appreciates innovative technical design and sophisticated machinery." The years may have passed but our opinion remains unchanged. This was a sports bike, luxuriously finished and much liked by road testers of the time. Other merits included crisp acceleration and powerful braking. Stability was exceptional, "worthy of a racing bike". Opinions were a little less enthusiastic about the noisy helical valve gear. The bike was also difficult to kick start when new

Specification

ENGINE: Four-stroke single-cylinder, vertical with 10° forward angle configuration. Air cooled. Single overhead camshaft, twin valves with gear shaft/helical valve gear. Bore: 74 mm. Stroke: 57.8. Capacity: 248.5 cc. Compression ratio: 8:1. Maximum power: 17,5 HP at 7.500 rpm. Dellorto UBF 24 BS carburettor (with air intake in calm area). Fuel tank capacity: 17 litres. Magneto flywheel and contact ignition. Lubrication: forced wet sump with 2 kg oil. Wet, multi-plate clutch. Gearbox: primary reduction by gears. Chain final drive. Four-speed gearbox. FRAME, FORKS AND RUNNING GEAR: Open cradle frame in tubular steel. Front telescopic forks. Swinging arm rear suspension with twin, 3-way adjustable shocks. Drum brakes: 180 mm (front) and 160 mm (rear). Tyres: 2.75 x 18" (front), 3.00 x 18" (rear). DIMENSIONS AND WEIGHT: Length: 2.000 mm. Width: 580 mm. Seat height: 750 mm. Wheelbase: 1.320 mm. Weight (dry): 120 kg. PERFORMANCE: Top speed 140 kph (to reach this speed Ducati advised a straight-through exhaust, a 43-tooth sprocket, a carburettor trumpet choke and a head-down riding position); 55 kph in 1st, 82 kph in 2nd, 105 kph in 3rd.

LEFT, 3-WAY ADJUSTABLE HYDRAULIC SHOCK ABSORBERS WITH LEVER ADJUSTMENT. ALSO VISIBLE IS THE 160 MM, SINGLE CAM, LIGHT ALLOY BRAKE DRUM. RIMS WERE CHROME STEEL. RIGHT, THE SVAMA SPEEDOMETER FITTED TO DIANA ROAD TESTED BY MOTOCICLISMO.

TOP, THE DIANA ENGINE WITH THE AIR INTAKE HOSE TAKING THE AIR FROM A CALM AREA UNDER THE SADDLE TO THE CARBURETTOR. MANY RIDERS REMOVED THE HOSE AND FITTED A SPORTIER CHOKE TRUMPET IN ITS PLACE. ABOVE, THE TOOL BOX WITH SCREW KNOB HOUSING A VERY COMPLETE TOOL KIT: 19-22 DOUBLE-ENDED BOX SPANNER, 21 BOX SPANNER WITH 14 SOCKET, 14 SPANNER WITH TYRE LEVER END, 10-11 SPANNER, SCREW DRIVER, 5-HEX SOCKET SPANNERS FOR INTERNAL NUTS AND A PUMP.

ANOTHER 250 DUCATI, THE AMERICANISED VERSION OF THE MONZA WITH CHARACTERISTIC HIGH HANDLE BARS AND SQUARE TANK. USED HERE BY FATHER CHRISTMAS IN PLACE OF THE TRADITIONAL REINDEERS AND SLEIGH, AT LEAST THAT WAS WHAT THE PHOTOGRAPHER WANTED TO SAY.

1962 And then there were mopeds

The new Italian Highway code in 1959 introduced a new class of light motorcycle — the moped. In Italy this meant, no number plate, no licence and a very low road fund licence fee. The popularity of the Ducati 48 spread. In 1958 Ducati were already producing the 48 Sport but for export only. In 1961 Ducati introduced three new models with two-stroke engines and a 3-speed, twist grip controlled gearbox. They were: the Brisk (simple and economic with a pressed steel and tubular frame), the Piuma (or Feather) with a pressed steel frame, and an export version, the Sport (top speed 80 kph) with a twin-tube cradle frame. Other versions followed, economy models, tourers, trail bikes and sports jobs. They sold well even though they lacked the soul of a real Ducati four-stroke.

Prove su strada 2

DUCATI "Piuma" 48

LEFT, AN EXPORT VERSION OF THE PIUMA. THE BRISK 50/1 HAD THE SAME RUNNING GEAR AND AN AUTOMATIC CLUTCH FIXED ONTO THE CRANKSHAFT.

THIS REAR VIEW SHOWS THE TAIL CLUSTER AND THE TELESCOPIC DAMPERS.

THE PIUMA 48 FEATURING BICYCLE PEDALS AND THREE-SPEED, TWIST-GRIP CHANGER.

ABOVE, THE 48 FALCON PRODUCED FOR THE AMERICAN MARKET. THE FINAL DRIVE RATIO COULD BE CHANGED BY LENGTHENING THE CHAIN (THE TOOL KIT INCLUDED THE EXTRA LINKS NECESSARY) AND FITTING A 60-TOOTH SPROCKET IN PLACE OF THE STANDARD 42-TOOTH SPROCKET. THE OPERATION WASN'T THAT EASY AND NEEDED HALF AN HOUR.

PREVIOUS PAGE, A HAWK-EYED HUNTER STALKING HIS PREY. HE ARRIVED ON A CACCIATORE (HUNTER) 48 TRAIL BIKE VERSION, DATED 1964.

THIS PHOTO OF 1962 SHOWS THE YOUNG MOTORCYCLING JOURNALIST OF *Motociclismo* MAGAZINE CARLO PERELLI ROAD TESTING THE PIUMA 48.

Sport 80

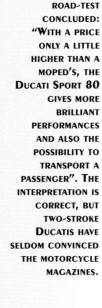

Ducati has always used the name Sport for its top of the range models. Here it was applied to a light motorcycle designed for export. The fact that the bike was designed for export explains the rather strange (for Italy) choice of cylinder capacity: 80 cc. Decidedly unpopular in Italy, 80 cc machines were much more widespread abroad. Marketed also under the name Setter, the 80 Sport gave some idea about what could be done with the 50 cc models of the time which by law were not allowed to exceed 40 kph. Not restricted by these legal limitations, the 80 was a sports moped, as the 18 mm carburettor feeding the two-stroke engine testifies. The 80 kph top speed promised by Ducati could be reached thanks to the 5.5 hp delivered. This lightweight weighed in at just 62 kg. In Italy the Sport 80 was competitively priced at 100,000 lire.

Motociclismo ROAD-TEST CONCLUDED: "WITH A PRICE ONLY A LITTLE HIGHER THAN A MOPED'S, THE DUCATI SPORT 80 GIVES MORE BRILLIANT PERFORMANCES AND ALSO THE POSSIBILITY TO TRANSPORT A PASSENGER". THE INTERPRETATION IS CORRECT, BUT TWO-STROKE DUCATIS HAVE SELDOM CONVINCED THE MOTORCYCLE MAGAZINES.

Specification

ENGINE: two-stroke single-cylinder, with 25° forward angle configuration. Air-cooled. Bore: 47 mm. Stroke: 46 mm. Capacity: 79.8 cc. Compression ratio: 9:1. Maximum power: 5.5 hp at 7,000 rpm. Dellorto UA 18 S carburettor. Lubrication: two-stroke, 5% oil/petrol mixture (6% mixture during the first 1,000 kilometres). Fuel tank capacity: 11.6 litres. Magneto flywheel ignition. Wet, multi-plate clutch. Gearbox: primary reduction by gears. Chain final drive. Three-speed gearbox with twist-grip control. FRAME, FORKS AND RUNNING GEAR: twin-tube, closed cradle frame in steel tubing. Front telescopic forks. Swinging arm rear suspension with twin shocks. Front and rear central drum brakes 118 mm. Tyres: 2.50 x 18". DIMENSIONS AND WEIGHT: Length: 1,780 mm. Width: 550 mm. Seat height: 750 mm. Wheelbase: 1,160 mm. Weight (dry): 62 kg. PERFORMANCE: top speed 80 kph. Maximum gradient fully laden with pillion passenger: 16%.

BELOW, THE CLEAN, UNCLUTTERED LINES OF THE SPORT 80. LEFT, THE VERY SLIM FRONT SECTION. OVERALL WIDTH FROM HANDLEBAR TIP TO HANDLEBAR TIP WAS JUST 550 MM. THE HANDLEBARS COULD BE ADJUSTED LIKE CLIP-ONS AND ARE SHOWN HERE IN THE FULLY OPEN POSITION. RIGHT, THIS 80 CC WAS NOT SUBJECT TO THE SAME SPEED RESTRICTIONS AS ITS SMALLER 50 CC BROTHER. THAT AND THE INCREASED CUBIC CAPACITY GUARANTEED AN ENJOYABLE RIDE.

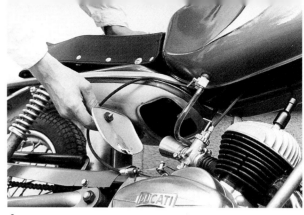

ABOVE, THE ELEGANT BUT AWKWARD TOOL BOX. BELOW, TWIST-GRIP GEAR CHANGING PROVIDED PLENTY OF WRIST EXERCISE, WITH A LONG TRAVEL FROM FIRST (TOP PHOTO) TO THIRD (BOTTOM PHOTO). TWIST-GRIP CHANGERS WERE WIDELY USED AT THE TIME. SCOOTERS HAD ACCUSTOMED BIKERS TO THIS METHOD, BUT THERE WERE STILL MANY SPORTS ENTHUSIASTS AROUND WHO LAY AWAKE AT NIGHT DREAMING OF A FOUR-SPEED BOX WITH A PEDAL CHANGER.

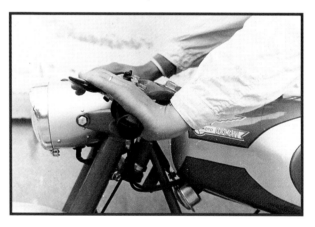

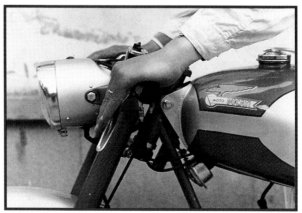

A BOLOGNA CITY SETTING FOR A BRIO 48 (LEFT) AND A PIUMA 48. FOR MANY ENTHUSIASTS THE NAME DUCATI IS SYNONYMOUS WITH SPORTS AND RACING BIKES. IT SHOULD NOT BE FORGOTTEN THAT WORK-A-DAY LIGHTWEIGHTS LIKE THESE TWO KEPT THE COMPANY'S HEAD ABOVE WATER IN THE CRISIS YEARS OF MOTORCYCLING.

1963/1964 The Brio Scooter

Ducati's return to the scooter was a long way from the technical sophistication of the Cruiser. The Brio, presented at the Milan Show in 1963 and followed a year later by a 100 cc model, was very basic. A pressed steel frame, a 2-stroke motor with forced air cooling, chain final drive and a three-speed gearbox made it very similar to the other scooters of the period. The Brio was a handy way to get about town, and the smaller version sold well. The 100 cc version was exported and also entered service with Italian public authorities; Bologna City traffic police, for example, used them for a long time.

TOP LEFT, THE BRIO CONTROLS: TWIST-GRIP CHANGER ON THE LEFT AND LIGHT SWITCH ON THE RIGHT. SECOND FROM TOP, THE BRIO 100 WAS LENGTHENED AT THE REAR TO MAKE ROOM FOR THE LARGER ENGINE AND A BIGGER SADDLE FOR A PILLION PASSENGER. THE MESH HOLDERS WERE AN ORIGINAL DUCATI ACCESSORY.

MOTOCICLISMO PROVE SU STRADA MOTOCICLISMO

DUCATI «Brio» 100

Prova effettuata sulla distanza di Km 260, in città e strade aperte di varia conformazione planimetrica e altimetrica, impiegando carburante Shell «Shellina con L.C.A.» al 5%.

Nella vasta gamma della propria produzione, che va dai ciclomotori utilitari alle 250 monoalbero, la Ducati ha recentemente inserito lo scooter «Brio» 100 due tempi tre marce. Questo nuovo modello deriva dallo scooterino di 48 presentato al motosalone di Milano del '63 e di cui conserva la stessa denominazione. Le ragioni che hanno spinto la Ducati a creare la versione di 100 sono presto spiegate: offrire alla clientela italiana e straniera uno scooter che pur essendo adatto come prestazioni ed abitabilità per l'uso a due non si discostasse sensibilmente come dimensioni, maneggevolezza e costo d'esercizio dal confratello di minor cilindrata.

AT THE END OF ITS CAREER, THE BRIO 48 WAS REPLACED BY THE BRIO 50 WITH A SLIGHTLY LARGER ENGINE (INCREASED FROM 47.6 CC TO 49.6) AND MORE LUXURIOUS TRIM. THE ENGINE WAS MOUNTED ON THIS PRESSED STEEL SWINGING ARM OF THE REAR SUSPENSION AND THUS FOLLOWED WHEEL MOVEMENTS. NOTE ALSO THE CHAIN TRANSMISSION AND THE PAIR OF SHOCKS. BELOW LEFT, THE TOOL KIT BAG FITTED TO THE INSIDE OF THE RIGHT-HAND SIDE PANEL.

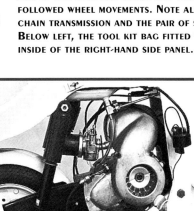

ABOVE, THE 100 CC ENGINE DELIVERING 6 HP AT 6,200 RPM. TOP SPEED WAS 76 KPH - 70 KPH WITH A PILLION PASSENGER.

viaggiate con Brio
senza targa
senza patente
fin dai 14 anni
di età
.....chi vuol esser
lieto sia
con
Brio
è un prodotto
DUCATI Brio 48
BOLOGNA
Tel. 49.16.01-2-3-4
MORE · BOLOGNA

THIS DUCATI BROCHURE EXTOLLED THE VIRTUES OF THE BRIO AND LISTED ALL THE ACCESSORIES NEEDED TO PRODUCE A CUSTOMISED VERSION.

1963/1964

125 Sport

Part of the Ducati range since 1957, the SOHC 125 Sport developed gradually over the years to become the dream of sports riders enthralled by its high revving engine. The 125 Sport remained part of the Ducati range until 1965, delivered 10 hp at 8,500 rpm and hit a top speed of 115 kph in the head down position. It was one of the best sports bikes in its class especially at the start of its career. In comparison with the original version, the 1963 model tested by *Motociclismo* had smaller brake drums but braked well just the same thanks to improvements in materials. The frame down tube from the steering head to the engine became rounder and larger and the characteristic ribbing of the first version disappeared. A close relation of the Sport was the sedate TS version aimed at those who were looking for something a little more stately. The TS was less powerful, down to 6.2 hp at 6,200 rpm, but had improved flexibility. There was also a Sport 100, almost identical except for a smaller bore and stroke (49 x 52 mm) and capacity (98.05 cc) and a lower power output (8 hp at 8,500 rpm).

THE DUCATI 125 SPORT TESTED BY *Motociclismo* IN 1963 WAS FITTED WITH A REV COUNTER. THIS WAS ONE OF THE FIRST EXAMPLES IN ITALY OF ROAD TESTING USING ADEQUATE INSTRUMENTATION.

Specification

ENGINE: Four-stroke single-cylinder, with 10° forward angle configuration. Air-cooled. Single overhead camshaft, twin valves with gear shaft/helical valve gear. Bore: 55.2 mm. Stroke: 52.8 mm. Capacity: 124.4 cc. Compression ratio: 8:1. Maximum power: 10 hp at 8,500 rpm. Dellorto UB 20 BS carburettor. Fuel tank capacity: 17 litres. Flywheel ignition with external contact breaker, 6 volt 13.5 Ah battery. Lubrication: forced wet sump with 2 kg oil. Wet, multi-plate clutch. Gearbox: primary reduction by gears. Chain final drive. Four-speed gearbox. FRAME, FORKS AND RUNNING GEAR: single-tube, open cradle frame in steel tubing. Front telescopic forks. Swinging arm rear suspension with twin shocks. Drum brakes: 158 mm (front) and 136 mm (rear). Tyres: 2.75 x 18" (front), 3.00 x 18" (rear). DIMENSIONS AND WEIGHT: Length: 1,910 mm. Width: 580 mm. Seat height: 750 mm. Wheelbase: 1,320 mm. Weight (dry): 100.5 kg. PERFORMANCE: top speed 112 kph.

ABOVE, THE 158 MM FRONT DRUM BRAKE COMPLETE WITH AIR SCOOP - ANOTHER RACE-BRED IMPROVEMENT.

ABOVE, CLOSE-UP OF THE ROUND-SECTION TUBULAR SWINGING ARM, REINFORCED WITH A TUBULAR CROSS PIECE. LEFT, THE ROCKER GEAR CHANGE PEDAL, WIDELY USED IN THE SIXTIES.

IN THESE PICTURES, THREE DETAILS FOR DUCATI SOHC ENTHUSIASTS. TOP, THE CONTACT BREAKER INSPECTION COVER. ABOVE, A FLIP-TOP, QUICK-RELEASE FUEL FILLER CAP, "JUST LIKE A RACER". RIGHT, THE CLUTCH COVER ON THE LEFT-HAND SIDE ENGINE CASING. WORKING ON DUCATIS OF THIS SERIES WAS NOT DIFFICULT, A CLEAR SIGN THAT THE DESIGNER HAD ALSO TAKEN MAINTENANCE NEEDS INTO CONSIDERATION.

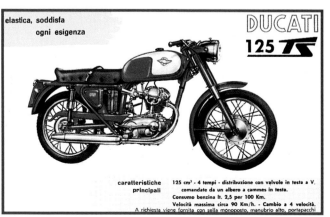

elastica, soddisfa ogni esigenza

DUCATI 125 **TS**

caratteristiche principali

125 cm³ - 4 tempi - distribuzione con valvole in testa a V. comandate da un albero a cammes in testa.
Consumo benzina lt. 2,5 per 100 Km.
Velocità massima circa 90 Km/h. - Cambio a 4 velocità.
A richiesta viene fornita con sella monoposto, manubrio alto, portapacchi

ORIGINAL PUBLICITY MATERIAL FROM THE SIXTIES: THE TS 125 OR "THE FLEXIBLE BIKE TO MEET ALL YOUR NEEDS". IT COULD BE ORDERED WITH HIGH HANDLEBARS, SINGLE SEATER SADDLE AND A LUGGAGE RACK.

The Apollo

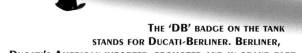

In 1963 a four-cylinder 1257 cc was could only be considered as real motorcycling madness given the depressed conditions of the Italian market. Fortunately things in the USA were a different matter. Ducati had close links with its American importer Berliner. Knowing that a high proportion of Ducati sales went to the USA, Berliner was in a position to insist on bikes being made to suit his market. At the beginning of the '60s H-D was the only American motorcycle manufacturer left and Berliner decided it was time to compete against them, especially in the lucrative police bike market. Ducati did not need asking and prepared a single prototype Apollo which was promptly shipped to the USA. The Apollo was a piece of mechanical architecture. A massive 90° V-4 with electric starter, chain final drive and a mixed tubular and box section frame. 80 hp at 6,000 rpm was claimed for the police model and the sports version (never seen in action) reputedly delivered 100 hp. The bike immediately had stability problems due mainly to the tyres. Attempts were made to remedy this by reducing power output to 65 hp but the bike just got worse. The

Apollo disappeared from view and nothing more was heard. Signs that some embers were still glowing under the ashes come from this article by Manfredo Giannotti on *Motociclismo* in 1964: "And may I now be allowed to make my one big wish and that is, that Ducati will decide to produce a 630 cc 90° V-twin made by splitting the Apollo engine in half ...". Prophetic words... You've not heard the last of this!

THE 'DB' BADGE ON THE TANK STANDS FOR DUCATI-BERLINER. BERLINER, DUCATI'S AMERICAN IMPORTER, PROMOTED AND IN GRAND PART FINANCED THE APOLLO PROJECT. NATURALLY ENOUGH HE WANTED TO SEE HIS NAME UP THERE. HE WHO PAYS THE PIPER ...

Specification

ENGINE: Four cylinder 90° V configuration. Air-cooled. Rocker arm and pushrod overhead valve gear. Bore: 84.5 mm. Stroke: 56 mm. Capacity: 1,257 cc. Compression ratio: 8:1. Maximum power: 80 hp at 6,000 rpm. Four Dellorto TT 24 carburettors. Lubrication: forced wet sump. Gearbox: primary reduction by gears. Chain final drive. Four-speed gearbox. FRAME, FORKS AND RUNNING GEAR: tubular and box section frame. Front telescopic forks. Swinging arm rear suspension with twin shocks. Drum brakes. Tyres: 5.00 x 16". WEIGHT (dry): 270.5 kg. PERFORMANCE: top speed not given.

DUCATI MANAGEMENT OFFICIALLY HANDING OVER THE APOLLO TO JOE BERLINER (CENTRE RIGHT IN A DARK SUIT SHAKING HANDS WITH DUCATI MD MONTANA). ALSO PRESENT, CALCAGNILE AND, YET AGAIN, TAGLIONI, DESIGNER OF THIS SUPER BIKE. A SPARE ENGINE STANDS READY ON THE STAND. THE BIKE IS NOW PART OF A JAPANESE COLLECTION. BELOW, THE APOLLO DISPLAYED AT THE DAYTONA SHOW IN 1965. COMPARED WITH THE FIRST PROTOTYPE THERE WERE A LOT OF CHANGES. THE COLOUR SCHEME, HORN, SADDLE UPHOLSTERY WERE DIFFERENT AND THE HANDLEBARS WERE LOWER. BELOW, LEFT, AN EXCELLENT VIEW OF THE POWER HOUSE. THE ELECTRICAL EQUIPMENT AND THE STARTER MOTOR WERE TAKEN FROM A CAR, A FIAT 1100.

GP 125 Four

In 1965 Ducati worked on a Grand Prix 125. This was not a desmo single but a four cylinder designed to combat the dominance of Japanese makers who had just entered the World Championship arena with great ambitions. Taglioni designed an air-cooled, DOHC straight four. Desmo valve gear was sacrificed for reasons of space. The engine had 16 valves, 4 per cylinder, actuated by springs and camshafts driven by a gear train. The trade press at the time reported that the four cylinder (with a twin-tube cradle frame) was shortly to race under the colours of Mototrans, Ducati's Spanish affiliate. The 125/4 was photographed at the Modena race track with Franco Farné riding as works tester. On the test bench the engine delivered 23 hp at 14,000 rpm. The project progressed slowly but the bike never made it to the starting line. In the meantime the Honda five cylinder had made its debut and the 125 Ducati slid into oblivion. The bike and its engine were displayed at international shows and then found its way into the Riga Technical Museum in the USSR.

In 1989 it was recovered by an Italian collector who also purchased the frame which inexplicably had ended up in Yugoslavia. A curious note to end on: the engine was fitted to a kart and there are those who say they see it flash by on Via C. Ducati.

ABOVE, MECHANIC AND WORKS TEST RIDER FRANCO FARNÉ DURING INITIAL TESTING OF THE 125 FOUR. THIS WAS THE FIRST TIME OUT FOR THE BIKE AS THE LACK OF A FAIRING AND THE RIDER'S WORKADAY OVERALLS SHOW. LEFT, TWO VIEWS OF THE DUCATI ENGINE. IN THE TOP PHOTO NOTE THE FOUR COILS FITTED TO THE FRAME DOWN TUBES AND THE MISSING IGNITION COVER. THE COVER APPEARS ON THE ENGINE IN THE BOTTOM PHOTO.

Specification

ENGINE: Four-stroke, four cylinder. Air-cooled. Bore: 34.5 mm. Stroke: 34mm. Capacity: 124 cc. Compression ratio: 12:1. Double overhead camshaft valve gear. Maximum power: 23 hp at 14,000 rpm. Battery and distributor ignition. Gearbox: primary reduction by gears. Chain final drive. Wet, multi-plate clutch. Eight-speed gearbox. Lubrication: forced wet sump. FRAME, FORKS AND RUNNING GEAR: twin-tube, cradle tubular steel. Front telescopic forks. Swinging arm rear suspension with twin shocks. Front and rear drum brakes. Tyres: 2.50 x 18" (front), 3.00 x 18" (rear). WEIGHT (dry): 85 kg.

HAIR BLOWING IN
THE WIND, BLUE
OVERALLS. WORKS
TESTER FRANCO
FARNÉ EXPERIENCES
THE THRILL OF
RIDING THE DUCATI
FOUR. FARNÉ WAS
ONE OF THE LUCKY
FEW BECAUSE THE
BIKE NEVER MADE IT
TO THE RACE TRACK.

1965

The motorcycles that made history

Mach 1 250

THE MACH 1 EPITOMISED ITALIAN SPORTS BIKES OF THE SIXTIES. SLIM, LIGHT AND NO FRILLS. NOTHING EXAGGERATED, JUST A GOOD, ALL ROUND BALANCE. THERE WERE NO SHORTAGE OF SUGGESTIONS FOR TUNING THE ENGINE. THE TOP SPEED OF THE PRODUCTION VERSION COULD BE PUSHED TO 170 KPH WITH THE TUNING OPTIONALS OFFERED BY DUCATI. TUNING ACCESSORIES INCLUDED A STRAIGHT-THROUGH EXHAUST AND A CAMSHAFT WITH "MEANER" CAM ANGLES.

Mach I is a term used in aeronautics to indicate the speed of sound. This splendid 250 series narrow sump was not that fast but it certainly did go. The engine was based on the well-known SOHC 175. The Mach I boasted a five-speed gearbox, something of a rarity at the time, and became the dream machine of thousands of sports bike fans. The Mach I had a clean, streamlined look, set-back footrests, clip-ons and a narrow sports saddle with a raised end enhancing the sports look. The shock absorbers were adjustable and the throttle grip had a set screw for adjusting the return speed. All in all, plenty of sports features at a time when there were not many around. The bike was uncomfortable to ride especially on rough roads but Mach I customers were more interested in the thrills of 24 hp at 8,500 rpm and a five-speed box. The first four ratios were close; fifth had a long ratio and was what was then known as a "cruising" or overdrive gear. The tyres seemed to be the wrong size and type but they were the same CEAT's that had been used on desmo machines until the end of the Fifties. On the straight and on narrow winding roads the Mach I had superb road holding, was a joy to handle and for many motorcyclists remains a wonderful memory. *Motociclismo*

DUCATI «Mach 1» 250

summed up its road test report with these words: "The latest model from this illustrious Marque is without doubt one of the best sports 250s available today, for its technical features, style and rideability. Particularly noteworthy are the powerful SOHC engine with five-speed gearbox, powerful acceleration, excellent road holding and efficient braking."

Specification

ENGINE: Four-stroke single-cylinder, with 10º forward angle configuration. Air-cooled. Single overhead camshaft, twin valves with gear shaft/helical valve gear. Bore: 74 mm. Stroke: 57.8 mm. Capacity: 248.5 cc. Compression ratio: 10:1. Maximum power: 24 hp at 8,500 rpm. Dellorto SS 29 A carburettor with choke trumpet intake. Contact breaker ignition with 6 volt 13.5 Ah battery. Gearbox: primary reduction by gears. Chain final drive. Wet, multi-plate clutch. Five-speed gearbox. FRAME, FORKS AND RUNNING GEAR: single, open cradle frame in tubular steel. Front telescopic forks. Swinging arm rear suspension with twin, 3-way adjustable shocks. Drum brakes: 180 mm (front) and 160 mm (rear). Tyres: 2.50 x 18" (front), 2.75 x 18" (rear). DIMENSIONS AND WEIGHT: Length: 2,000 mm. Width: 590 mm. Seat height: 760 mm. Wheelbase: 1,350 mm. Weight (dry): 116 kg. Performance: top speed 170 kph (with sports tuning); 65 kph in 1st, 96 kph in 2nd, 122 kph in 3rd, 150 in 4th.

ABOVE LEFT, THIS REAR VIEW OF THE MACH 1 CLEARLY SHOWS JUST HOW SMALL AND NARROW THE REAR TYRE WAS:

2.75 x 18". ABOVE RIGHT, THE SLIM LINE FRONT SECTION ALSO ENABLED THE BIKE TO REACH **140** KPH IN FOURTH; FIFTH GEAR RATIO WAS TOO LONG AND SERVED MAINLY AS AN "OVERDRIVE".

ABOVE, THIS SIDE VIEW SHOWS THE CONTORTED SHAPE OF THE KICK START, NECESSARY TO AVOID THE SET-BACK FOOTREST: THE LARGE STAND SEEMS TO CLASH WITH THE OTHERWISE LEAN SPORTS LINES OF THE BIKE. BELOW LEFT, THE VERY NARROW (**59** CM) CLIP-ONS AND THE STEERING DAMPER MOUNTED ON THE STEERING HEAD. INSTRUMENTATION WAS REDUCED TO THE BASICS,

JUST THIS SPEEDO/REV COUNTER, A TYPICAL DESIGN CHOICE FOR THE TIMES. RIGHT, FRANCO FARNÉ ON A PROMOTIONAL TOUR IN THE UNITED STATES, HERE RIDING A **250** RACING RIG. THE ENGINE HAS A LARGE NON-STANDARD SUMP WHICH EXPLAINS THE TWIN-TUBE CLOSED CRADLE FRAME.

BRUNO SPAGGIARI RACES TO VICTORY AT BILBAO ON HIS 125 DESMO TWIN.

70

1966 The Spanish connection

In business since 1957, Mototrans was more than just a Ducati importer. Encouraged by successful sales (in the mid-'60s it was close on the heels of Bultaco and Montesa), it developed its own bikes, inspired by the Ducatis, including the "narrow crank case" SOHC single-cylinders and, the "wide crank case" versions, especially the 250 and 350 cc models, sold until 1982. Also worthy of notice were ambitious projects such as the 4-cylinder GP and the single-cylinder 24 Horas and "256", with bore and stroke different to those used by Ducati. Mototrans has always worked on two-stroke engines, proposing light-weight motorcycles and mopeds for the Spanish market. Its sporting interests are notable: from the '60s, Mototrans bikes dominated the Spanish racing circuit, with riders Farné, Villa and Spaggiari. The Ducatis won at Bilbao, La Coruna, Vallodolid and Seville, but above all in the 24 Hour Montjuich race.

L'attività della Ducati spagnola

ABOVE, ANOTHER EXAMPLE OF INDEPENDENT WORK FROM MOTOTRANS: THE 4-VALVE SOHC CYLINDER HEAD WITH TWIN CARBURETTOR. DUCATI DIRECTLY SUPPLIED COMPETITION MATERIAL. MANY SPECIAL "COMPONENTS" FROM THE DUCATI RACING DEPARTMENT WERE SENT TO SPAIN FROM THE SIXTIES ONWARDS.

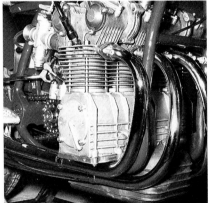

ABOVE, THE GRAN PREMIO FOUR-CYLINDER BIKE DEVELOPED BY SPANISH FIRM MOTOTRANS IN 1965, IN THE 250 AND 350 CC VERSIONS, WITH DOHC VALVE GEAR. DESIGNED BY ITALIAN ENGINEER AULO SAVELLI, THIS BIKE, WHICH NEVER GOT PAST THE PROTOTYPE STAGE, IS NOT CONSIDERED A DUCATI, BUT RATHER AN INDEPENDENT CREATION FROM THE SPANISH FIRM. RIGHT, ANOTHER VIEW OF THE 250 GRAN PREMIO. EVEN THE GREAT ANGEL NIETO, JUST STARTING OUT ON HIS CAREER, RACED FOR MOTOTRANS DURING THOSE YEARS.

THE JUNIOR 50 WITH FORCED AIR COOLING, DESIGNED AND MANUFACTURED IN SPAIN UNDER THE DUCATI MARQUE. RIDDEN "SIN MATRICULA, SIN CARNET", ROUGHLY TRANSLATED: "WITH NEITHER A NUMBER PLATE NOR A LICENCE".

Monza Junior 160

Designed mainly with the US market in mind, rather than a racebike, the Monza 160 was a small custom bike which arrived on the scene way ahead of its time. Around the SOHC engine, characterised by a bore and stroke measuring 61 x 52 mm (151 cc), Ducati fitted running gear and fairings to suit the tastes of the North American public. The bike has "Western" or "cow-horn" handlebars and a square 15 litre fuel tank. The Monza Junior used 16" tyres — a truly unusual choice for Ducati during that period. Despite the modifications to adapt it to the US style, this single-cylinder bike retains the "true" Ducati features, with optimum handling on and off the road, and safe braking. The engine, derived from the 125 SOHC, had a maximum power of 11 hp. *Motociclismo* pointed out that in '66 Ducati was the only Italian manufacturer whose catalogue included a bike with this type of valve gear. Other manufacturers tended towards simpler, cheaper solutions, such as rocker arms and pushrods, or two-stroke engines.

DUCATI «Monza Junior» 160

EASY RIDER - THE CULT FILM FOR FANS OF THE FREEDOM OF BIKE TRAVEL - HAD STILL NOT BEEN MADE, BUT A SMALL CUSTOM BIKE WAS ALREADY INCLUDED IN THE DUCATI CATALOGUE. TOP, THE "COW-HORN" HANDLEBARS WHICH LITERALLY SCANDALISED PURIST SUPPORTERS OF THE ITALIAN-STYLE BIKE, USED TO HANDLING THE AWKWARD "CLIP-ON HANDLEBARS" ON ALL OF THE DUCATI SPORT BIKES WHICH WERE SOLD IN ITALY AND EUROPE.

Specification

ENGINE: Four-stroke single-cylinder, with 10° forward angle configuration. Light alloy cylinder head and block (with cast-iron liner). Bore: 61 mm. Stroke: 52 mm. Capacity: 151.97 cc. Compression ratio: 9:1. Single overhead camshaft, twin valves with gear shaft/helical valve gear. Dellorto UB 22 BS carburettor with 22 mm choke. Fuel tank capacity: 15 litres. Maximum power: 11 hp at 8,500 rpm. Torque: not available. Contact breaker ignition with HT coil. Electrical equipment with 6V-30W alternator and 6 volt 13.5 Ah battery. Wet sump forced lubrication with gear pump, 2.4 litres oil. Wet, multi-plate clutch. 4-speed gearbox. FRAME, FORKS AND RUNNING GEAR: Simplex open cradle tubular steel frame. Front hydraulic telescopic forks. Swinging arm rear suspension with hydraulic shocks. Full width drum brakes. Tyres: 2.75 x 16" (front), 3.25 x 16" (rear). DIMENSIONS AND WEIGHT: Length: 1,915 mm. Width: 800 mm. Seat height: 785 mm. Wheelbase: 1,300 mm. Weight (dry): 108 kg. PERFORMANCE: Top speed 110 kph; 40 kph in 1st, 68 kph in 2nd, 95 kph in 3rd. Max gradient: 26%.

DUCATI
OUTBOARD ENGINES FOR SPORT AND FISHING BOATS. WITH THE EXCEPTION OF THE CUCCIOLO 5, A TWO-STROKE, SINGLE-CYLINDER 94 CC ENGINE, ALL OF THE OTHER ENGINES WERE TWO-STROKE TWINS. BELOW, THE SIDE STAND MOST APPRECIATED BY AMERICAN BIKERS REAPPEARED ON THE SCRAMBLER.

RIGHT, THE TOP CUBIC CAPACITY REACHED BY NARROW CASE ENGINES WAS REPRESENTED BY THE SEBRING 350 CC, ANOTHER BIKE WITH AMERICAN TRIM. THE VERSION SEEN HERE WAS RESERVED FOR "PUBLIC SERVICES", ACCORDING TO THE CAPTION USED THIRTY-FIVE YEARS AGO BY AN ANONYMOUS ARCHIVE WORKER. NOTICE THE TOP, ANTI-DAZZLE SECTION OF THE WINDSCREEN, THE LIGHT FITTED THROUGH THE WINDSCREEN'S WATER RESISTANT CANVAS AND THE CRASH BARS.

ABOVE, THE SPORTY 50 SL/1, WITH ITS INCREDIBLE EXTENDED FUEL TANK WHICH HAS TWO BAYONET CLIP CAPS AND A BREATHER WHICH CARRIES OIL RESIDUES FROM THE STURDY TWO-STROKE ENGINE AWAY FROM THE RIDER.

1968 SAW THE RETURN OF THE MOTOGIRO, ALTHOUGH IT WAS VERY DIFFERENT TO THE RACE WHICH CAPTURED THE IMAGINATION OF THE NATION A DECADE EARLIER. MORE THAN ANYTHING, IT SEEMED TO BE AN OFF-ROAD BIKE RACE, SPICED UP BY SPECIAL TRACK TRIALS. AGAIN, THE DUCATIS DID WELL.
IN THE PHOTO: MASSIMO VARIATI, FOURTEENTH OVERALL AND WINNER OF GROUP C ON A PRACTICALLY STANDARD DUCATI 250. ON THIS OCCASION, VARIATI WAS HAILED AS A REVELATION, SINCE HE HAD NO PRIOR RACING EXPERIENCE.

1967 Racing singles

During these years, although Ducati did not show an official interest in World Championship races, its bikes abounded at the start lines of many Italian and international competitions. Customised bikes, interesting Special models, updated Gran Premio versions — these were the tools of the trade for a generation of riders which fought it out with the Japanese machines which continued to appear on the tracks in ever increasing numbers. Courageous duels and memorable sporting feats came thick and fast, thrilling the public and contributing to the Ducati legend. In the opinion of many mechanics, it was impossible for "the same engine" to be used on a racebike and on the more subdued touring models. Yet Borgo Panigale's mechanics and the team of experts in the sector who used Ducati materials managed to reconcile the requirements with this "miracle". It was, perhaps a "lesser" historical achievement, but was fascinating all the same.

1965, CERVIA - MILANO MARITTIMA TRACK: SPAGGIARI (DUCATI NUMBER 54) AHEAD OF THE BECCACCINO 125 RIDDEN BY FRANCESCO VILLA (LAPPED THREE TIMES DUE TO MECHANICAL PROBLEMS) AND MEDRANO'S BULTACO.

ABOVE, OFFICIAL PHOTO OF THE DELIVERY OF NEW DUCATIS TO THE VIGILI URBANI (MUNICIPAL POLICE) OF BOLOGNA, ALWAYS LOYAL CUSTOMERS OF THE BORGO PANIGALE FIRM.

TOP PHOTO, EUGENIO LAZZARINI IN ACTION ON THE PESARO TRACK IN '65. AT THE END OF THE RACE HE WAS SECOND IN THE 125 CATEGORY.

RIGHT, A BEAUTIFUL 1966 SPECIAL, THE FIVE-SPEED SOHC BIKE WITH TWIN IGNITION ON WHICH FACTORY TESTER FRANCO FARNÉ RACED. THE ENGINE WAS SAID TO DEVELOP A MAXIMUM POWER OF 32 HP AT 10,500 RPM AND THE BIKE WEIGHED-IN AT JUST 87 KG.

THE NEW GEAR FOR THE CLUTCH ON THE SINGLE-CYLINDER SOHCs, AS ADVERTISED BY US IMPORTER BERLINER MOTOR CORPORATION.

Cadet 125

"We would like to begin by pointing out that the Ducati Cadet, at a cost of 149,000 lire, ex-works, is the cheapest 4-stroke of this class available on the Italian market." This was the start of Roberto Patrignani's report on the road test published by *Motociclismo* in 1967. Thus, no technical or sporting reference to the Ducati Marque: this was the people's bike, a safe 125 for the trip to work or school. The special feature of the engine with rocker arm and pushrod valve gear is the presence of parallel valves (the other Ducati with this technical feature was the Cucciolo moped). At a truly competitive price, close to those of the more sophisticated sporty mopeds, here was a reliable bike that would travel 37 km on one litre of fuel and reach speeds of 90 km/h. The engine was flexible and silent, although the tester at the time, who already boasted good sporting results, probably preferred a hp at least double that of the Cadet. Its steady engine didn't top 5 hp at 6,500 rpm!

Specification

ENGINE: Four-stroke single-cylinder, with 25° forward angle configuration. Light alloy cylinder head and block (with cast-iron liner). Bore: 53 mm. Stroke: 55 mm. Capacity: 121.3 cc. Compression ratio: 9:1. Twin parallel valves with rocker arm and pushrod valve gear. Dellorto ME 18 BS carburettor with 18 mm choke. Fuel tank capacity: 11.6 litres. Maximum power: 5 hp at 6,500 rpm. Torque: not available. Magneto flywheel ignition with HT coil. Electrical equipment with 6V-28W alternator and 6 volt 13.5 Ah battery. Wet sump forced lubrication with gear pump, 0.8 kg oil. Wet, multi-plate clutch. 4-speed gearbox. FRAME, FORKS AND RUNNING GEAR: Duplex closed cradle tubular steel frame. Semi-hydraulic/mechanical forks. Swinging arm rear suspension with hydraulic shocks. Full width drum brakes. Tyres: 2.50 x 18" (front), 2.75 x 18" (rear). DIMENSIONS AND WEIGHT: Length: 1,790 mm. Width: 660 mm. Seat height: 770 mm. Wheelbase: 1,165 mm. Weight (dry): 72 kg. PERFORMANCE: Top speed 95 kph; 29 kph in 1st, 48 kph in 2nd, 70 kph in 3rd. Max gradient: 25%.

DEAR DUCATI FANS,
IT'S SOMETIMES DIFFICULT TO RECOGNISE
THE SPECIFICATIONS OF A MODEL
WITH OUR FAVOURITE MARQUE. THE
PROTOTYPES AND PREPRODUCTION
MODELS WERE OFTEN VERY DIFFERENT TO
THE FINAL ONES - OR OFFICIAL PHOTOS
WERE HEAVILY RETOUCHED,
WHILST OTHERS SHOWED MODELS
DESIGNED FOR FOREIGN MARKETS.
TOP LEFT, THE "LUSSO" MODEL WITH
ROUND HEADLIGHT, THREE COLOURS
AND REAR-VIEW MIRROR. NOTICE THE
FUEL TANK'S BAYONET CLIP CAP,
FITTED BACK-TO-FRONT IN THE
INTERESTS OF SAFETY. THE LONG
LEVER POINTING IN THE DIRECTION
OF THE RIDER WAS NOT ACCEPTED IN
ALL COUNTRIES.
LEFT, A PREPRODUCTION MODEL ON
DISPLAY IN A SHOWROOM IN '66: THE
BIKE IS BLACK AND WHITE, WITH A
POLISHED TAPPET COVER AND
PAINTED CYLINDER. TOP RIGHT, THE
CADET 125 USED FOR OUR TESTS

AND, BELOW, THE ENGINE WHICH, DUE TO
THE CASING, RESEMBLES THE TWO-STROKES
OF THAT PERIOD. THE MOST UNUSUAL
FEATURE OF THIS ENGINE IS THE POSITION
OF THE (PARALLEL) VALVES, AN UNUSUAL
CHOICE FOR DUCATI.

77

1968 The arrival of the "wide casings"

In '68 Ducati made official a radical change that began in '66: a new generation of single-cylinder SOHC bikes had arrived, the "wide case". Whilst the basic architecture of the engine remained similar to that of its predecessors, the two crankcase halves (in aluminium alloy) were larger. The new engines could be recognised by the wider fittings for the rear frame and the bigger oil sump (2.5 kg as opposed to 2). The starting mechanism and many internal components also changed, and resembled those of the "narrow case" engines in appearance only (bench bearings, clutch, valve drive shaft). The "wide case" engines went down in history as the most powerful, advanced Ducati singles. They were produced for a long period, which extended into the early Eighties, thanks to Mototrans, and were soon fitted with a desmo head, which made this engine the best single of its time.

ABOVE, THE RARE 1968 VERSION WITH DIFFERENT CENTRAL SECTION OF THE FRAME.

ABOVE, THE PROTOTYPE OF THE T/TS 450. CHARACTERISED BY THE "WIDE CASE" ENGINE AND TOURING TRIM, THIS BIKE BECAME THE MODEL USED FOR MANY YEARS BY THE "GUFI" (OWLS), THE BOLOGNESE NICKNAME FOR THE MUNICIPAL POLICE. BELOW, A RARITY: THE CONDOR 350, A SWISS BIKE MADE FOR THE LOCAL ARMY. ALTHOUGH THE BIKE BORE THE MARQUE OF THE SWISS COMPANY ON THE CRANKCASE, IT WAS IN FACT A DUCATI. CONDOR ALSO BUILT OTHER MILITARY BIKES, USING AN 800 CC BOXER TWIN INSPIRED BY BMW. THE 350 APPEARED DURING THE FIRST HALF OF THE SEVENTIES.

RIGHT, THE MAGNIFICENT 1969 MARK 3 D VERSION WITH DESMODROMIC HEAD. A FINE IMPRESSION IS MADE BY THE TWO FUEL TANK FILLER CAPS, THE REV COUNTER (ON SOME MODELS), SPEEDO AND A FAIRING SUPPORT - ALREADY SEEN ON THE RARE MARK 3 WITH VALVE SPRINGS - AND THE HEADLIGHT COVER WITH MINI WINDSCREEN.

"WONDERFULLY SPARTAN", A SLOGAN STILL VALID MANY YEARS ON. THIS BIKE WAS ONE OF THE MOST BEAUTIFUL "WIDE CASE" ENGINES EVER MADE, THE 1971 DESMO.

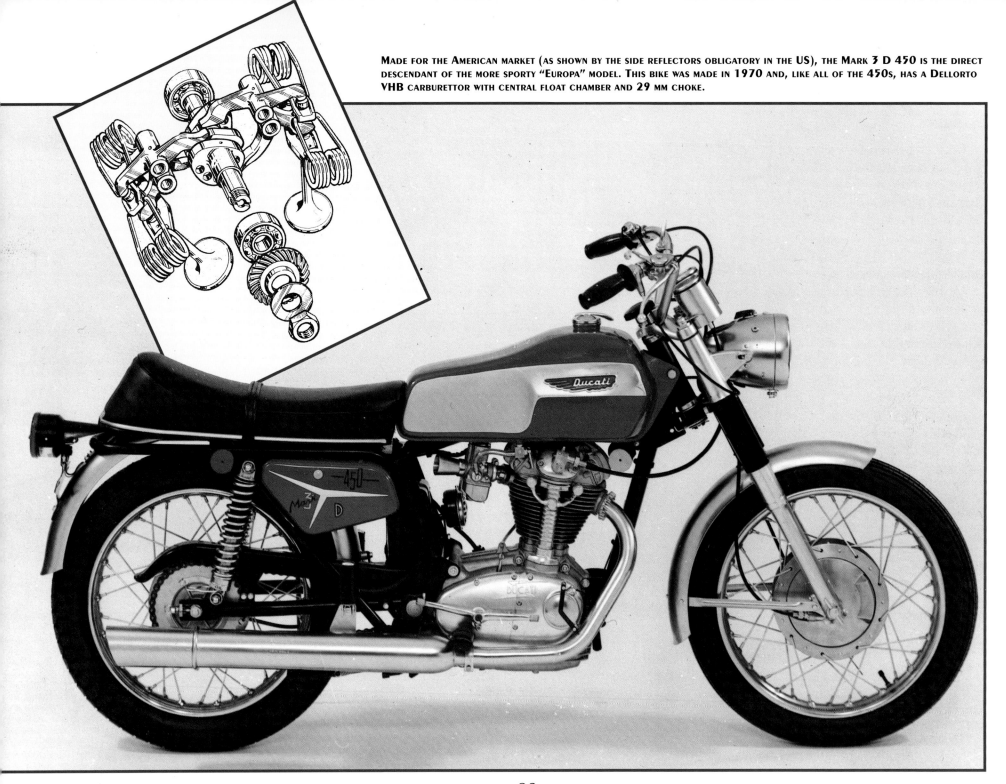

MADE FOR THE AMERICAN MARKET (AS SHOWN BY THE SIDE REFLECTORS OBLIGATORY IN THE US), THE MARK 3 D 450 IS THE DIRECT DESCENDANT OF THE MORE SPORTY "EUROPA" MODEL. THIS BIKE WAS MADE IN 1970 AND, LIKE ALL OF THE 450s, HAS A DELLORTO VHB CARBURETTOR WITH CENTRAL FLOAT CHAMBER AND 29 MM CHOKE.

1968 Scrambler and Desmo arrive

The long-awaited news arrived midway through the year: Ducati was to manufacture and sell to the public the latest "wide case" version of its SOHC bikes, fitting them with a desmo cylinder head. The first to arrive on the market was the Mark 3, in the spring of '69; the 350 version, with rev counter (although not all bikes had one... this being one of the mysteries of the time), broke many hearts. This was a crucial period for the Company, as demonstrated by the arrival of similar 250 and 450 cc versions. But Ducati's fervour didn't stop here: the prototype of a 500 twin-cylinder bike with slanting engine and rocker arm and pushrod valve gear had been known of for some time. Meanwhile, the Scrambler debuted, a bike with revolutionary design, dubbed by some the usual "American-style". Not long afterwards, the critics were forced to publicly recognise their mistake: the Scrambler turned out to be one of Ducati's all-time best sellers.

"Desmo" e bicilindriche in programma alla Ducati

FARNÉ, LEFT, AND SPAGGIARI "CHECK OVER" THE PROTOTYPE OF THE 500 TWIN SLANTING ENGINE MODEL WITH ROCKER ARM AND PUSHROD VALVE GEAR. THIS BIKE WEIGHED 180 KG, DEVELOPED A MAXIMUM OF 36 HP AND TOPPED SPEEDS OF 160 KM/H. THE PROTOTYPE OBVIOUSLY WASN'T TOO CONVINCING, AND WAS SOON SET ASIDE. THE "PARALLEL TWIN" DESIGN REAPPEARED IN ANOTHER FORM SEVERAL YEARS LATER, AGAIN WITH LITTLE SUCCESS.

LEFT, THE '69 EUROPEAN VERSION SCRAMBLER 450. COMPARED WITH THAT MADE FOR THE US, THIS VERSION HAD DIFFERENT REAR LIGHT AND A SMOOTH RATHER THAN GROOVED AIR FILTER CASING. IT WAS AN OVERWHELMING SUCCESS ON BOTH SIDES OF THE ATLANTIC. THE CYLINDER HEAD WAS CONVENTIONAL RATHER THAN DESMODROMIC.

ABOVE, THE MARK 3 D 250 FROM 1970, WITH CARBURETTOR WITH CENTRAL FLOAT CHAMBER. THE EARLY MODELS HAD A DELLORTO SSI WITH SIDE FLOAT CHAMBER AND 27 MM CHOKE.

WITH THE EXCEPTION OF A FEW SPECIALS MADE IN RECENT YEARS, THE PEAK IN THE SPORTING DEVELOPMENT OF THE SINGLE-CYLINDER DESMO WAS THIS 450 PREPARED FOR BRUNO SPAGGIARI, WHO USED IT DURING THE 1970 RACING SEASON. NOTICE THE 42 MM SS CARBURETTOR AND THE SWINGING ARM SUSPENSION WITH RIBBED BRACING.

NINETEEN SIXTY NINE, CESENATICO TRACK, 350 CLASS: ON THE LONG STRAIGHT OF THE SEA-FRONT, SPAGGIARI LEADS THE
AERMACCHIS RIDDEN BY BERGAMONTI AND MILANI. THE MAIN DANGER WAS THE PINE TREE'S ROOTS (WHICH DEFORMED THE ASPHALT,
CAUSING SUBSIDENCE) AND RESIN, FACTORS WHICH REALLY PUT A BIKE'S RUNNING GEAR TO THE TEST.

1968 The Romagna Time Trials

The races run at the start of the season at Cesenatico, Cervia, Rimini, Riccione, but also at Modena and Imola (with an Autumn extra at Sanremo) were a unique occasion for manufacturers and riders who wanted to experiment with new developments, or get back into the swing of things after the winter. The best Italians raced (fighting it out for the national title), against the best foreigners, drawn to the Riviera in search of glory and contracts. At last, it was possible to take a closer look at the increasingly competitive Japanese bikes which challenged Italian models and riders. Whilst their presence in the World Championship was increasingly limited, the Ducatis participated en masse in these races, especially the 250 and 350 categories, with state of the art SOHC singles. Miracles do happen! For example, Spaggiari on a 4-stroke SOHC managed to stay ahead of Phil Read on the two-stroke Yamaha.

LEFT, A SPLENDID ACTION PHOTO OF BRUNO SPAGGIARI, AN EXPERT RIDER WHO EVEN UNSETTLED PASOLINI AND AGOSTINI WITH HIS DUCATI 350, ESPECIALLY ON THE MORE WINDING TRACKS OR WHERE GRIP WAS LIMITED.

TOP RIGHT, AN EXAMPLE OF SPORT SPONSORSHIP IN THE SIXTIES: THE DUCATI 250 RIDDEN BY PARLOTTI, A MEMBER OF THE SCUDERIA AMARO MONTENEGRO TEAM. RIGHT, BRUNO SPAGGIARI (54) AND BRITISH CHAMPION PHIL READ ON THE YAMAHA IN A THRILLING DUEL ON THE WET ASPHALT OF THE IMOLA TRACK, 1968.

ABOVE, SPAGGIARI COMPETES AGAINST TEAM-MATE PARLOTTI AT RICCIONE.

THE DUCATIS WERE TOPS EVEN AT "LOWER" SPEEDS: HERE WE SEE BARONCINI, WINNER OF THE JUNIOR CLASS 250 CHAMPIONSHIP HELD IN MODENA IN '69. THESE YEARS SAW THE ARRIVAL OF THE BEST DUCATI ENGINE SPECIALISTS; SOME RIDERS RACED THEIR BIKES UNTIL THE END OF THE SEVENTIES. THESE INCLUDED BRETTONI AND PERUZZI, EXPERT TUSCAN "HILL-CLIMBERS".

Mark 3 Desmo 350

THE FIRST VERSION OF THE MARK 3 DESMO, TESTED BY *MOTOCICLISMO* IN APRIL 1969. THE STYLE IS SPLENDID: NOTICE THE PROTECTED REV COUNTER SUPPORT AND THE NUMBER PLATE WITH SMALL TRANSPARENT WINDSCREEN. UNDER IDEAL CONDITIONS, THIS BIKE REACHED CLOSE ON 165 KM/H.

"This bike is obviously not intended for a vast public, being a rare example of sporting mechanics, which only the motorcycle élite deserve to own. Those who do obtain one must preserve it with care: in the distant future, as a vintage bike, it will be priceless, since it will go down in history as one of the most famous desmodromics ever sold". These were the words of *Motociclismo*'s prophetic tester, surprised when he started up the Mark 3. He expected a bike that would be difficult to handle, surly and disagreeable, yet kick-starting proved easy, the idling speed low and well timed. On the move, it was a true sport bike, with a very quick engine and running gear that withstood even the most difficult conditions. The Mark 3 Desmo had powerful brakes, was perhaps not so quiet and vibrated, but was a pleasure to ride. The single-cylinder series with desmo head was improved upon year-by-year: '71 saw the arrival of the beautiful Desmo (with metallised silver paintwork), whilst '73/74 brought the latest version (in bright yellow ochre) with electronic ignition (although the kick-starter remained) and, as an optional, with 280 mm Brembo disc front brake. This bike was an excellent starting point for the sport Specials.

Specification

ENGINE: Four-stroke single-cylinder, with 10° forward angle configuration. Light alloy cylinder head and block (with cast-iron liner). Bore: 76 mm. Stroke: 75 mm. Capacity: 340.2 cc. Compression ratio: 9.5:1. Desmodromic SOHC camshaft, twin valves with gear shaft/helical valve gear. Dellorto SSI 29D carburettor with 29 mm choke. Fuel tank capacity: 13 litres. Maximum power: 30 hp at 8,000 rpm. Torque: not available. Contact breaker ignition with HT coil. Electrical equipment with 6V-70W alternator and 6 volt 13.5 Ah battery. Wet sump forced lubrication with gear pump, 2.5 litres oil. Wet, multi-plate clutch. 5-speed gearbox. FRAME, FORKS AND RUNNING GEAR: Simplex open cradle tubular steel frame. Front hydraulic telescopic forks. Swinging arm rear suspension with adjustable hydraulic shocks. Full width drum brakes. Tyres: 2.50 x 18" (front), 3.00 x 18" (rear). DIMENSIONS AND WEIGHT: Length: 2,000 mm. Width: 590 mm. Seat height: 735 mm. Wheelbase: 1,360 mm. Weight (dry): 128 kg. PERFORMANCE: Top speed 165 kph; 65 kph in 1st, 96 kph in 2nd, 122 kph in 3rd, 145 kph in 4th.

Two views of the beautiful Mark 3; the front view clearly illustrates the narrow profile which allowed this bike to reach high speeds. The carburettor is a Dellorto SSI 29, whilst sports riders substituted the original silencer with larger versions to gain extra power. Below, a moment from the road test published by *Motociclismo* in '69. At the time, the rider's clothing was not as professional as that used today, but when the bikes were pushed to the limit on the track at Monza, biking leathers and helmet were worn.

Above, the engine with desmodromic valve control which, according to Ducati, developed 30 HP at 8,000 RPM. During tests with a less restrictive silencer, much higher power ratings were recorded: over 36 HP at the crankshaft! This engine could be pushed to 10,000 RPM without mechanical problems.

1969/1975 The development of the Desmo singles

Despite the great success of the Japanese 4-cylinders which had invaded world markets from the start of the Seventies, the charm of the desmodromic singles still had a hold on many enthusiasts. Therefore, Ducati, although starting new projects, continued to develop the Desmos derived from the Mark 3. Nineteen seventy one saw the arrival of the Desmo, with its characteristic and, if the truth must be told, a little garish, metallised silver livery, followed, two years later by a bike with identical name, but painted in an attractive bright yellow and slightly modified. With the exception of the Mototrans bikes, on the scene since the Eighties, these were the last two Ducati sport singles produced.

LEFT, ON THE '71 MODEL, THE FOOT RESTS AND REAR BRAKE LEVER CAN BE FOLDED TO ALLOW THE PASSAGE OF THE STARTER LEVER.

BELOW, THE DESMO 350 (LIKE THE 250 AND 450) FROM '71 HAD A HIGH-CLASS MECHANICAL, RACING-STYLE VEGLIA BORLETTI REV COUNTER, CHOKE LEVER, TOMMASELLI THROTTLE AND A TWIN BRAKE LEVER FOR THE 4-CALIPER FRONT BRAKE. NOTICE THE CARBURETTOR WITH "NON-REGULATION" SIDE-MOUNTED FLOAT CHAMBER FITTED ON THIS MODEL.

IN '73 AN IMPORTANT CHANGE WAS MADE TO THE BOLOGNESE SINGLES: ELECTRONIC IGNITION WAS FITTED. ABOVE, THE CONTROL UNIT FIXED TO THE FRAME. ANOTHER DETAIL WAS THE IGNITION KEY ON THE HEADLIGHT. AS TO ITS PERFORMANCE, THE 350 DESMO WAS SAID TO HAVE A TOP SPEED OF 160 KM/H. WITH A STRAIGHT-THROUGH EXHAUST IT APPROACHED 170.

TOP, THE DESMO, WHICH REMAINED IN THE CATALOGUE - ALSO UPDATED - WITH THE 250, 350 AND 450 CC VERSIONS OF THE MARK 3. FITTED WITH ELECTRONIC IGNITION, THIS WAS THE LAST DUCATI TO EMPLOY THE ROCKER ARM GEAR CHANGE.

THE SINGLES PRODUCTION LINE WAS TRANSFERRED TO MOTOTRANS IN SPAIN DURING THE MID-SEVENTIES.

SHINY AND
SPARKLING, THE
SCRAMBLER
125 WAS
READY TO TAKE
ON THE LIGHT-
WEIGHT OFF-
ROAD RIVALS.
THE ENGINE
WAS A SOHC
WITH HELICAL
VALVE GEAR AND
A MAXIMUM
POWER OF
10 HP AT
8,000 RPM AT
THE AXLE,
ACCORDING TO
MOTOCICLISMO.
BUT THE GREAT
DIVIDE THAT
SEPARATED IT
FROM THE TWO-
STROKES THAT
RACED AND
WON IN OFF-
ROAD TRIALS
(AND OUTSIDE
THE HIGH
SCHOOLS...)
WAS
SIGNIFICANT,
AND SO IT DID
NOT SELL WELL.

1970

The little Scramblers and American fever

The start of the Seventies was a dynamic period at Ducati. The company continued to produce its sport bikes, but realised that something new was needed, and that it had to extend its range. Increasingly varied requests arrived from the US. The period of the gigantic Apollo had come to an end, and people wanted fast, responsive off-road bikes, this being the case in Italy too. By retouching some components and modifying others, Ducati managed to build two bikes of the same name but with significant differences, that were powered by very different engines: one was a two-stroke, the other a four-stroke! This certainly extended the range of products, but was not considered sufficient, and it was decided that a custom Ducati should be built, as a taste of things to come...

DUCATI E MULLER:
novità per il fuori-strada

Sempre più impegnata nel settore fuori-stradistico competitivo, la Muller ha realizzato anche una bella 125 da cross col motore Zündapp cinque marce, 19 CV a 7500 giri che ha già vittoriosamente esordito col prototipo. La strumentazione ciclistica è classica e robusta, col forcellone posteriore a sezione rettangolare. Pneumatici 2.50-21 ant. e 3.00-18 post., peso 98 chilogrammi, prezzo 520.000 lire.
Sulla linea della recente «RT-450, la Ducati ha invece creato la «Scrambler» 125 col famoso monoalbero a coppie coniche, ora potenziato a 10 CV a 8000 giri (alla ruota) e provvisto di cambio a cinque rapporti e carburatore a vaschetta incorporata. Anche in questo caso, il telaio è di classica e robusta impostazione; pneumatici 2.50-19 ant. e 3.50-18 post., peso 105 chilogrammi, prezzo 350.000 lire, strumentazione compresa.

La versione definitiva della Müller • Cross • 125.

La nuova Ducati • Scrambler • 125 col motore monoalbero.

MANY BIKERS DREAM OF THE MAGNIFICENT SPECIAL ON WHICH SPAGGIARI DUELLED WITH AGOSTINI'S MV, AND SOME DECIDED TO GO TO WORK ON THE DREAM.

IN '71 JOURNALIST BRUNO DE PRATO PREPARED THIS MARK 3 450 D, FITTING IT WITH FAIRINGS, CAMPAGNOLO FRONT DISC BRAKES (A RARITY AT THAT TIME) AND TUNING THE ENGINE. THE CARBURETTOR (ABOVE) WAS A "HUGE" DELLORTO SS 40, AND THE BASE OF THE FUEL TANK HAD TO BE MODIFIED IN ORDER TO FIT IT.

TOP, PHOTO FROM 1959: JOSEPH BERLINER, A US DUCATI IMPORTER, WELCOMED BY MONTANO, DUCATI GENERAL MANAGER. THE

BERLINER BROTHERS SIGNIFICANTLY INFLUENCED DUCATI HISTORY. PRESSURE ON THEIR PART LED TO FAILURES SUCH AS THE APOLLO, BUT ALSO SUCCESS STORIES SUCH AS THE SCRAMBLER. IN 1970, THE CLEVER COMBINATION OF PARTS FROM KNOWN BIKES CULMINATED IN THE PREPARATION OF TWO DELIGHTFUL SCRAMBLERS WITH A TWO-STROKE ENGINE, SPECIALLY MADE TO CASH IN ON THE NAME OF THE LARGER PREDECESSOR WHICH WAS, AT THAT TIME, SELLING LIKE HOT-CAKES. THE CADET FRAME WAS COMBINED WITH THE ENGINE OF THE 50 (SL TYPE) TO CREATE TWO BIKES: THE BORE AND STROKE OF THE 50 MEASURED 38.8 x 42 MM AND ITS CAPACITY WAS 49.66 CC. THE 100 HAD A BORE AND STROKE OF 52 x 46 AND CAPACITY 97.6 CC. THE POWER RATINGS WERE 4.5 HP FOR THE 50 (EXPORT VERSION) AND 7 HP FOR THE 100. THE TWO WERE PRACTICALLY IDENTICAL, THE 100 WEIGHING JUST 3 KG MORE THAN THE MOPED!

ANOTHER BIKE THAT ARRIVED FROM THE STATES WAS THE RT 450, INITIALLY DESIGNED AS A TRAIL BIKE, THEN CONVERTED FOR ROAD USE. AROUND 30 EXAMPLES OF A 350 CC VERSION WERE ALSO MADE, AT THE REQUEST OF ITALIAN DEALERSHIPS, BUT THE RT 350 NEVER APPEARED IN THE DUCATI CATALOGUE.

Scrambler 450

UNUSUAL AND ELEGANT, THE SCRAMBLER 450 (THE PHOTO SHOWS THE MODEL TESTED BY *MOTOCICLISMO* IN FEBRUARY 1970) FUELLED THE IMAGINATION OF ENTHUSIASTS WORLD-WIDE. ALSO MADE WITH 250 AND 350 CC ENGINES, ITS SALES FIGURES ROCKETED INTO THE THOUSANDS.

The Ducati Scrambler, designed for the US market, was much admired even in Italy. It was a fashionable bike, still popular today: thanks to an excellent engine, with satisfying performance and flawless running gear. Marcello Peruzzi, one of the top riders of Ducati singles during the '70s, had this to say about the running gear: "After unsuccessful trials with a special chrome-molybdenum frame, the engine, suspension, wheels and fairings were fitted on a Scrambler frame. It was immediately competitive." The Scrambler goes back a long way: in '62 the 200 Motocross version made its first appearance. Derived from a "wide case" road version, it was followed by the 250 Scrambler, again for Berliner, which was developed year after year and sold in Italy from '65 onwards. Nineteen sixty eight saw the arrival of the "wide casing" bikes, and the Scrambler's market success. The first models sold were 250 and 350 cc, characterised by carburettors with side float. In '69 – although Spaggiari began testing the prototype in '68 – the 450 cc version was brought out and was an immediate success. The explanation was simple: the Scrambler was attractive, easy to ride, with good handling both on and off the road. It was a bike that couldn't be pigeon-holed, yet today we would describe it as an enduro, but it hit the market ten years before its time. It was termed "a pleasant mix between the American and European schools of motorcycling...". How true!

DUCATI «Scrambler» 450
IMPRESSIONI DI GUIDA

Specification

ENGINE: Four-stroke single-cylinder, with 10° forward configuration. Light alloy cylinder head and block (with cast-iron liner). Bore: 87 mm. Stroke: 75 mm. Capacity: 436 cc. Compression ratio: 9.3:1. Single overhead camshaft, twin valves with gear shaft/helical valve gear. Dellorto VHB 29AD carburettor with 29 mm choke. Fuel tank capacity: 11 litres. Maximum power: 27 hp at 6,500 rpm. Torque: not available. Coil ignition. Electrical equipment with 6V-70W alternator and 6 volt 13.5 Ah battery. Wet sump forced lubrication with gear pump, 2.2 litres oil. Wet, multi-plate clutch. 5-speed gearbox. FRAME, FORKS AND RUNNING GEAR: Simplex open cradle tubular frame. Front hydraulic telescopic forks. Swinging arm rear suspension with adjustable shocks. Full width drum brakes. Tyres: 3.50 x 19" (front), 4.00 x 18" (rear). DIMENSIONS AND WEIGHT: Length: 2,120 mm. Width: 940 mm. Seat height: 770 mm. Wheelbase: 1,380 mm. Weight: 145 kg. PERFORMANCE: Top speed 130 kph; 45 kph in 1st, 65 kph in 2nd, 85 kph in 3rd, 110 in 4th.

WITH AGILE, YET STABLE RUNNING GEAR (THE WHEELBASE WAS 1,380 MM) AND A POWERFUL ENGINE (MAXIMUM POWER 27 HP AT 6,500 RPM IN 1970), THIS WAS A GUARANTEED ENJOYABLE RIDING EXPERIENCE, EVEN THOUGH THE VIBRATIONS WERE EVIDENT. AS TO THE BRAKING, MANY JAPANESE ENDURO BIKES PRESENTED TEN YEARS ON HAD MUCH INFERIOR BRAKING... TOP LEFT, "TOP" VIEW OF THE DASHBOARD, CLEARLY SHOWING THE INCREDIBLE HANDLEBARS, NO LESS THAN 94 CM WIDE. THE INSTRUMENTS WERE MADE BY BRITISH FIRM SMITHS. IT WAS ALSO FITTED WITH A STEERING DAMPER AND FOAM HANDLEBAR GRIPS TO REDUCE THE VIBRATIONS. SIDE, THE AIR FILTER WITH PAPER FILTER. SOME MODELS HAD THE DELLORTO F 20 FILTER WITH STEEL WOOL.

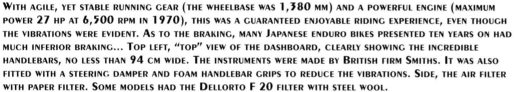

ABOVE, ONE OF THE FIRST SCRAMBLERS, THE 250 WITH NARROW CASE ENGINE AND UNUSUAL TRIM. NOTICE THE STRAIGHT-THROUGH EXHAUST AND THE FUEL TANK STILL WITHOUT THE CHARACTERISTIC CHROME SIDE-PANELS. LEFT, THE SHOCK SPRING PRELOADING COULD BE ADJUSTED BETWEEN THREE POSITIONS USING THE SPECIAL LEVER. BELOW, THE IMPOSING 436 CC SINGLE (WITH BORE AND STROKE 86 x 75 MM), WITH THE DELLORTO VHB 29 AD CARBURETTOR AND THE DECOMPRESSOR CLEARLY SHOWN. ALL OF THE 450S WERE FITTED WITH CARBURETTORS WITH CENTRAL FLOAT CHAMBER. IT WAS RELATIVELY EASY TO START THE 250 AND 350 ENGINES. THE PROCEDURE FOR STARTING THE MODEL WITH A LARGER ENGINE WAS DECIDEDLY PROFESSIONAL, ALWAYS REQUIRING USE OF THE DECOMPRESSOR AND ACCURATE ADJUSTMENT OF THE SPARK ADVANCE.

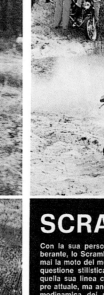

SCRAMBLER

Con la sua personalità scanzonata ed esuberante, lo Scrambler DUCATI è ora più che mai la moto del momento e non solo per una questione stilistica e di moda derivante da quella sua linea così fresca, estrosa e sempre attuale, ma anche perché l'efficienza termodinamica dei motori di cui può essere equipaggiato assicura prestazioni brillanti e consumi decisamente modesti in assoluto ed ancora più in relazione alla cilindrata.
E poi perché nonostante i limiti di velocità lo Scrambler è sempre una macchina godibile fino in fondo, per la sua brillante accelerazione e per la sua manegevolezza e stabilità.
Sul misto è favolosa.
E anche in città, per affrancarsi dalla morsa del traffico, per avere più tempo libero, per reagire alla nevrosi che ci attanaglia quando siamo lì, in fila, chiusi dentro le nostre scatolette a 4 ruote.
E se poi si vuole andare in campagna, per i sentieri, per i prati, in completa libertà lo Scrambler sa fare anche questo.
Lo Scrambler dà uno stile nuovo alla nostra personalità, alla nostra libertà.

1970 Ducati Power

"Fabulous on and off the road. In town, too. For more spare time. To escape the vice-like grip and neurosis of town traffic as others sit there trapped in 4-wheeled boxes ... The Scrambler is style and freedom". This text reads more like a political manifesto or a philosophical tract and comes from a Ducati brochure describing a bike which has become a cult object and a collector's item. Ducati bikes of the period were advertised with the slogan "Ducati Power" inserted in the circle and arrow of the biological male symbol. The message was clear: Men only! "Politically correct" times were still a long way off. The lads (and lassies) of the wild bunch roaring around on their Scramblers certainly seemed to be having fun.

Prezzo invariato per la rinnovata DUCATI "SCRAMBLER" 450

Questa nota macchina della Casa bolognese è stata notevolmente migliorata all'avantreno e in altri particolari senza subire aumenti di prezzo.

La nuova versione della Ducati "Scrambler" 450

Le nuove fiancate, montonare fra i lati del telaio, rendono più pulito e piacevole l'esterno del mezzo

Particolare dell'avantreno completamente rinnovato

ON THE **350** AND **450** THE **4**-LEADING SHOE FRONT BRAKE AND LIGHT-ALLOY RIMS WERE BY BORRANI. THE ENGINE HAD STRENGTHENED CON-RODS AND ELECTRONIC IGNITION.

THE LAST VERSION OF THE **450** SCRAMBLER WAS PRODUCED IN **1973-74** BUT SOME VERSIONS WERE BUILT LATER FROM STOCK PARTS. THE MOST OBVIOUS DIFFERENCES WERE THE STIFF FIBREGLASS SIDE PANELS AND THE FORK WITH UNCOVERED CAMS.

ABOVE, THE **250** SCRAMBLER. LEFT, THE LAST VERSION OF THE **350** PRODUCED IN **1974**.

THE **250** WAS ALMOST TOTALLY PRODUCED BY MOTOTRANS USING SPANISH PARTS (AMAL CARBS AND TELESCO SUSPENSION). MANY **350**s PRODUCED AT BORGO PANIGALE HAD SPANISH ENGINES. THE **450**, ON THE OTHER HAND, WAS **100%** ITALIAN.

Ducati
MECCANICA S.p.A.
Via A.C. Ducati, 3 - Cas. Post. 313
40100 Bologna - Italia
Tel.: (051) 40.50.49 - Telex 51492

SCRAMBLER
ACCENSIONE ELETTRONICA

BELL-BOTTOM JEANS AND TIGHT-FITTING T-SHIRTS, UNMISTAKABLE SEVENTIES STYLE ON THE FRONT PAGE OF THIS BROCHURE FOR THE SCRAMBLER.

ON THE PESARO RACE CIRCUIT IN 1971, THE VETERAN RIDER SPAGGIARI ON THE DUCATI 500 GP LEADING SEVENTIES ACE AGOSTINI ON A MV THREE CYLINDER.

94

1971 The 500 GP twin

Ducati's sporting exploits had not progressed since the time of the singles ridden by Spaggiari and company. This changed in 1971-72 with the arrival of a promising 500 GP twin. Based around a sand-cast crankcase, the engine had two cylinders from the 250 Desmo and two Dellorto SS 40 carburettors. The 500 touched 70 hp at 12,000 rpm but there were also rumours of 63 hp at 11,500 rpm. Four-valve heads were discussed and design engineer Armaroli also tried a belt driven valve gear. At least two types of frame were available: a standard frame produced in Bologna and a special built by Colin Seeley in England. These bikes disappeared into obscurity after 1972 but the experience gained with the 500 GP proved to be invaluable in later years. The bike never actually won a race but was always well-placed.

NOVITA' NEL MONDO DELLE CORSE

LA DUCATI TORNA IN GRANDE STILE CON UNA 500 BICILINDRICA

Realizzata sullo schema della 750 di imminente lancio, questa nuova macchina, che verrà anch'essa commercializzata, è un banco-prova «viaggiante» destinato al miglioramento della produzione di serie.

La limitata sezione frontale, pari a quella di una monocilindrica.

HAILWOOD WITH SPAGGIARI (IN BLACK OVERALLS) AT THE SILVERSTONE PITS WITH A **747.9** CC TWIN IN A SEELEY FRAME; A CLEAR HINT AT DUCATI'S PROSPECTIVE ENTRY INTO **200** MILE RACING.

PHIL READ WAS ANOTHER **500** TWIN RIDER, COMING SECOND IN A **1971** ITALIAN CHAMPIONSHIP RACE ON THE SANREMO-OSPEDALETTI CIRCUIT AND FOURTH AT MONZA.

RIGHT, THE FIRST VERSION OF THE **500** WITH A DUCATI FRAME VERY SIMILAR TO THAT ON THE PRODUCTION VERSION. NOTE THE REAR DRUM BRAKE.
OPPOSITE, COLIN SEELEY POSES ALONGSIDE THE FIRST VERSION OF HIS FRAME, WITH TWO LONG RAILS JOINED AT THE STEERING HEAD. THIS VERY ADVANCED SOLUTION INSPIRED OTHER SIMILAR FRAMES. TOP RIGHT, A LATER VERSION OF THE **500** WITH DISC BRAKING ALSO IN THE REAR WHEEL.

ABOVE, DESIGN ENGINEER TAGLIONI, WITH THE EVER-PRESENT CIGARETTE, KEEPING A CLOSE WATCH ON THIS TEAM.

BELT-DRIVEN VALVE GEAR DESIGNED BY ARMAROLI WAS ALSO TRIED ON THE **500** GP. THIS IS THE ONLY SURVIVING VERSION AND BELONGS TO AN ITALIAN COLLECTOR.

GT 750

Nineteen seventy one was the year of the big bikes and Ducati was ready and waiting, thanks to Taglioni's instinct for spotting market trends. He used the cylinders and the valve gear (with modification) of the SOHCs in a 90° Vee configuration. The front cylinder of the V-twin was nearly parallel with the ground and this engine layout was soon renamed "L-twin". Other experiments included Dellorto SS 35 carbs (the final version mounted 30 mm Amal Concentrics), a large diameter Fontana brake drum and a 230 mm Grimeca drum; the standard GT had a 280 mm disc with a Lockheed caliper and brake cylinder derived from the Morris Mini. The prototype fork had a straight head; the production version has a raked pin and Marzocchi forks with 38 mm stanchions. The frame and styling were redesigned and when the bike finally arrived on the market it managed to carve a niche for itself between the Guzzis, Laverdas and Hondas.

DUCATI "GT" 750

Specification

ENGINE: Four-stroke 90° V-twin configuration. Light alloy head and cylinders (with cast-iron liner). Bore: 80 mm. Stroke: 74.4 mm. Capacity: 748 cc. Compression ratio: 8.5:1. Desmodromic single overhead camshaft driven by gear shaft/helical gear, 2 valves per cylinder. Two Amal Concentric 930 carburettors with 30 mm choke. Fuel tank capacity: 17 litres. Maximum power: 60 hp at 8,000 rpm. Torque: n.a. Distributor ignition with HT coil. Electrical equipment with 12V-150W alternator and 12 volt 12 Ah battery. Wet sump forced lubrication with gear pump, 4.5 litres oil. Wet, multi-plate clutch. 5-speed gearbox. FRAME, FORKS AND RUNNING GEAR: Duplex open cradle tubular frame. Front hydraulic telescopic forks. Swinging arm rear suspension with adjustable hydraulic shocks. 280 mm disc front brake. Full width drum rear brake. Tyres: 3.60 x 19" (front), 4.10 x 18" (rear). DIMENSIONS AND WEIGHT: Length: 2,250 mm. Width: 760 mm. Seat height: 800 mm. Wheelbase: 1,500 mm. Weight (dry): 185 kg. PERFORMANCE: 200 kph.

LEFT, THE GT 750, FINAL VERSION, JUDGED BY *MOTOCICLISMO* TO BE A SUCCESSFUL COMPROMISE BETWEEN A SPORT AND A TOURING BIKE. THE TUBULAR FRAME WAS CLOSED AT THE BOTTOM BY THE ENGINE.

TOP LEFT, THE 1970 PROTOTYPE; NOTE THE FRAME, THE FONTANA BRAKE AND THE PARALLEL PIN FORK (AN ITEM WHICH DISAPPEARED ON THE FINAL VERSION) AND THE SS CARBS. LEFT, A PROTOTYPE SURPRISED AT THE FACTORY GATES AT THE START OF A TEST WITH AN ELEGANT WORKS TESTER. ABOVE, THE LAST 750 GTS, WITH SPECIAL TRIM FOR BOLOGNA CITY MUNICIPAL POLICE. RIGHT, DETAIL OF THE ENGINE WITH THE IGNITION CONTACT BREAKER HOUSING AND ONE OF THE TWO AMAL CONCENTRIC CARBURETTORS.

Smart (16) ahead of Spaggiari (9); this was the finishing order at the end of the race. The Italian was unable to try a flying finish, having practically consumed all of the fuel in his tank. Much has been said about this episode, and rumours abound even today: the riders confirm the official version.

1972 Triumph at Imola

The moment of glory arrived. Ducati enthusiastically accepted Checco Costa's proposal to bring the races reserved for large cylinder capacity bikes to Imola, officially involving both the manufacturers and riders. In the US, the Honda, Triumph and BSA teams fought it out with a Rocket 3 entrusted to Mike Hailwood. At Imola, Giacomo Agostini on his MV 750 with shaft drive, challenged Walter Villa's Triumph, the Guzzis, the Nortons and the Japanese. The racing department applied itself to the task with a vengeance, employing a strong element of logic: the running gear closely resembled that of the GT, whilst the engine was fitted with desmodromic cylinder heads (anticipating the standard SS). The race ended in victory: Smart and Spaggiari on the podium with Walter Villa, who came in third on the Triumph. Its competitors beaten, Ducati was back in fighting style!

SMART AND SPAGGIARI LAPPING A SLOWER RIVAL ON A LAVERDA 750: NOTICE THE BRITISH RIDER'S SPECTACULAR RACING STYLE. HE SOON BECAME A FAVOURITE OF THE ITALIAN PUBLIC, THANKS TO HIS AGGRESSIVE RIDING AND GENEROSITY OF SPIRIT. IN 1973 DUCATI ATTEMPTED TO REPEAT THIS VICTORY AT IMOLA WITH THE RENEWED 750, A BIKE THAT WAS HIGHLY DEVELOPED AND MUCH EASIER TO HANDLE THAN ITS PREDECESSOR. THE RACE WAS RUN IN TWO HEATS AND WAS WON BY JARNO SAARINEN ON THE YAMAHA TZ 350, A TWO-STROKE TWIN-CYLINDER GRAND PRIX BIKE ALLOWED BY THE NEW RULES.

TOP RIGHT, BRUNO SPAGGIARI AND PAUL SMART CELEBRATE ON THE WINNER'S PODIUM AFTER THEIR TRIUMPHANT 200 MILE RIDE. THE ITALIAN, RIGHT, PUT IN AN IMPRESSIVE PERFORMANCE, DESPITE THE FACT THAT HIS 40TH BIRTHDAY WAS FAST APPROACHING, WHILST THE ENGLISHMAN RODE LAPS WHOSE TIMES COMPARED FAVOURABLY WITH THOSE OF THE 500 GRAND PRIX BIKES.

SPAGGIARI, ABOVE, TOOK SECOND PLACE, WHILST THE OTHER DUCATI RIDER, THE SWISSMAN BRUNO KNEUBULER, FELL AS HE ATTEMPTED TO ROB SAARINEN OF THE LEAD, INFURIATING TAGLIONI.

THE BEAUTIFUL FAITHFUL REPLICA OF SMART'S BIKE, OWNED BY GIULIANO PEDRETTI, A HISTORIC FIGURE AT DUCATI. INSET: PEDRETTI SHOWS OFF THE "CERTIFICATE OF AUTHENTICITY", SIGNED BY NONE OTHER THAN TAGLIONI.

1972 Anatomy of 750 "Imola"

The Ducati 750 "Imola" — this being the unofficial, yet commonly used name — was closely derived from the standard model. Despite the experience gained with the 500 GPs and the 750 with Seeley frame tested by Hailwood, it used assembly line components. The crankcases were even numbered, whilst the frames (with lugs for the stand) came from the GT 750. The engine had desmo valve gear with 40 mm intake valves and 36 mm exhaust valves. The carburettors were the new Dellorto PHF with central float chamber. The maximum power developed was 84 hp at 8,800 rpm; but developed 70 hp at 7,000 rpm.

An inside view, revealing the secrets of the bike that won at Imola. For example, the frame is standard, as is the crankcase; yet the valve gear is a SOHC desmo, not available on standard models at that time. These photos reveal three classic features: top left, the crank breather protected by a flap; right, the fuel tank quick-release filler cap and transparent tank sides to allow inspection of the fuel level; above, the battery quick-release terminals.

The "Imola" was fitted with the new Dellorto PHF 40 carburettor with central float chamber (above right), which had dangerous-looking choke trumpets. Above left, the hydraulic brake master cylinder, which controlled the Brembo 280 twin front discs, gripped by AP Lockheed 2-piston calipers - and the rear unit with its 230 mm disc.

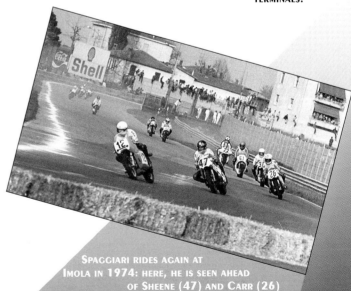

Spaggiari rides again at Imola in 1974: here, he is seen ahead of Sheene (47) and Carr (26) on the Suzukis, followed by Woods, Gütner, Williams, Tchernine and Pons. A fine mixture of 2- and 4-stroke bikes!

RT 450

In 1970, at the request of US importer Berliner, a new Ducati off-road bike was made, even its name evoking the American trim. It was dubbed the RT (road and track). Relatively small numbers were produced for US off-road riders, who used them mostly in their trail races run on fast southern US tracks. This bike had no silencer or lights, yet, in response to demand, a version with the said features was prepared and even arrived in Italy. The bike was built around an open simplex cradle, the engine closing the lower structure, and had little in common with the Scrambler. The engine was a single-cylinder 450 with desmodromic head, capable of developing 36 hp at 6,500 rpm. Compared with the European off-road bikes, its basic trim limited its agility on the trails where Italian off-road races were run, although this did not prevent the RT from being used by the Italian team at the '71 International Six Day Trial on the Isle of Man, from which they returned with several medals. The RT was produced from '70 to '73, including the rare 350 cc version, which remains the most specialised off-road bike, at least with a four-stroke engine, ever to come out of the Ducati works. Not easy to start, it was fitted with "Spagna" (i Sevilla) type Pirelli tyres, with their characteristic deep tread.

THE DUCATI RT 450 WAS HARD ON RIDERS BUT NEVERTHELESS TODAY DUCATI'S MOST SPECIALISED SINGLE-CYLINDER OFF-ROAD BIKE IS MUCH SOUGHT AFTER BY COLLECTORS WORLD-WIDE.

Specification

ENGINE: Four-stroke single-cylinder, with 10° forward angle configuration. Light alloy head and cylinders (with cast-iron liner). Bore: 86 mm. Stroke: 75 mm. Capacity: 436 cc. Compression ratio: 9.3:1. Desmodromic SOHC camshaft driven by gear shaft/helical valve gear. Dellorto VHD 29 AD carburettor with 29 mm choke. Fuel tank capacity: 10 litres. Maximum power: 36 hp at 6,500 rpm. Torque: not available. Distributor ignition with HT coil. Electrical equipment with 6V-70W alternator and 6 volt 13.5 Ah battery. Wet sump forced lubrication with gear pump, 2.5 kg oil. Wet, multi-plate clutch. 5-speed gearbox. FRAME, FORKS AND RUNNING GEAR: Simplex open cradle tubular frame. Front hydraulic telescopic forks. Swinging arm rear suspension with adjustable hydraulic shocks. Centre drum brakes. Tyres: 3.00 x 21" (front), 4.00 x 18" (rear). DIMENSIONS AND WEIGHT: Length: 2,181 mm. Width: 940 mm. Seat height: 820 mm. Wheelbase: 1,450 mm. Weight (dry): 128 kg. PERFORMANCE: Not available.

SEVERAL DIFFERENCES BETWEEN THE RT CROSS AND THE ROAD VERSION WITH NUMBER PLATES. LEFT, THE FORMER HAS A DIFFERENT TYPE OF AIR FILTER FITTED UNDER THE SIDE-PANEL, INTO WHICH THE CRANK CASE BREATHER FUMES FLOWED. NOTICE THE INCREDIBLE STRAIGHT-THROUGH EXHAUST AND THE CONTAINER FOR THE CHAIN OILER. EVEN THE FOOTRESTS ARE DIFFERENT; THE ARROW INDICATES THE DECOMPRESSOR. RIGHT, THE "EUROPEA" RT WITH LOW EXHAUST PIPE AND DIFFERENT AIR FILTER.

LEFT, IN THE DEPTHS OF WINTER, VETERAN DALL'ARA TACKLES A TRAIL ON HIS RT 450, CLASSED AMONG THE "OVER 175s". BOTTOM LEFT, THE RT 450 WITH "CROSS" TRIM WHICH DEBUTED ON THE US MARKET IN 1970. MILAN'S KOELLIKER DEALERSHIP, ALWAYS AN "EXOTIC" BIKE ENTHUSIAST, SOLD SEVERAL IN ITALY BEFORE DUCATI HOMOLOGATED THIS TOUGH OFF-ROAD BIKE.

TO MAKE THE RT TRULY SUITABLE FOR TOUGH TRIALS OR OFF-ROAD RACES, ONE STEP COULD NOT BE AVOIDED: THE BEAUTIFUL HIGH TWIN EXHAUST PROPOSED BY DUCATI AS AN OPTIONAL EXTRA (SEE PHOTO ABOVE) HAD TO BE FITTED. LEFT, THE RT'S FRAME WAS VERY DIFFERENT TO THAT OF THE SCRAMBLER - AND MUCH STRONGER. NOTICE THE BOXED SECTION IN WHICH THE SHOCKS WERE ATTACHED: THERE WAS A CHOICE OF FOUR DIFFERENT FITTINGS FOR THE TOP END, TO ADJUST SUSPENSION ACCORDING TO THE TRAIL TO BE COVERED, OR TO SUIT THE RIDER'S STYLE.

BENJAMIN GRAU IN
ACTION ON THE
DUCATI 860 AT THE
MONTJUICH TRACK
IN BARCELONA,
1973. THE BIKE,
PREPARED FOR THE
SPANISH LONG
DISTANCE RACE, WAS
CHARACTERISED BY
ITS HIGH EXHAUSTS,
FUEL TANK WITH
"TRANSPARENT"
INSPECTION WINDOW
AND THE UNUSUAL
AIR INTAKE FOR THE
CALIPER OF THE
REAR DISC BRAKE.
THE 860 WEIGHED
LESS THAN 180 KG
IN RACING TRIM.

1973 Racing to glory: endurance and off-road

Montjuich is a demanding road track in the centre of Barcelona, used for endurance races and the exhausting 24 Horas. With the support of Mototrans, Ducati always obtained optimum results with its single-cylinder bikes, but 1983 also saw the triumph of the "L" twins, with the victory of Spaniards Benjamin Grau and Salvador Canellas. The bike was prepared by the Ducati racing department, based on the experience gained from the "short stroke" 750, by then excluded due to homologation of the 4-cylinder Yamaha TZ 700 and the other GP two-strokes. By increasing the capacity to 860 cc, the engine was capable of incredibly low revs, was easy to handle and developed a power as high as 85 hp. It was fitted in a frame very similar to the standard version and the bike was ridden without any fairings. This was Ducati's response to the endurance races which continued to gain popularity, and from '73 onwards the Italian twins were increasingly present on tracks world-wide.

ABOVE, TWO-MAN TEAM PEDRINI AND MIGNANI ON THE MODENA TRACK WITH THEIR DUCATI L-TWIN SIDECAR. THE RIDERS WHO CAME TO FAME WITH THE 750 INCLUDED JOURNALIST NICO CEREGHINI, LEFT, DURING A RACE AT MISANO IN 1973.

ABOVE, THE OLD SOHC 200 STILL RACED IN '71, USED IN THE ICE SPEEDWAY BY SPECIALIST SISTO BELLODIS. BUT DUCATI NEVER LOST SIGHT OF THE OFF-ROAD BIKE: IN 1971 IT SUPPLIED ITS RT TO THE ITALIAN TEAM COMPETING IN THE TOUGH INTERNATIONAL SIX DAY TRIAL (ISDT), RUN ON THE ISLE OF MAN. PHOTO RIGHT, A TRICKY MOMENT FOR EDOARDO DOSSENA.

A SYSTEM PERFECTED BY THE MECHANICS FOR ENDURANCE RACES: TWIN CONDENSERS ON THE IGNITION CIRCUIT. ONLY TWO CONDENSERS WERE USED, BUT THE SECOND PAIR WAS ALWAYS READY IN CASE OF EMERGENCIES.

1973
Sport 750

WITH ITS SINGLE-SEATER SADDLE, LONG FUEL TANK AND SET-BACK FOOT-RESTS, THE SPORT 750 WAS MUCH ADMIRED BY BOY RACERS, WHO DREAMED OF SMART AND SPAGGIARI'S BIKES.

In some people's opinion the Sport 750 was a waste of time, or a stage that could have been omitted, passing from the first GT to the Super Sport 750 — the direct descendant of Smart's bike that won at Imola, enhanced with a desmo head and racing trim. Sport bikes were not a favourite of the management at that time, anxious as they were to challenge the other manufacturers in the touring sector. Yet the very essence of Ducati is firmly rooted in sport, and it is certainly not only due to the critics if, with few exceptions, Ducati's "legendary" bikes are all sport models. The Sport was presented in 1972 and the major objections that arose were to its appearance: the over-long look, the excessively bright yellow, the low quality handlebar controls and instruments. In contrast, the running gear, engine and riding position were praised. The engine, supplied by the Dellorto PHF 32 with pump, worked perfectly even at low revs, proving very reliable. The tester of the time commented as follows: "It's clear how this engine, backed up by a frame with optimum characteristics and a suitably rigid, efficient suspension, heightens a rider's enthusiasm for speed". The bike did not have a desmodromic valve gear.

La rude
Ducati Sport 750
ha un motore molto elastico
e un telaio veramente stabile

Specification

ENGINE: Four-stroke 90° L-twin configuration. Light alloy cylinder head and block (with cast-iron liner). Bore: 80 mm. Stroke: 74.4 mm. Capacity: 748 cc. Compression ratio: 9:1. Single overhead camshaft driven by gear shaft/helical gear, two valves per cylinder. Two Dellorto PHF carburettors with 32 mm choke. Fuel tank capacity: 19 litres. Maximum power: not available Torque: n.a. Distributor ignition with HT coil. Electrical equipment with 12V-150W alternator and 12 volt 12 Ah battery. Wet sump forced lubrication with gear pump, 5 litres oil. Wet, multi-plate clutch. 5-speed gearbox. FRAME, FORKS AND RUNNING GEAR: Duplex open cradle tubular frame. Front hydraulic telescopic forks. Swinging arm rear suspension with adjustable hydraulic shocks. 180 mm disc front brake. Rear 280 mm centre drum brake. Tyres: 3.50 x 19" (front), 4.00 x 18" (rear). DIMENSIONS AND WEIGHT: Length: 2,250 mm. Width: 670 mm. Seat height: 840 mm. Wheelbase: 1,500 mm. Weight (dry): 186 kg. PERFORMANCE: Not available.

ABOVE, THE RIGHT FOOT REST HAD TO BE FOLDED UPWARDS IN ORDER TO START THE ENGINE; NOTICE THE BENT SHAPE OF THE REARSET GEAR LINKAGE ROD. WITH A MINIMUM OF PRACTICE, THIS OPERATION WASN'T TOO COMPLICATED, BUT IT WAS TO BE A LONG TIME BEFORE ELECTRIC IGNITION WAS INTRODUCED.

LEFT, A PHOTO TO SET YOUR IMAGINATION RUNNING: IT MAKES YOU WANT TO JUMP ON THE SADDLE, REACH OVER THE FUEL TANK, GRIP THE HANDLEBARS AND TAKE OFF... ABOVE, ENGINE WITH CONVENTIONAL HEAD (SOHC WITH HELICAL GEARS AND VALVE SPRINGS). ALSO SHOWN: ONE OF THE TWO DELLORTO CARBURETTORS WITH PUMP AND CHOKE TRUMPETS PROTECTED BY A MESH GUARD.

LEFT, THE CERIANI FORKS WITH LEFT FORK LEG READY FOR FITTING OF A SECOND DISC, AVAILABLE AS AN OPTION. RIGHT, THE SECRET OF THE BREMBO CALIPER REVEALED. THANKS TO THIS BRAKING UNIT, THE SPORT GAINED A REPUTATION AS AN EXCELLENT BIKE FOR LATE BRAKING.

Top and bottom, two photos of the first type of off-road bike, characterised by the large exhaust which runs under the frame's cradle, and the cylinder with characteristic radial finning, considered optimum for two-stroke air-cooled bikes at the time. Colour photo: a *Motociclismo* tester lands after a jump during the ISDT.

1974 Two-stroke off-road bikes

From the early '70s, there was a boom in the production of off-road bikes that reached incredible proportions, only to be halted at the end of the decade. The roots of this success lay in the emergence of the new two-stroke bikes (Puch, KTM, SWM) which, thanks to their racy performance, attracted the younger buyers. In Italy dozens of Companies, often only assemblers using Sachs engines, put out their own models. From '74, Ducati perfected a bike destined for this market segment, the Regolarità 125. In '77, thanks to the work of Italo Forni, champion of the cross 500 category, the more powerful and advanced Six Days was unveiled. These bikes were not a great success and were quite different: the former was closer to a touring model, with a wider range of applications, the latter being a true competition bike.

Grosse novità in casa DUCATI per la strada e il fuori strada

Si tratta di una bicilindrica 350-500 monoalbero a catena con avviamento elettronico e di una 125 monocilindrica due tempi sei marce; entrambe hanno l'accensione elettronica. Dovrebbero essere presentate ufficialmente in primavera.

1977: WITH THE AID OF ELECTRONIC TIMING, THE *MOTOCICLISMO* TEST CENTRE THRASHES THE SIX DAYS 125 AT THE PIRELLI TRACK IN VIZZOLA TICINO.

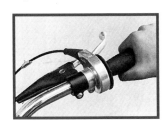

BELOW, GROUP PHOTO AROUND THE REGOLARITÀ: FROM LEFT, DE ECCHER (MANAGER OF DUCATI IN '75), RIDER ITALO FORNI, MASSIMO BACCHETTI (CURRENTLY DIRECTOR OF *MOTOCICLISMO*), DUCATI MARKETING MANAGER COSIMO CALCAGNILE AND EDOARDO GRANATA, WHO WROTE FOR THE MAGAZINE.

ABOVE, THE SIX DAYS WITHOUT ITS SADDLE AND FUEL TANK. NOTICE THE REDESIGNED FRAME AND THE EXHAUST PIPE THAT PASSES HIGH OVER THE ENGINE. THANKS TO FORNI'S EFFORTS, THE MAXIMUM POWER WAS INCREASED TO 25 HP AT 10,250 RPM.

DETAIL, TOP, A CULT ITEM FOR THE YOUTH OF THAT PERIOD: THE GERMAN MAGURA'S THROTTLE TWIST GRIP. THE CABLE HAS AN OILER, AND THE LEVERS AND VINYL GUARDS ARE AGAIN MAGURA PRODUCTS. ABOVE, THE

REGOLARITÀ'S CLOSED DUPLEX CRADLE FRAME AND ENGINE WITH RADIAL FINNING. THE RATED MAXIMUM POWER WAS 21.8 HP AT 9,000 RPM; A 5% OIL-PETROL MIXTURE WAS USED FOR LUBRICATION.

A DETAIL OF THE SIX DAYS 125: THE MARZOCCHI ZTI FORKS WITH MAGNESIUM FORK LEGS AND 35 MM RODS.

1974 The motorcycles that made history

Super Sport 750

TO SAY THAT THE SUPER SPORT 750 WAS ONE OF THE MOST BEAUTIFUL SPORT BIKES EVER MADE IS NO EXAGGERATION; IT MAY BE CONSIDERED AMONGST THE MOST SIGNIFICANT MOTORCYCLE DESIGNS OF ITS TIME.

"It must immediately be pointed out that, although offering breathtaking performance, this bike has a set of features which are rarely seen together on a sport- or racebike. The Super Sport starts with the docility of a utility bike, has no vibrations, runs at high speeds, at low revs and even maintains idling speeds!" Testing the Super Sport 750 in '74, *Motociclismo* repeatedly emphasised one of the many aspects of this super sport model. This was the engine, able to satisfy the demands made on it by all riders, even for racing purposes, without requiring special modifications. The secret of so many positive features was the result of an uncompromising layout, targeted work to improve both the running gear and engine, and the craftsmanship that went into its construction. The SS combined the great potential of the twin-cylinder engine with a mechanical configuration that, at last, presented the general public with the characteristics of Spaggiari and Smart's 750 "Imola" once more. It had a desmodromic head, Dellorto PHM 40 carburettors, larger valves and beautiful single-piece con-rods, a Marzocchi fork with axle pin, new plates, full disc braking system and a great look.

The result? Today, as then, the SS750s are much sought after (and so extremely expensive). 450 examples were made in the first series, presented here, with frame numbers 75,000 to 75,450.

Specification

ENGINE: Four-stroke 90° V-twin configuration. Light alloy head and cylinders (with cast-iron liner). Bore: 80 mm. Stroke: 74.4 mm. Capacity: 748 cc. Compression ratio: 10:1. Desmodromic single overhead camshaft driven by gear shaft/helical gear, 2 side valves per cylinder. Two Dellorto PHM carburettors with 40 mm choke. Fuel tank capacity: 20 litres. Maximum power: not available. Torque: not available. Distributor ignition with HT coil. Electrical equipment with 12V-150W alternator and 12 volt 12 Ah battery. Wet sump forced lubrication with gear pump, 5 litres oil. Wet, multi-plate clutch. 5-speed gearbox. FRAME, FORKS AND RUNNING GEAR: Duplex open cradle tubular frame. Front hydraulic telescopic forks. Swinging arm rear suspension with adjustable hydraulic shocks. 280 mm twin disc front brake. 280 mm disc rear brake. Tyres: 3.50 x 18" (front), 3.50 x 18" (rear). DIMENSIONS AND WEIGHT: Length: 2,250 mm. Width: 670 mm. Seat height: 800 mm. Wheelbase: 1,500 mm. Weight (dry): 192 kg. PERFORMANCE: not available.

110

THIS IS THE PROTOTYPE OF THE **SS 750**: NOTICE THE FRONT DISC BRAKE SUPPORT WITH **18** HOLES, THE LOW-MOUNTED REAR DISC CALIPER AND THE TRANSPARENT STRIP ON THE FUEL TANK, MUCH WIDER THAN THAT ON THE STANDARD VERSION.

THE **SS 750** IN THE PHOTOGRAPHER'S SIGHTS AND MONITORED BY THE ELECTRONIC TIMING FOR *MOTOCICLISMO'S* READINGS DURING THE **1974** ROAD TEST.

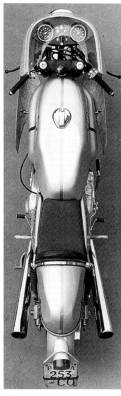

THE LINE IS ROBUST (AND BRINGS TO MIND THAT OF PAST MODELS...) EVEN TODAY, SINCE IT COMBINES ESSENTIAL FORMS AND UNUSUAL CHROMATIC FEATURES FRAMING THE EXTRAORDINARY MECHANICS. THE EXPLODED DIAGRAM ILLUSTRATES THE "BEAUTIFUL MECHANICS" WHICH WERE A FUNDAMENTAL INGREDIENT OF THE **SS 750**. FOR THE FIRST TIME, THE DESMO SINGLE OVERHEAD CAMSHAFT WAS AVAILABLE FOR SALE TO THE PUBLIC ON A TWIN-CYLINDER BIKE.

STRANGE DESTINY: THIS BIKE WAS NOT DESIGNED BY A GREAT ENGINEER, BUT WAS A COMPOSITE OF VARIOUS COMPONENTS, PUT TOGETHER WITH A STRONG DOSE OF GOOD TASTE.

THE **SS** CAPTURED THE ENTHUSIASM OF *MOTOCICLISMO*'S TESTERS, USED TO THE BIG BIKES OF THE TIME WHOSE PERFORMANCE WAS BY NO MEANS IMPECCABLE, ESPECIALLY IN TERMS OF SPEED: "THE STEERING HAS A GOOD LINEAR RESPONSE, EVEN UNDER CRITICAL CONDITIONS, THANKS TO ITS TRULY SUPERIOR STABILITY. THE IMPRESSION OF OPTIMUM SAFETY IS MAINTAINED EVEN AT HIGH SPEEDS".

1974 Secret kits and details

An engine hardly muffled by the fabulous Conti silencers, a secret compartment closed by a zip, a pair of con-rods which deserve to be exhibited at a modern art show — these are just a few of the little secrets of this incredible twin-cylinder bike. For sporting customers, who increasingly raced their SSs world-wide, there was also a tuning kit, designed, perfected and, finally, put on sale, by the Borgo Panigale Company.

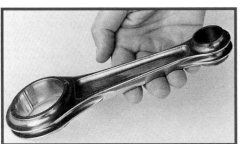

LEFT, THE BEAUTIFUL SINGLE-PIECE CON-ROD, A TRUE MODERN SCULPTURE. BELOW, THE KIT DESIGNED BY DUCATI FOR THE MANY CUSTOMERS WHO RACED THE SS.

TOP, A TOOL COMPARTMENT CLOSED BY A ZIP WAS CREATED AT THE REAR. THIS FEATURE WAS NOT PARTICULARLY APPRECIATED AT THE TIME, YET TODAY IS CONSIDERED A REFINED PIECE OF CRAFTSMANSHIP. ABOVE, THE RAPID OPENING THROTTLE TWIST GRIP HAS A "KNURLED" FINISH, TO ALLOW THE RIDER A BETTER GRIP.

REAR VIEW OF THE SS 750, OFTEN THE ONLY VIEW EVER SEEN BY COMPETITORS! THIS IS A PREPRODUCTION MODEL.

THE REAR VIEW. DISC BRAKE CONTROLLED BY A LOCKHEED CALIPER. THE MENACING CONTI MEGAPHONE SILENCER, WHICH PRODUCED A SOUND INSTANTLY RECOGNISABLE TO ENTHUSIASTS.

860 GT

The management of the period identified another "gap" in the Ducati range: given the decline of the GT, the archetypal "L-twin", a new, large cylinder capacity touring bike was needed. Italdesign was contacted, this being the company owned by Giugiaro, designer of the first VW Golf, who rose to the challenge. The result was an unusual prototype with new, original lines that were decidedly outside the normal motorcycle standards. With a few changes, dictated by the need to contain costs (for example, the fancy light casing disappeared), the design was accepted and entered production. The mechanics applied themselves to both the mechanisms and the running gear. The first model had bore and stroke measuring 86 x 74.4 mm, resulting in a capacity of 864 cc. It was also decided that the engine should have a conventional head, with valve springs. The ignition was electronic and, for the first time on a Ducati twin, the starter was electric, this choice obliging the designers to exercise their skills to the limit in order to position the starter motor. In the end, it was the attractive crankcase which suffered. The running gear was fitted over a duplex open cradle frame; the swinging arm suspension was made by Ceriani, the shocks adjustable between no less than 5 positions. The engine developed 65 hp at 6,500 rpm with a robust, linear torque, but on the road the GT felt the effects of the 1,550 mm wheelbase. Just a few months after their release, several details of the GT 860s were updated: twin front discs were fitted, the electrical system, often paralysed by water infiltration, was redesigned and even a new saddle was fitted. But the 860 had got off to a bad start...

A FOGGY WINTER SETTING FOR THE **860 GT** DURING THE *MOTOCICLISMO* ROAD TEST.

Specification

ENGINE: Four-stroke 90° V-twin configuration. Light alloy head and cylinders (with cast-iron liner). Bore: 86 mm. Stroke: 74.4 mm. Capacity: 863.9 cc. Compression ratio: 9.2:1. Desmodromic single overhead camshaft driven by gear shaft/helical gear, 2 valves per cylinder. Two Dellorto PHF carburettors with 42 mm choke. Fuel tank capacity: 19 litres. Maximum power: not available. Torque: not available. Electronic ignition. Electrical equipment with 12V-200W alternator and 12 volt 36 Ah battery. Wet sump forced lubrication with gear pump, 4.5 litres oil. Wet, multi-plate clutch. 5-speed gearbox. FRAME, FORKS AND RUNNING GEAR: Duplex open cradle tubular frame. Front hydraulic telescopic forks. Swinging arm rear suspension with adjustable hydraulic shocks. 280 mm disc front brake. Centre drum rear brake. Tyres: 3.50 x 18" (front), 120/90 x 18" (rear). DIMENSIONS AND WEIGHT: Length: 2,200 mm. Width: 900 mm. Seat height: 800 mm. Wheelbase: 1,550 mm. Weight (dry): 229 kg. PERFORMANCE: not available.

TIMED TESTS RECORDED **13.5** SECONDS AS THE PERIOD REQUIRED TO COVER **400** METRES FROM A STANDING START. A GOOD TIME: JUST HALF A SECOND SLOWER THAN THE **S 750**, **43** KG LIGHTER. LEFT, THE OMNIPRESENT FARNÉ POURS WATER OVER THE FRONT SECTION TO DEMONSTRATE THAT THE CHANGES MADE HAD RENDERED THE ELECTRICAL SYSTEM WATER-TIGHT.

THE FIRST VERSION OF THE **GT 860** HAD A SINGLE DISC; A TWIN UNIT WAS SOON FITTED, AGAIN MEASURING **280** MM AND WITH BREMBO CALIPER. BELOW LEFT, A RARITY: THE **860**'S LEFT CRANKCASE ON THE VERSION WITHOUT ELECTRIC STARTER, WHICH SOON DISAPPEARED FROM THE SCENE. ABOVE, THE COMPLEX STARTER SYSTEM, WITH STRAIGHT-TOOTH CROWN COUPLING AND CHAIN IN AN OIL BATH. THIS WAS NOT TO BE REMEMBERED AS A STROKE OF FUNCTIONAL GENIUS.

RURAL SETTING FOR THE GTL 500: THIS PHOTO WAS TAKEN DURING A PAUSE IN *MOTOCICLISMO*'S 1976 TESTS.

1976 The parallel twins

The 350 and 500 cc parallel twins can certainly not be defined "great success stories". The slanting twin often reappeared in Ducati history from '57 onwards. In '74, the company had a poor assortment, the single-cylinder Desmo and Scrambler being at the end of their careers, and the sporty 750s too élitist. Even the petrol crisis seemed to condemn the thirsty big sport bikes. Thus, the "parallel twin" project was begun, resulting in the production of the GTL 350 and 500. The origin of the engine is steeped in legend: some say that the design was purchased by Ricardo in Great Britain, but the official version is that the GTL was the product of a study by design-engineer Tumidei, based on the 1965 500. The "parallels" were not a success, due to their excessive weight, vibrations and their appearance derived from Giorgetto Giugiaro's 860 design. The updated 350 and 500 with desmo head and new running gear, which gave them a more attractive look, were more successful several years later.

TOP TO BOTTOM, THE HEAD SEEN FROM ABOVE AND, BELOW, AND THE CYLINDERS. THE TIMING GEAR SOHC WAS CHAIN-DRIVEN, AN UNUSUAL CHOICE, BUT RIGHT CONSIDERING THE NEED TO PRODUCE LOW-COST ENGINES.

IN THE PHOTO OF THE ENGINE, DOMINATED BY THE LARGE MASS OF THE CRANKCASES, A CERTAIN SIMILARITY WITH THE '65 PROTOTYPE WITH ROCKER ARMS AND PUSHRODS IS EVIDENT.

THE GTL 350 WAS IMMEDIATELY RECOGNISABLE DUE TO THE SINGLE FRONT DISC, AS OPPOSED TO THE TWO MOUNTED ON THE 500. DESPITE THE WIDESPREAD USE OF ELECTRONICS ON DUCATI BIKES, THE GTLs STILL HAD CONTACT-BREAKER IGNITION.
THE INSTRUMENTS (SHOWN IN THE DETAIL ABOVE) WERE COMPLETE AND WERE ENHANCED BY A SET OF WARNING LIGHTS; NOTICE THE STEERING DAMPER, A TECHNICAL FEATURE OFTEN ADOPTED BY DUCATI.

THE GTL 350-500s WERE SOLD IN THREE COLOURS: BLUE, GREEN AND RED. A NEW LOGO APPEARED ON THE FUEL TANK.

117

1976 Racing the twins

Speed races, 24 hour long-distance challenges: Ducati's sporting activities were rife during the mid-Seventies. The company did not compete officially, yet the right bikes, special frames and engines perfected by Taglioni & Co. appeared on the tracks. This was the Scuderia Spaggiari team period: the old champion continued his activities in the racing world as sports manager and talent-scout. He provided young riders with perfectly tuned SS bikes and launched Franco Uncini. Other riders who used the Ducati "twins" included Sabbatini, Perugini, Ferrari and Saltarelli. In '78 a young American called Freddie Spencer finished third in the Daytona 100 Mile race on a 900 SS. He was the only rider to win in two World Championship categories during the same season (in '85 with Honda). Ducati had given him an excellent grounding!

BELOW, IN '77 A GERMAN PREPARED THIS BIG ENDURO, WHICH ARRIVED ON THE SCENE AHEAD OF THE CAGIVA-DUCATIS THAT WENT ON TO WIN THE AFRICAN "RAID" OF THE '80s.

BELOW, FIRST RACE FOR A FUTURE WORLD CHAMPION IN THE 500 CATEGORY: ON THE VALLELUNGA TRACK FOR THE BIASCHELLI TROPHY RACE, FRANCO UNCINI LEADS THE PACK WITH HIS 750 FROM THE SCUDERIA SPAGGIARI.

ANOTHER EXCELLENT RACER WHO EMERGED THANKS TO DUCATI WAS CARLO SALTARELLI, TOP, IN ACTION IN 1976. ABOVE, THE YOUNG FRANCO UNCINI ON THE STARTING GRID AT MISANO IN THE '75 MAGNANI TROPHY CUP WITH HIS SS 750.

IN FRANCE THE ENDURANCE RACES WERE MORE POPULAR THAN THE GRAND PRIX WORLD CHAMPIONSHIPS; IN PARTICULAR, THE THRILLING BOL D'OR. DUCATI ALWAYS WORKED HARD FOR THESE RACES. PHOTO OPPOSITE PAGE, A FRENCH TEAM PREPARES FOR THE RACE. ABOVE, ONE OF THE GREAT RIDERS WHO USED THE DUCATI TWINS WAS VIRGINIO FERRARI, WHO RAN THE MUGELLO 1,000 KILOMETRE RACE ON THE 900.

A DREAMY EXPRESSION AND INTERESTING POSE STRUCK BY A MODEL IN AN "OFFICIAL ADVERTISING CAMPAIGN" FOR THE 860.

PHOTO OF THE *MOTOCICLISMO* TESTERS WITH THE *500* TWIN, WHICH THEY PUSHED TO ITS LIMITS ON BOTH ROAD AND TRACK.

1976 GTL 350 - GTL 500

In '76 *Motociclismo* tested the parallel twins which broke with the Ducati motorcycling tradition. "The general line is similar to that introduced by Giugiaro on the 860 GT. Yet the architecture of the engine does not have fluid, modern lines. The crankcase is large. The exteriors are too rough. But the Ducati people were bent on building a completely reliable camshaft and con-rods. Even the top performance was above average (on the 500), and in both curves and on the straight, this bike could easily hold its own against 2- or 4-cylinder bikes with the same size engine. This was also partly thanks to its easy handling". Less impressive, were the troublesome vibrations and tricky maintenance (the engine had to be removed from the frame in order to take off the head). Basically, this touring-utility bike, built to complete the range, had its pros and cons. But Ducati remembered Leopoldo Tartarini, former rider and raidman for the company, manufacturer and designer. He was asked to develop a new line for the "parallels", which were also fitted with desmo valve gear.

THIS TOP VIEW OF THE GTL 500 SHOWS ITS BOXY, ANGULAR LINE, WHICH WAS BECOMING VERY POPULAR AT THE TIME. NOTICE THE GEAR CHANGE, WITH THE LEVER ON THE LEFT. THE JAPANESE-GERMAN SCHOOL GOT THE BETTER OF ITS BRITISH RIVALS, WHO HAD DOMINATED SINCE THE SIXTIES WITH A RIGHT-HAND GEAR CHANGE LEVER AND LEFT-HAND REAR BRAKE.

THANKS TO LEOPOLDO TARANTINI'S ATTENTIONS, THE TWIN WAS COMPLETELY REDESIGNED IN A SPORTING VEIN. DESMO VALVE GEAR WAS ALSO FITTED AND IMPROVED THE BIKE'S PERFORMANCE: THE GTL 350

REACHED 160 KM/H, WHILST THE 500 DESMO SPORT ARRIVED AT 180. LEFT, THE FRONT WHEEL RISES OFF THE GROUND ON THIS DIFFICULT PASSAGE: EVEN THE GTL ALLOWED THE RIDER SOME ACROBATICS.

RIGHT, RETOUCHING THE MAINTENANCE; WITH A SPECIAL KEY, THE CURIOUS ECCENTRIC ON THE SWINGING ARM PIVOT ALLOWS PRACTICAL ADJUSTMENT OF THE CHAIN TENSION.

MAINTENANCE AGAIN: THE PADS OF THE DISC BRAKES ARE EASILY REPLACED BY REMOVING THE COVERS. BREMBO CALIPERS ARE USED.

EUGENIO INGLESE, WEARING THE HELMET, ABSORBS TAGLIONI'S INSTRUCTIONS BEFORE TESTING THE NEW "500 L-TWIN": THIS WAS THE FIRST NAME USED BY *MOTOCICLISMO* FOR THE BIKE THAT WENT ON TO BE CALLED THE PANTAH.

1977 The novel drive-belt

During this period Ducati was part of the Efim group, a State finance corporation which controlled the Bolognese Marque, but did not particularly admire motorcycles. Ideas for relaunching the company and cost reduction would doubtless have led to the close of production. Ducati's success had a name — Fabio Taglioni — who continued to design authentic masterpieces, without allowing himself to be demoralised by the lack of means available or the limitations imposed from on high. At the end of the summer of '77, *Motociclismo* reported on two prototypes, a single-cylinder 350 cc and the new "L" twin 500 cc. The former never got past the experimental stage, whilst the latter began on a course of development which extends to the present day. Immediately noticeable were the SOHC desmo valve gear, driven by a rubber belt. This bike went on to be called the Pantah.

Provate in anteprima le nuove **Ducati 350-500 ad L**
di Eugenio Inglese

THE **500**'S TESTERS WERE ENTHUSIASTIC: THEY APPRECIATED THE ENGINE'S CONSIDERABLE POWER, ESPECIALLY ABOVE **3,000** RPM (RAPIDLY REACHING **9,000**...), AND SIGNIFICANT TOP-END PERFORMANCE: THE BIKE EASILY REACHED **190** KM/H. THE BIKE'S APPEARANCE WAS A THROW-BACK TO THE SADDLE-TANK UNIT OF THE "PARALLEL" DESMO **500**, DERIVED FROM THE GTL TOURING MODEL.

THE BACK OF THIS PHOTO STILL BEARS THE INSCRIPTION "EMPHASISE THE LEAN". THE JOURNALIST IMMEDIATELY TOOK TO THE NEW **500**, DEMONSTRATING THE POTENTIAL OF THIS NEW DUCATI. OF COURSE, THE **350** SINGLE-CYLINDER WAS ECLIPSED BY THIS MORE POWERFUL MODEL.

THE **500** ENGINE ON THE TEST-BENCH: THE BORE AND STROKE MEASURED **74 x 58** MM, THE SAME AS FOR THE **GP** TWINS SEVERAL YEARS PREVIOUSLY. THE COMPRESSION RATIO WAS **9.5:1** AND THE MAXIMUM POWER **50** HP. DURING ITS DEVELOPMENT, THIS ENGINE REACHED INCREDIBLE LIMITS.
ABOVE, THE PROTOTYPE OF THE **500** DURING PREPARATION. AN OPEN-BASED SPACE FRAME WAS PREPARED FOR THIS BIKE, WITH THE ENGINE "SUSPENDED" AT THREE POINTS. THE CRANKCASE ALSO HOUSED THE PIN OF THE SWINGING ARM SUSPENSION. THE WHEELBASE OF THIS PROTOTYPE WAS **1,450** MM, THE SAME AS THAT OF THE PANTAH. DETAIL, TOP LEFT, ANOTHER PROTOTYPE OF THE **500**: IN THE BACKGROUND, THE INCREDIBLE NUMBER OF SEPARATE COMPONENTS USED BY THE DEPARTMENT TO CREATE THE NEW MODEL.

THEIR TECHNICAL AND AESTHETIC FEATURES REVIEWED AND CORRECTED, THE **350** AND **500** "PARALLELS" WERE MARKETED AGAIN FOR THOSE BIKERS READY FOR A FAST RIDE WITH A PASSENGER, KITTED OUT WITH ONE-PIECE RACING LEATHERS AND FULL-FACE HELMET.

Super Sport 900

Much of the aura of fame which has, for years, been synonymous with Ducati is owed to the splendid Super Sport 900, a development on the earlier SS 750 with an engine derived from the GT 860. This is a bike with austere finish, perhaps "underdone" in terms of details, yet a pleasure to ride, impeccable in fast curves and when changing direction, and suitable for competition racing with a minimum of modifications. It was a triumph of substance over form and even impressed *Motociclismo*, which defined it "a well-mannered beast". The SS combined the advantages of good, high-performance mechanics with running gear that was classic but not obsolete. Another point in its favour was the fact that it weighed-in at under 200 kg, whilst its rivals (BMW R1000RS, Kawasaki Z 900, Laverda 1000 and Guzzi Le Mans) were much heavier. The engine performed perfectly between 3,000 and 9,000 rpm, being reliable and with negligible vibration. Below 3,000 rpm, the engine tended to "hunt" a little, and the wide turning circle and very long first gear made the 900 slightly clumsy in traffic. Yet this performance was acceptable for a bike designed for sporting use, far from the chaos on the city streets. The engine remains a splendid example, with desmo SOHC driven by gear shaft/helical gear and 90° V configuration.

A SPLENDID EXAMPLE OF AN ITALIAN SPORT BIKE, THE SUPER SPORT 900 IS ONE OF THE DUCATIS BEST LOVED BY COLLECTORS.

Specification

ENGINE: Four-stroke 90° V-twin configuration. Light alloy head and cylinders (with cast-iron liner). Bore: 86 mm. Stroke: 74.4 mm. Capacity: 863.9 cc. Compression ratio: 9.5:1. Desmodromic single overhead camshaft driven by gear shaft/helical gear, 2 valves per cylinder. Two Dellorto PHM carburettors with 40 mm choke. Fuel tank capacity: 19 litres. Maximum power: not available. Torque: not available. Electronic ignition. Electrical equipment with 12V-200W alternator and 12 volt 12 Ah battery. Wet sump forced lubrication with gear pump, 4.5 litres oil. Wet, multi-plate clutch. 5-speed gearbox. FRAME, FORKS AND RUNNING GEAR: Duplex open cradle tubular frame. Front hydraulic telescopic forks. Swinging arm rear suspension with adjustable hydraulic shocks. 280 mm twin disc front brake. 280 mm disc rear brake. Tyres: 3.50 x 18" (front), 460 x 18" (rear). DIMENSIONS AND WEIGHT: Length: 2,210 mm. Width: 675 mm. Seat height: 770 mm. Wheelbase: 1,500 mm. Weight (dry): 196 kg. PERFORMANCE: Top speed (measured) 225 kph. Average fuel consumption (measured) 14 km/lt.

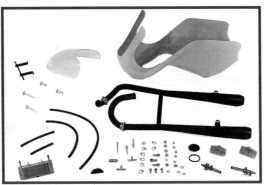

FAIRING, EXHAUSTS, OIL COOLER, STEEPER CAM ANGLES AND CLIP-ONS WERE ALL PART OF A KIT OF SPECIAL PARTS SOLD BY DUCATI AND INTENDED FOR THE 900 SS USED FOR TRACK RACES. BUT SOME PEOPLE USED THE KIT FOR STREET RIDING. THE 900 SS IS A FAVOURITE AMONG COLLECTORS. BUT, IF YOU'RE LUCKY ENOUGH TO OWN ONE, DON'T KEEP IT IN THE GARAGE: IT'S STILL A THRILLING RIDE! SEE-THROUGH DIAGRAM, THE SECRETS OF THE "L" TWIN ENGINE AND ITS LUBRICATION SYSTEM.

DEDICATED TO FANS OF GOOD MECHANICS, THREE PHOTOS TO DREAM OF: TOP, THE BEAUTIFULLY FABRICATED STEEL TUBE FRAME, A CLASSIC EXAMPLE OF DUCATI FRAMES FROM THAT YEAR. BELOW, SHAFT AND HELICAL GEARS WHICH DRIVE THE VALVE GEAR. BOTTOM, THE COMPLETE CON-ROD SET - NOTICE THE ROLLER-BEARINGS.

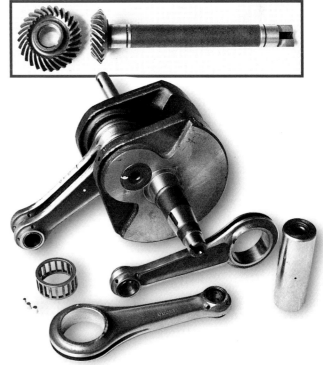

A DETERMINED MIKE HAILWOOD IMMORTALISED BY THE CAMERA DURING A RACE. HIS VICTORY AT THE TT CAUSED A SENSATION THE WORLD-OVER: THE LIKEABLE RIDER'S FAME (WELL DESERVED, THANKS ALSO TO HIS GENEROUS SPIRIT) WAS ALWAYS CONSIDERABLE, DESPITE THE FACT THAT HE HAD ALREADY LEFT THE HIGH-LEVEL RACE CIRCUIT SOME TIME EARLIER.

1978 Hailwood returns

In 1978, Hailwood decided to rejoin the Ducati team. The objective was to win the TTI World Championship. Mike obtained help from Taglioni and Farné and the support of the NCR team. He was provided with a bike that resembled a 900 "Special", one of the most advanced versions of the large cylinder capacity bikes with "helical gears". The large twin-cylinder bike developed 90 hp. The bike had special Dellorto PHM carburettors, modified by Malossi with a 41 mm choke and an engine protected by a sand-cast crankcase, from a limited edition made for endurance races. A dry clutch was fitted. The frame, similar to that of the standard model, but much lighter, was made by Bologna firm Daspa; the shocks were made by Girling. This work culminated in the conquest of the World Championship title by Ducati and Mike's victory over the exhausting distance covered by six laps on the Isle of Man track. The bike was painted red, white and green, the colours of Castrol, the rider's sponsor.

Piega bene
scatta meglio la
Ducati 350 SD

THE FINAL VERSION OF THE SD (SPORT DESMO): THE 500 HAD A DETERMINED LINE AND A HIGH-PERFORMANCE ENGINE, THANKS TO THE DESMODROMIC HEAD. THE BOTHERSOME VIBRATIONS AND ROUGH FINISH REMAINED, BUT THE POWER (37 HP AT 8,800 RPM) AND OPTIMUM HANDLING IMPROVED THE TESTER'S VERDICT.

DUCATI 125 Six Days

BELOW, A RADIANT HAILWOOD WITH HIS DUCATI: THE BRITISH RIDER WON NINE WORLD CHAMPIONSHIP TITLES; ONE EUROPEAN F2 AUTOMOBILE CHAMPIONSHIP AND RACED IN F1 WITH ADMIRABLE RESULTS UNTIL '74. HE DIED ON 22 MARCH 1981, HIS CAR BEING HIT BY A LORRY AS HE RETURNED FROM THE FISH AND CHIP SHOP WITH HIS TWO CHILDREN: HIS YOUNG DAUGHTER MICHELLE ALSO DIED, WHILST HIS SON, DAVID, MIRACULOUSLY SURVIVED.

BELOW, THE FAMOUS CELEBRATORY PHOTOGRAPH OF MIKE HAILWOOD'S VICTORY AT THE TOURIST TROPHY RACE: THE HISTORIC DATE WAS 2 JUNE 1978. AT LAST DUCATI WON ITS FIRST TITLE, AFTER MANY ATTEMPTS.

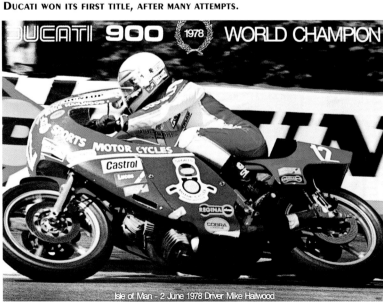

DUCATI 900 1978 WORLD CHAMPION

Isle of Man - 2 June 1978 Driver Mike Hailwood

TO RENDER THE 125 SIX DAYS MORE ATTRACTIVE, THE BROCHURE MADE USE OF THE ACROBATIC TALENTS OF ITALO FORNI, A DUCATI TESTER AND FORMER ITALIAN CROSS CHAMPION.

127

DON'T BE FOOLED BY THE PINT OF RED WINE: THE **NCR** WORKSHOP ATMOSPHERE WAS INFORMAL AND DOWN-TO-EARTH, BUT CARACCHI AND NEPOTI WORKED WITH A PRECISION COMPARABLE TO THAT OF THE BEST SWISS WATCHMAKERS. THEIR BIKES CAN BE CONSIDERED AUTHENTIC WORKS OF ART.

1978 900 NCR

Rino Caracchi and Giorgio Nepoti worked on Ducati bikes for almost 30 years and both have been in retirement since 1995, but the legend lives on. A glance at the photographs of one of their many creations, the 900 endurance, created in a limited edition and winner of many races with riders such as Vanes Francini, Carlo Perugini and Mauro Ricci, shows why the motorcycling world owes so much to this type of people. NCR was established in via Signorini in 1967. The abbreviation derives from the surnames of Nepoti, Caracchi and Rizzi, although from the moment in which the third partner left the firm, the "R" stood for Racing. Franco Farné, Mario Recchia and Piero Cavazzi, all Ducati employees, co-operated with NCR. The link between Ducati and NCR began in '72, with the 200 Mile race at Imola and, from '73 onwards the team was considered an external Ducati racing department. NCR produced the bikes ridden by Hailwood, the endurance bikes, the TT2 on which Rutter won the TTF2 World Championship, those of Polen in World Superbike and an infinite series of Specials, prototypes and "replicas".

Il grande MIKE HAILWOOD torna alle corse con la DUCATI 900 NCR

LEFT, THE INGENIOUS QUICK-RELEASE SYSTEM FOR THE **900 SS** WHICH WON THE SILHOUETTES CATEGORY AT THE LE MANS 24 HOUR RACE WITH RIDERS CANELLAS AND GRAU. BELOW, THE DRY CLUTCH AND BEAUTIFUL ADJUSTABLE FOOT RESTS: NCR TOOK GREAT PRIDE IN ATTENTION TO DETAIL, CONFIRMED BY THE INCREDIBLE RADIAL DRILLING ON THE DISCS (SMALL PHOTO, BELOW).

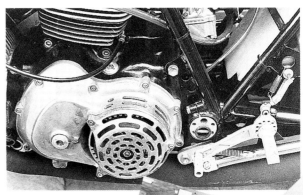

ABOVE AND RIGHT, TWO **900**S PREPARED BY **NCR**; NOTICE THE LARGER OIL SUMP (CAPACITY: **4** KG) THAN ON THE STANDARD MODELS AND THE DIFFERENT WAY IN WHICH THE FRONT BRAKE CALIPERS, EXHAUSTS AND REAR SHOCKS ARE MOUNTED ON THE TWO VERSIONS.

ABOVE, THE FRAME OF THIS BIKE WAS MADE BY BOLOGNESE FIRM DASPA IN CR-MO TUBES WITH MEASUREMENTS VERY SIMILAR TO THE ORIGINAL. HOWEVER, THIS MODEL WEIGHED **7** KG LESS THAN THE STANDARD VERSION. THE **900** NCRs WEIGHED **160** KG, COMPARED WITH THE **194** KG STANDARD VERSIONS.

FROM LEFT, GIORGIO NEPOTI, *MOTOCICLISMO*'S TESTER EUGENIO INGLESE AND RINO CARACCHI IN THE NCR MACHINE SHOP. AS CAN BE SEEN, THERE WERE NO MIRACLE SOLUTIONS, JUST PLAIN HARD WORK! NCR CLOSED AT THE END OF '95, LEAVING A VOID FOR MANY DUCATI FANS.

WITH FANTASTIC POWER AT LOW AND MEDIUM REVS, THE DARMAH WAS A PLEASURE TO RIDE AND VERY PRACTICAL, THANKS TO THE NEW ELECTRIC STARTER. THE PURISTS WERE NOT UPSET: THE INSTRUMENTS AND HANDLEBAR CONTROLS WERE MADE IN JAPAN, BUT THIS WAS NECESSARY, CONSIDERING THE MEDIOCRE CHARACTERISTICS OF SIMILAR ITALIAN COMPONENTS.

1979 The Darmah roars

Darmah is the name of the tiger in Sandokan, the famous Far-Eastern character in Salgari adventure books. This bike represents one of the final chapters in the history of the 900 road bikes, which started with the 860 GT and ended with the beautiful Mike Hailwood Replica and the less well-known S2. The Darmah was designed as the SS series meets the 860 GT. In contrast to its predecessor, its appearance derived from the 500 and 350 Desmo "Parallels". The frame was similar to that of the 860, although 5 cm lower and wider at the mid-point. The engine descended from that of the 860, taking the latter's pistons, con-rods and gearbox (although the selector and gearshift were on the left). Desmodromic heads were fitted, but with smaller intake manifold; the carburettors measured 32 mm rather than the 40 mm on the SS 900. The electronic ignition was made by Bosch.

Desmo comoda e vigorosa la nuova
DUCATI DARMAH 900

Questa esclusiva maximoto vanta la sportivissima distribuzione desmodromica unita alla comodità al tiro e alle finiture di una gran turismo. Si guida magnificamente sul misto, consuma relativamente poco ma accusa qualche oscillazione in curva a forte velocità. Frena veramente bene.

MOTOCICLISMO

ABOVE, A PROTOTYPE OF THE DARMAH 900 SPORT. EVEN THE WHEELS WERE OF A DIFFERENT DESIGN TO THOSE OF THE FINAL BIKE, AS WERE THE FRONT TWIN DISCS - AND GRAPHICS.

RIGHT, THE DARMAH FRAME DERIVED FROM THAT OF THE 860 BUT WAS LOWERED, ESPECIALLY AT THE CENTRE. THIS 900 WAS THE FIRST STANDARD BIKE FITTED WITH MAGNESIUM ALLOY WHEELS, PREVIOUSLY RESERVED FOR COMPETITION MODELS.

"WEAR THE COLOURS OF YOUR DUCATI", WAS THE SLOGAN FOR THIS LINE OF CLOTHING AND ACCESSORIES AVAILABLE FOR FANS OF THE ITALIAN COMPANY.

1979

The motorcycles that made history

CHARACTERISED BY A MORE CONVINCING LINE, THE PANTAH BORROWED FROM THE LINES OF THE DUCATI SPORTS MODELS, RESHAPING THEM IN A MODERN VEIN: IT WAS WELCOMED WITH GREAT ENTHUSIASM, AND RIGHTLY SO.

Pantah 500

"Nothing in the world is more powerful or faster than the Pantah". This was how *Motociclismo* described the 500 Ducati. A truly breathtaking bike that immediately won the hearts of many fans, but which marked the starting point for the history of Ducati during the busy period from the end of the Seventies to the subsequent decade.

The new desmo SOHC twin design was very modern at the time, and all due credit must be paid to the Ducati designers for their excellent work (the team consisted of the "guru" Taglioni, Luigi Mengoli, Giuseppe Bocchi and Federico Martini). The Pantah convinced the testers of that period: "Almost 50 hp at the wheel and 200 km/h are the exceptional results of our tests. The new twin has a high torque, great stability and low consumption. It is also distinguished by its exclusive technical features. Greater attention could, however, be paid to the details." In addition, it was the first Ducati twin with silent mechanisms (thanks to the valve gear controlled by the drive belt which substituted the helical gears).

But some things still had to be perfected... For example, the clutch tended to swell under stress, making it difficult for the rider to find neutral, whilst the hard saddle and stiff suspension made it a little uncomfortable — and the fuel tank filler cap leaked. But these oversights were forgiven. This engine brought Ducati victories in both speed and off-road races; the engine with "drive belt" was, in fact, the secret of success for dozens of bikes.

Specification

ENGINE: Four-stroke 90° V-twin configuration. Light alloy head and cylinders (with Gilnisil liner coating). Bore: 74 mm. Stroke: 58 mm. Capacity: 498.9 cc. Compression ratio: 9.5:1. Desmodromic single overhead camshaft driven by gear shaft/helical gear, 2 valves per cylinder. Two Dellorto PHF 36AS carburettors with 36 mm choke. Fuel tank capacity: 18 litres. Maximum power (at axle): 45 hp at 9,050 rpm. Torque: 4.1 kgm at 6,300 rpm. Electronic ignition. Electrical equipment with 12V-200W alternator and 12 volt 14 Ah battery. Wet sump forced lubrication with gear pump, 3 litres oil. Wet, multi-plate clutch. 5-speed gearbox. FRAME, FORKS AND RUNNING GEAR: Tubular space frame. Front hydraulic telescopic forks. Swinging arm rear suspension with adjustable hydraulic shocks. 260 mm twin disc front brake. 260 mm disc rear brake. Tyres: 3.25 x 18" (front), 350 x 18" (rear). DIMENSIONS AND WEIGHT: Length: 2,150 mm. Width: 675 mm. Seat height: 700 mm. Wheelbase: 1,450 mm. Weight (dry): 180 kg. PERFORMANCE: Top speed (measured) 198 kph.

THE *MOTOCICLISMO* TESTER IS READY FOR THE OFF... BUT BEFORE STARTING THE INSTRUMENT READINGS, THERE'S JUST ENOUGH TIME FOR A WELL-POSED PHOTO, WITH THE SHINY ENGINE (MADE COMPLETELY OF LIGHT ALLOY) IN FULL VIEW.

ONCE THE CASING IS REMOVED, THE EVOLUTION IN THE VALVE GEAR IS OBVIOUS: THE TOOTHED BELTS MADE OF REINFORCED RUBBER CONTROL THE MOVEMENTS OF THE CAMSHAFTS. THE CYLINDERS ARE MADE OF A LIGHT ALLOY, THE RODS TREATED WITH A NICKEL-SILICON CARBIDE LINER.

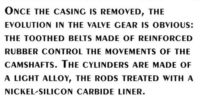

THE SPACE FRAME WAS STARTING TO BE ONE OF THE CHARACTERISTICS OF DUCATI BIKES. THE ENGINE WAS SUSPENDED FROM THE STRUCTURE AT THREE ANCHORING POINTS. LEFT, THE STEERING GEAR WITH MARZOCCHI FORKS WITH 35 MM RODS AND THE 260 MM BREMBO CALIPER WHICH GUARANTEED SURE-FOOTED BRAKING.

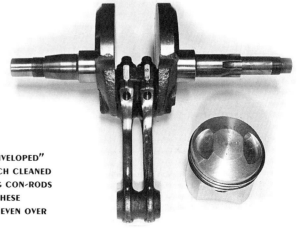

THE PIN OF THE SWINGING ARM SUSPENSION "ENVELOPED" BY THE CRANKCASE, A RATIONAL SOLUTION WHICH CLEANED UP THE LINE OF THE FRAME. RIGHT, THE STRONG CON-RODS AND PISTON. IT IS IMMEDIATELY OBVIOUS THAT THESE IMPORTANT COMPONENTS CAN TAKE THE STRAIN EVEN OVER LONG DISTANCES.

133

THE BEAUTIFUL RED/SILVER VERSION OF THE BIKE TESTED BY *MOTOCICLISMO* IN **1979** WAS IN THE STANDARD COLOURS OFFERED BY THE COMPANY. THIS BIKE HAS A **24** LITRE FUEL TANK, OFFERED AS AN OPTIONAL IN PLACE OF THE STANDARD **18** LITRE TANK.

1979 The Pantah and its rivals

According to *Motociclismo*'s readings, the Pantah developed 48.8 hp at 9,000 rpm, making it the fastest 500 around in '79; its maximum torque of 4.02 kgm at 6,750 rpm was second only to that of the Honda CX: in fact, this was the only defeat suffered by the Ducati twin at the hands of its competitors. In the 400 m from standing start test, the bike reached 156.5 km/h in just 13.3 seconds, and its top speed of 198 km/h was more than 10 km/h faster than that of its closest rival, whilst in terms of fuel consumption only the more subdued and famously thrifty Morini 500 went one better. In a word, rather than a test, *Motociclismo* published a triumphant article, confirmed by other specialised magazines which sang the praises of the Ducati twin. Today, the remaining Pantahs are sought after by collectors, but are difficult to come by. This bike is still great to ride on the streets, as many happy enthusiasts will tell you.

THE FINAL PHOTOS WHILE A MECHANIC CHECKS THAT EVERYTHING IS OK. THE MAN WITH THE MOUSTACHE IS MARCO CUPPINI, THEN DUCATI PRESS OFFICER.

BELOW, A WHEELIE AT THE START LINE, AFTER FITTING THE OPTIONAL 43 TOOTHED SPROCKET WHICH DECIDEDLY SHORTENED THE FINAL RATIO.

TOP, THE PANTAH'S ENGINE SEEN FROM THE VALVE GEAR SIDE. ABOVE, THE TAIL SECTION WITH SINGLE-SEATER SADDLE. A TWO-SEATER SADDLE WAS ALSO AVAILABLE; THE TAIL SECTION HAS A BUILT-IN TOOL COMPARTMENT.

THE NIPPODENSO INSTRUMENTS; THE DECISION TO FIT JAPANESE-MADE COMPONENTS GAVE GOOD RESULTS AND AN INTERNATIONAL FLAVOUR. HOWEVER, SOME PEOPLE SUBSTITUTED THE INSTRUMENTS WITH A WELL-CRAFTED VEGLIA BORLETTI REV COUNTER.

THE "OFFICIAL" TT WITH FULL FAIRING, TOGETHER WITH THE HALF-FAIRING VERSION DESIGNED FOR PRIVATE RIDERS.

1980 Pantah: on the road to victory

There had hardly been time to get used to the new twin when Ducati began working on the Pantah with the aim of creating a winning bike and, at the end of 1980, it had clocked up numerous victories on both European and American tracks. But the best was still to come — when just one year later Tony Rutter won the World Championship title. Ducati prepared two bikes: the official version with full fairing, with obvious NCR traits, and a "kitted-out" version for sport riders. The transformation envisaged new bore and stroke measurements (80 x 58 mm), a 582.7 cc capacity, 2 into 1 exhaust pipe and camshafts with steeper angle. Thus transformed, the Pantah developed 70 hp at 9,800 rpm. The running gear, on the official version, included a Marzocchi front fork with magnesium alloy fork legs, gas shocks (also by Marzocchi), Brembo racing brakes and Michelin slick tyres. The fairing and saddle-fuel tank unit were the result of experience with the 900 NCR endurance bike. The "Kit box" for private riders cost 1,368,000 lire, although today its value has soared.

Ducati Pantah protagonista sulle piste di due continenti

Alla sua prima stagione di gare, la vivacissima bicilindrica bolognese ha confermato le promesse imponendosi nettamente in numerose gare per moto di serie in Europa e negli USA Le versioni TT, TT2 e il gruppo di potenziamento.

MOTOCICLISMO - 180

A TOUGH CHAMPIONSHIP SPEED RACE WAS RUN IN PERU, DOMINATED BY TWO ITALIAN RIDERS WHO LIVED IN LIMA: LEFT, CLAUDIO SOLI (WITH MOUSTACHE), PERUVIAN CHAMPION IN '78 WITH THE DUCATI SS 900, AND THE OTHER "DUCATISTA" GIAMPAOLO BARBIERI, CLASSIFIED SECOND. THE TWO RIDERS, MEMBERS OF THE "PIEGA RACING TEAM", HAD TWO BIKES PREPARED IN BOLOGNA. THEY WERE THE ONLY DUCATIS IN PERU!

ABOVE, THE OFFICIAL TT READY FOR THE '81 SEASON AND, RIGHT, THE "KIT" VERSION. INSIDE THE KIT BOX SOLD BY DUCATI, THE PRIVATE RIDER FOUND CYLINDERS, PISTONS, AN EXHAUST PIPE, THREE SPROCKETS, CARBURETTOR JETS AND STEEP-ANGLE CAMSHAFTS. THE ORIGINAL FAIRINGS USED ON THE STANDARD MODEL WERE APPLIED ON THIS BIKE.

DUCATI SUPPLIED ITS BIKES TO THE DETERMINED BOLOGNA VIGILI URBANI TEAM, WHICH OFTEN WON ITS CATEGORY AT THE RACE MEETINGS: HERE THE TEAM MEMBERS ARE SEEN IN A PHOTO AT THE DUCATI FACILITY WITH TAGLIONI, FOLLOWING THEIR VICTORY AT PAVIA IN '78. THE MOUSTACHED MUNICIPAL POLICEMAN AT THE CENTRE (BETWEEN BIKES 14 AND 6) HAS OFTEN SHOWN GREAT LENIENCY TO ONE OF THE AUTHORS OF THIS BOOK, CAUGHT WHILE PULLING SPORTING STUNTS NOT ALWAYS COMPATIBLE WITH THE HIGHWAY CODE...

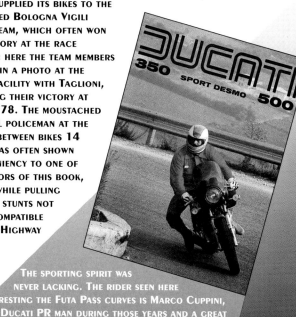

THE SPORTING SPIRIT WAS NEVER LACKING. THE RIDER SEEN HERE CRESTING THE FUTA PASS CURVES IS MARCO CUPPINI, DUCATI PR MAN DURING THOSE YEARS AND A GREAT SPORTING FIGURE: HE WAS AN EXCELLENT BASKETBALL PLAYER, AND WASN'T AT ALL BAD ON A MOTORCYCLE.

Mike Hailwood Replica 900

To celebrate its first World Championship title, Ducati produced a splendid sport bike, the Mike Hailwood Replica, which was the latest development on the 900 Super Sport. Tall and imposing, painted brightly in the Italian colours, red, white and green, this bike was a dream for the more "fanatical" fans of the Ducati marque; not even fitted with an electric starter, it was a bike for "real" men! It was not easy to ride (it required strength, especially on hairpin bends and tight curves), but those who managed to get to grips with this bike were never disappointed. Many Japanese big bikes were faster and easier to handle, but this bike stood the test of time. Try buying one today, it'll cost you a fortune! It had some novelties compared with the 900 SS: the fairings, new alloy hubs, a Brembo racing-style braking system and new Pirelli Phantom tyres. The tester of the time had this to say about the bike: "At 3,000 rpm the engine torque is 6 kgm and is the same at 8,000 rpm, after passing through a top value of 7.63 kgm at 5,250 rpm... It's always ready to take off, whatever gear you're in and wherever you are on the rev range..." And it consumed very little: covering 16 kilometres per litre at a speed of 170 km/h! The MHR was the penultimate bike with "helical gear"-driven camshaft to be mass produced. The last was also a MHR, but was a 1,000 cc.

A ROMANTIC AND ANACHRONISTIC SPORT BIKE, PAINTED IN THE COLOURS OF THE ITALIAN FLAG, OR A FANTASTIC TWIN WITH HIGH TORQUE AND PROVEN STABILITY? A DIFFICULT DECISION, AND ONLY TIME WILL TELL...

Specification

ENGINE: Four-stroke 90° V-twin configuration. Light alloy head and cylinders (with cast-iron liner). Bore: 86 mm. Stroke: 74.4 mm. Capacity: 863.9 cc. Desmodromic single overhead camshaft driven by gear shaft/helical gear, 2 valves per cylinder. Two Dellorto PHM carburettors with 40 mm choke. Fuel tank capacity: 18 litres. Maximum power (at crankshaft): 80 hp at 7,000 rpm. Torque: 8.5 kgm at 5,800 rpm. Electronic ignition. Electrical equipment with 12V-200W alternator and 12 volt 14 Ah battery. Wet sump forced lubrication with gear pump, 4.5 litres oil. Wet, multi-plate clutch. 5-speed gearbox. FRAME, FORKS AND RUNNING GEAR: Duplex open cradle tubular frame. Front hydraulic telescopic forks. Swinging arm rear suspension with adjustable hydraulic shocks. 280 mm twin disc front brake. 229 mm disc rear brake. Tyres: 100/90 x 18" (front), 110/90 x 18" (rear). DIMENSIONS AND WEIGHT: Length: 2,200 mm. Width: 700 mm. Seat height: 750 mm. Wheelbase: 1,510 mm. Weight (dry): 194 kg. PERFORMANCE: Top speed (measured) 213.88 kph. Average fuel consumption (measured) 15 km/lt.

THE MHR 900 IN ITS PREFERRED SURROUNDINGS, FAST WIDE CURVES, IN WHICH IT DEMONSTRATED GREAT STABILITY. THE ARRIVAL OF PIRELLI PHANTOM TYRES FURTHER IMPROVED ITS ROADHOLDING. THE FRAME, LIKE THE ENGINE, WAS DERIVED FROM THAT OF THE WELL-KNOWN SS 900. NOTICE THE CONTI EXHAUST PIPES, A "MUST" FOR THE MORE TENACIOUS DUCATI FANS.

THESE COMPONENTS WERE FAMOUS FOR THEIR "TOLERANCE" OF THE ENGINE, AND ISSUED A POWERFUL ROAR. OBSERVE THE CAMSHAFT DRIVEN BY GEAR SHAFT/HELICAL GEAR, CHARACTERISTIC OF A LENGTHY PERIOD IN DUCATI'S HISTORY. ONCE THE MHR 900 AND 1000 WERE RETIRED FROM THE SCENE, THIS SYSTEM WAS NO LONGER USED. BOTTOM LEFT, THE IMPRESSIVE CHOKE OF THE

DELLORTO PHM 40 CARBURETTOR, READY TO SUPPLY THE FRONT CYLINDER. DESPITE APPEARANCES, THE MHR DID NOT CONSUME LARGE QUANTITIES OF FUEL. THE STEERING GEAR (BELOW) USED A MARZOCCHI FORK WITH 38 MM RODS AND A MULTI-HOLE TWIN DISC BREMBO BRAKING SYSTEM WITH TWIN PISTON "GOLD SERIES" CALIPERS.

WOULD THE "HELICAL GEAR ENGINES" HAVE HAD A FUTURE? ACCORDING TO MANY DUCATI EXPERTS, THE ANSWER IS "YES". IT SEEMS THERE WAS ALREADY A DESIGN THAT WOULD HAVE ENHANCED THE FAMOUS "POMPONE", BRINGING IT UP TO 1,200 CC. THE STANDARD VERSION DEVELOPED A MAX. OF 83 HP AT 6,700 RPM; THE RACING VERSION, WITH STRAIGHT-THROUGH EXHAUST, REACHED 90 HP AT 7,500 RPM.

140

1980 MHR Mille, the last "helical gear"

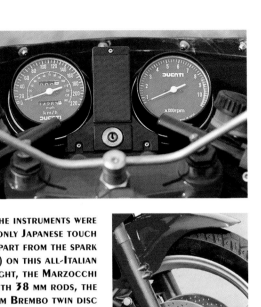

The beautiful, monumental Mike Hailwood Replica Mille closed a chapter in Ducati technical history, that of the "helical gear engines". Some insist that the extinction of these engines was caused by excessive production costs, by the insuperable technical difficulties encountered when attempts were made to fit them with electronic injection systems, and even a kind of boycott by the new proprietor. Yet the MHR 1000 remains a monument to motorcycling: a beautiful, rare, imposing and high-performance bike, one of the best models of the Eighties. But the 1000 did not just have "the look". Redesigned by design-engineer Bordi (the rising star of the period) and Mengoli, it had new bore and stroke measurements, completely renewed crankcases, a single-piece engine shaft, enhanced oil pump and cylinders with incorporated liners. A redesigned gearbox was fitted (the earlier "overdone" model used on the 900 disappeared). The Dellorto PHM 40 carburettor remained, but new exhaust pipes arrived, with a wonderful "2 in 1" model, inspired by those of NCR.

ABOVE, THE INSTRUMENTS WERE THE ONLY JAPANESE TOUCH (APART FROM THE SPARK PLUGS) ON THIS ALL-ITALIAN BIKE. RIGHT, THE MARZOCCHI FORKS WITH 38 MM RODS, THE 280 MM BREMBO TWIN DISC AND FPS ALLOY WHEELS.

KNOWN TO FANS AS THE "POMPONE" ("BIG PUMP"), THE MIKE HAILWOOD REPLICA MILLE ENGINE HAD MANY FEATURES ALREADY SEEN IN THE 900, BUT IMPORTANT DEVELOPMENTS WERE MADE ON THE CRANK-CASE, CYLINDERS AND CLUTCH. THE BEST FEATURE OF THIS ENGINE WAS THE HIGH TORQUE: 9 KGM AT LESS THAN 6,000 RPM. ALL THINGS CONSIDERED, IT WAS A JOY TO RIDE.

FOR FANS OF THE "POMPONE", SWISSMAN GERALD VOGEL, OWNER OF MOTO FASZINATION, PROPOSED A SPECIAL BASED ON THE MHR 1000. NOTICE THE TRANSPARENT COVER ON THE HELICAL GEARS, AUTOGRAPHED BY TAGLIONI. PURE DEVOTION!

141

1981/1982 Limited edition, unlimited victories

When considering "exotic" motorcycles, that is to say, high-tech yet limited editions, the Pantah TT2 is a classic example. Around thirty examples of this bike were hand-built in a joint project by the racing department and specialists (NCR, Verlicchi frames, Paioli and Marzocchi suspension, Campagnolo wheels). The TT2 was at the same time magnificent and competitive. It won many races in Italy, but is best remembered as the unbeatable machine ridden by Tony Rutter, the British racer, four times winner of the TT Formula Two World Championship. Strangely, due to the racing rules, this bike mounted 41 mm carburettors in Italian races and 36 mm ones in the World Championship races. The TT2 concept soon developed into another magnificent racebike, the TT1, less fortunate on the track, but no less interesting from the technical viewpoint. It was also a good test bench for new running gear: it was the first Ducati to be fitted with the 16" front wheel, requested by Italian racer Walter Cussigh.

CHARACTERISED BY ITS COMPACTNESS - TALLER RIDERS HAD TROUBLE GETTING TO GRIPS WITH THIS MODEL - THE TT2 HAS A CR-MO STEEL SPACE FRAME MADE BY VERLICCHI, WEIGHING JUST 8 KG. THE REAR SUSPENSION WAS A CANTILEVER SINGLE-SHOCK MODEL.

TOP, THE DIAMETER OF THE AIR INTAKE ON THE HEADS, WITH DESMO VALVE GEAR, WAS MODIFIED COMPARED WITH THE STANDARD VERSIONS (41 MM COMPARED WITH THE STANDARD 35); THE CAMSHAFT HAD A STEEPER ANGLE, BUT THE REST WAS ALL STANDARD! ABOVE, THE MULTI-DISC DRY CLUTCH WITH HYDRAULIC CONTROL AND ITS MAGNESIUM COVER. THE PRIMARY DRIVE SPROCKET HAD STRAIGHT-CUT TEETH. THE DELLORTO PHM 41 CARBURETTOR HAD NO PUMP. THE FRONT VIEW AT CENTRE-PAGE REVEALS THE BIKE'S COMPACTNESS AND THE PRESENCE OF THE OIL COOLER.

OPPOSITE, THANKS TO THIS BIKE, TONY RUTTER, A BRITISH RACER APPROACHING HIS FORTIES, BECAME THE MAN TO BEAT IN THE TT2 CATEGORY.

THE REAR CALIPER HAD A TWIN MOUNTING: THIS DETAIL WAS DESIGNED TO FIT TWO CALIPERS ON THE SAME DISC; ONLY ONE WAS USED DURING RACES.

143

TUCKED BEHIND THE LOW HANDLEBAR FAIRING, TO IMPROVE THE AERODYNAMICS, THE *MOTOCICLISMO* TESTER REACHED ALMOST **200** KM/H DURING A TRACK TEST.

1981/1982 Right on track with the Pantah 600

Take a step back in time, to the designing of the Pantah engine: this twin was originally made in the 600 cc version, then reduced to 500 cc for marketing reasons. After its initial success, the Pantah returned to its former capacity, demonstrating that the original calculations were spot on; the new 600 had more torque and was much easier to handle at low revs. The new 600 was also fitted with a new low handlebar fairing, hydraulic clutch and wider rear fairing (4.00" rather than 3.50"). The *Motociclismo* testers who tried it out during track sessions at Monza and Imola found it precise, easy to handle, with sure-footed braking and a sharp engine. The maximum power rating was 52.8 hp at 8,500 rpm, whilst the actual top speed was just under 200 km/h.

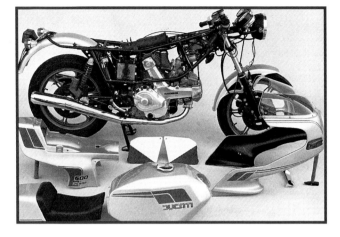

Con la Ducati Pantah 600 e la Kawasaki GP 550 sulle piste di Imola e Monza

Primi contatti con queste due attese novità sportive, a Imola per la Ducati e Monza per la Kawasaki. La Ducati ha guadagnato soprattutto i riscoppia nei confronti della già affermata versione di 500. La Kawasaki ha dimostrato di non temere il confronto con le 650-750.

di Riccardo Tellarini

THE TUBULAR SPACE FRAME, WHICH WAS TO BE A CHARACTERISTIC OF DUCATI BIKES EVEN IN THE FUTURE. THE FUEL TANK IS THE ONLY COMPONENT MADE OF SHEET METAL; ALL OF THE OTHER PARTS WERE MADE OF FIBREGLASS.

ABOVE, THE PANTAH 600 ON THE TEST BENCH: ITS MAX POWER (52.86 HP) WAS DEVELOPED AT 8,500 RPM. BELOW, THE 2-SEATER SADDLE COULD BE TRANSFORMED INTO A SINGLE-SEATER THANKS TO A TAIL SECTION EXTENSION SUPPLIED WITH THE BIKE.

THE PANTAH 600 LINE WAS CHARACTERISED BY THE NEW LOW HANDLEBAR FAIRING WITH SPOILER, DESIGNED TO "HOLD DOWN" THE STEERING GEAR AT HIGH SPEEDS AND DIRECT AIR TO THE CYLINDERS.

THE PANTAH 600 WAS MORE THAN JUST A SPORT BIKE: FOR EXAMPLE, IT WAS ALSO THE FIRST CHOICE OF THE MUNICIPAL POLICE FORCE.

THE LAST **900**, THE **S2** WITH DESMO VALVE GEAR, IN A POSED PHOTO DURING THE *MOTOCICLISMO* TESTS.

1983 A crucial year

If there was a moment that threw Ducati fans into a panic, this was in '83. Owned by the Società Finmeccanica — therefore, the State — and part of the VM Group, at the time Ducati was considered almost exclusively a "production unit" with a vast facility. The management thought little of motorcycles, whilst the company's new horizons opened onto large diesel and boat engines. Yet enthusiasts the world over dreamed of the Bolognese bikes, Rutter won with the TT2, Walter Villa challenged the Japanese with the TTI at the Bol D'Or... Luck would have it that a joint-venture was set up with a newly established but determined Italian motorcycle manufacturer, Cagiva, which was in search of new engines and 4-stroke technology. More about Cagiva later...

THERE WERE ALSO DESIGN STUDIES BASED ON THE HELICAL GEAR ENGINE: THIS PHOTO SHOWS THE PROJECT 900, CHARACTERISED BY A BOXY LINE THAT WAS - AND NOT WITHOUT REASON - SAID TO BE "HACKED OUT WITH AN AXE"!

THE S2 900, ALSO MADE IN A 1000 CC VERSION, WAS THE LAST OF THE "HELICAL GEAR ENGINE" MOTORCYCLES. THIS BIKE, MAINLY MADE FOR EXPORT, WAS CHARMING, FAST AND HAD SURE BRAKING, BUT IS REMEMBERED FOR ITS UNCOMFORTABLE RIDING POSITION, DIFFICULT HANDLING AND "DIRTY" CARBURATION. BELOW, THE "HELICAL GEAR ENGINE" BIKES DEFEND DUCATI'S HONOUR ON AMERICAN TRACKS, DOMINATING THE BATTLE OF THE TWINS, IN PARTICULAR WITH JAMES ADAMO, SEEN WITH THE 900 NCR ON WHICH HE WON THE '82 DAYTONA RACE.

THE DERBY CONTINUES: DUCATI SOLD MANY SPORT BIKES TO THE MORE HARDENED SPEED FREAKS AND SUPPLIED THE PANTAH 600 TO THE VIGILI URBANI. BUT THE HIGH-PERFORMANCE BIKES WENT TO THE FORMER...

DUCATI 900 S2 DESMO

EMPHASISED BY THE BLACK LIVERY WITH RED, ORANGE AND YELLOW COACHLINES, THE 900 S2 DESMO SHOWS OFF ITS AGGRESSIVE FRONT PROFILE.

XL 350 and TL 600

The engine is the most interesting feature of a bike, and often identifies it. We often forget the designers of this fundamental component, who present valid designs which, once put into production, do not always win over the public. This was the destiny of the TL 600, basically a Pantah 600 with touring-oriented trim and form, proposed with a large side fairing which completely hid the rear cylinder. The TL convinced the testers only when ridden as a sport bike, that is to say, when the positive features inherited from the Pantah were revealed. In contrast, the XL 350 was a typical product of Italian tax laws, which impose a high level of VAT on bikes with a capacity above 350 cc. This explains the Italian tendency to prefer bikes of that capacity and the examples of this category, such as the 350 Ducati and Aermacchi singles, and the Morini twins. The Pantah engine was intended for this capacity right from the design stage, thus the 350 Ducatis' impeccable performance. The XL, although marred by a most unfortunate styling, had an engine capable of smooth power delivery from 2,500 to 10,000 rpm and excellent performance, combined with impressive road holding. Its powerful braking and low consumption should also be noticed. Defects included: the poor finish, its weight (comparable to that of a "500") and over-long gear ratios. But the XL and TL's real problem was their look.

SIDE VIEW OF THE **XL** AND A PHOTO OF THE BIKE IN USE, WITH FRONT WHEEL FOR THE **TL 600**: THESE TWO BIKES, REDESIGNED AND CORRECTED, PASSED OVER TO THE CAGIVA CATALOGUE.

MOTORE, TELAIO, FRENI I TRE NERBI DELLA NUOVA DUCATI XL 350

Specification

ENGINE: Four-stroke 90° V-twin configuration. Aluminium alloy head and Gilnisil barrel liners. Air-cooled. Bore: 66 mm. Stroke: 51 mm. Capacity: 349.6 cc. Compression ratio: 10.5:1. Desmodromic single overhead camshaft, belt driven, two 60° side valves per cylinder. Two Dellorto PHF 30 carburettors with pump. Fuel tank capacity: 19 litres. Maximum power: 38.5 hp at 9,000 rpm. Max. torque: 3.1 kgm at 8,750 rpm (measured). Bosch BTZ electronic ignition. 12V-200W electrical equipment with 12 volt 14 Ah battery. Wet sump forced lubrication, 3 litres oil. 5-speed gearbox. FRAME, FORKS AND RUNNING GEAR: Tubular steel space frame. Paioli front telescopic forks with 35 mm stanchions. Swinging arm rear suspension with 2 adjustable hydraulic shocks. Brembo 260 mm twin disc front brake. 260 mm disc rear brake. Tyres: 3.00 x 18" (front), 3.50 x 18" (rear). DIMENSIONS AND WEIGHT: Length: 2,160 mm. Width: 710 mm. Seat height: 820 mm. Wheelbase: 1,450 mm. Weight (dry): 187 kg. PERFORMANCE: Top speed (measured) 165.2 kph.

ABOVE, THE TL 600, WITHOUT THE BODYWORK, REVEALS ITS DIRECT DESCENT FROM THE PANTAH 600. BELOW, THE INSTRUMENTS SET INTO A DASHBOARD.

TOP LEFT, THE XL IS PUSHED TO ITS TOP SPEED: DURING *MOTOCICLISMO'S* TESTS, THE BIKE REACHED OVER **165** KM/H, A TRULY IMPRESSIVE RESULT FOR ITS CATEGORY. DESPITE THE TOURING TRIM, THE TL 600 (LEFT) WAS NO SLOW COACH: IT EASILY REACHED **180** KM/H WITH THE RIDER IN AN AERODYNAMIC POSITION. THE SIDE VIEW HIGHLIGHTS THE "DISAPPEARANCE" OF THE REAR CYLINDER, HIDDEN BY THE SIDE FAIRING.

TOP LEFT, TWO DETAILS OF THE XL: THE CHAIN TENSIONER GUIDE AND THE VALVE FOR ADJUSTING THE PRESSURE OF THE SHOCKS. ABOVE, THE INSTRUMENTS: THIS IS A UNIT WITH ROUNDED DIALS, ALREADY SEEN ON THE PANTAH.

SPECIALS CONSTRUCTED AROUND DUCATI BASES HAVE ALWAYS EXISTED, SINCE THE PERIOD OF TAMAROZZI AND HIS CUCCIOLO, BUT THE REAL BOOM STARTED IN THE MID-EIGHTIES. JAPANESE COMPANY YAJIMA BUILT AN ALUMINIUM BOX-SECTION TUBULAR FRAME AROUND AN 860, WITH 16" WIDE FRONT WHEEL.

1984/1985 The great comeback

This was a period of contrasting reports: word (and print) had it, perhaps deliberately, that Ducati was to cease production of motorcycles in order to concentrate on manufacturing engines for Cagiva. Meanwhile, the Italian Marque's cult spread like wildfire in Japan, thanks to inspired specialists who created refined Specials. Amid all the confusion, there was one certainty: the Pantah 750 F1, then the news that the Italian company would continue its production of 1,000 cc helical gear engines, the S2 and MHR spread. The situation seemed unfathomable, yet some decisions had been made: Bordi was the new technical director, his task to guide Ducati into the Nineties, whilst Cagiva began work in earnest and its Elefant 650, with Pantah engine, debuted in Morocco. This attractive bike demonstrated the universal application of Ducati engines, competitive on the race tracks, but also on the African trails littered with sand and stones.

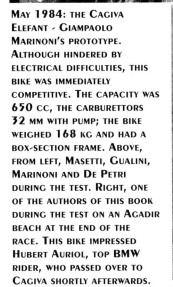

MAY 1984: THE CAGIVA ELEFANT - GIAMPAOLO MARINONI'S PROTOTYPE. ALTHOUGH HINDERED BY ELECTRICAL DIFFICULTIES, THIS BIKE WAS IMMEDIATELY COMPETITIVE. THE CAPACITY WAS 650 CC, THE CARBURETTORS 32 MM WITH PUMP; THE BIKE WEIGHED 168 KG AND HAD A BOX-SECTION FRAME. ABOVE, FROM LEFT, MASETTI, GUALINI, MARINONI AND DE PETRI DURING THE TEST. RIGHT, ONE OF THE AUTHORS OF THIS BOOK DURING THE TEST ON AN AGADIR BEACH AT THE END OF THE RACE. THIS BIKE IMPRESSED HUBERT AURIOL, TOP BMW RIDER, WHO PASSED OVER TO CAGIVA SHORTLY AFTERWARDS.

IN ORDER TO COMPETE IN THE TT1 (UP TO 750 CC), DUCATI PREPARED A SPLENDID BIKE WHICH REACHED A TOP POWER RATING OF 748 CC THANKS TO A BORE AND STROKE MEASURING 88 x 61.5 MM. THE MODIFICATIONS MADE FORCED THE ENGINEERS TO REDESIGN THE CRANKCASE. THE REAR SUSPENSION WAS A RISING RATE SINGLE-SHOCK. THIS BIKE WAS ENTERED IN BOTH SPEED AND ENDURANCE RACES, EVEN WITH A NEW FOUR-VALVE HEAD DESIGNED BY BORDI, NEWLY APPOINTED TECHNICAL DIRECTOR AT DUCATI. ABOVE, THE BIKE DURING TESTS AT MISANO ON A COLD WINTER'S DAY, SEEN WITH THE MEN FROM THE RACING DEPARTMENT AND, FINALLY, DISASSEMBLED.

WITH THE PANTAH 600 TL, DUCATI PROMOTED ITS TOURING MODELS AGAIN.

WHAT DO YOU NEED TO RACE AT 180 KM/H ON THE SANDS OF NORTH AFRICA? THE ANSWER IS SIMPLE: A POWERFUL, SOLID DUCATI 750. IN THE PHOTO, HUBERT AURIOL, ALREADY WINNER OF TWO PARIS-DAKAR RACES, IN ACTION WITH THE CAGIVA-DUCATI IN 1985.

1984/1985

The arrival of the elephant

As already indicated, from June 1983 there was an agreement between Cagiva and Ducati, which saw the latter supply twin cylinder engines to the newly established Company (1978), which was already doing very well on the small cc market. This period was followed by a more solid relationship and, in 1985 Cagiva, represented by brothers Claudio and Gianfranco Castiglioni, acquired control of the majority shareholding in Ducati from Finmeccanica, thus extracting the Bolognese company from the VM Group. Ducati's entry into the Cagiva Group immediately provided at least one certainty: it would continue to produce high level motorcycles, even for racing. Much criticism was aimed at the Castiglioni management, yet if Ducati held its present position and won across the board in Superbike and Supersport competitions, at the Pharaohs' Rally and in the Paris-Dakar, it would be thanks to the little elephant (Cagiva's trade-mark) that began to appear on the fairings of the bikes from Borgo Panigale from '85 onwards — especially on one of the best ever 750 sport models: the F1. Meanwhile, the 350 and 600 cc engines of the Pantah provided the basis for two touring bikes bearing the Cagiva Marque.

Cagiva e Ducati insieme

MASSIMO BORDI, GENERAL MANAGER OF DUCATI. AWARDED A DEGREE IN ENGINEERING AT BOLOGNA IN '75 WITH A THESIS ON "THE 4-VALVE HEAD WITH DESMODROMIC CONTROL", AND AN EMPLOYEE OF THE COMPANY SINCE '78, HE WORKED HIS WAY UP FROM DESIGNER TO TOP MANAGER. HE'S CONSIDERED THE "FATHER" OF THE MODERN DUCATI BIKES.

LEFT, THE "SYNERGIES" BETWEEN DUCATI AND CAGIVA LED TO THE PRODUCTION OF THE ALAZZURRA 350 AND 650 WITH PANTAH ENGINE. THIS RELIABLE TOURING BIKE WAS ALSO TURNED INTO A CURIOUS "AMBULANCE BIKE".

THE ORIGINAL CAPTION FOR THIS PHOTO READ: "1983, UNION OF CAGIVA-DUCATI"; IN REALITY, THIS OCCASION ONLY SAW THE SIGNING OF AN AGREEMENT TO SUPPLY BIKES. FROM LEFT, LAZZATI, GIANFRANCO AND CLAUDIO CASTIGLIONI AND BRIGHIGNA; IN THE BACKGROUND, A TL 600.

ABOVE, CLAUDIO CASTIGLIONI ON THE BIKE USED FOR THE PARIS-DAKAR. HE NEVER HID HIS GREAT PASSION FOR MOTORCYCLES. FAMOUS FOR THE ENTHUSIASM AND DETERMINATION WITH WHICH HE FOLLOWED THE RACES, HE MADE A SIGNIFICANT CONTRIBUTION TO THE RELAUNCHING OF DUCATI.

THE MHR 1000 WAS STILL PRODUCED EVEN AFTER DUCATI ENTERED THE CAGIVA GROUP. THE LITTLE ELEPHANT, SYMBOL OF THE NEW PROPRIETOR, APPEARED ABOVE THE DUCATI MARQUE.

1985
The motorcycles that made history

F1 750

When talking about "Italian-style bikes", thoroughbred sport models (which are difficult to ride), sources of incredible satisfaction and pride for their owners, the conversation inevitably turns to one of that period's most magnificent creations, the F1. Derived from the experience gained using works bikes, it was — for better or for worse — one of the most highly customised bikes of its time, and even today is still much in demand among collectors, but also among racers attracted by its spartan style. This is the key-concept when talking about the F1 — there is nothing superfluous; perhaps the instruments are out of date and the black painted exhaust looks like a boiler tube, but the toughness conveyed by every detail is obvious even to the untrained eye. There are no doubts about the quality of the components (suspensions, brakes, wheels). Nor are there about its handling: "The F1 750 is a beautiful bike, we've waited years for it and it faithfully reproduced the characteristics of racebikes without leaving room for gadgets or fashionable items." This was *Motociclismo's* opinion at the time of the test, although the magazine also pointed out the difficulties of every-day riding on the F1. But this was not an "every-day" bike, nor was it suited to all riders. Painted red, white and green (this time the colours of the Italian flag, not those of the sponsor) its sales rocketed abroad.

Specification

ENGINE: Four-stroke 90° V-twin configuration. Aluminium alloy head and Cermetal NC20 barrel liners. Air-cooled. Bore: 88 mm. Stroke: 61.5 mm. Capacity: 748.1 cc. Compression ratio: 9.3:1. Desmodromic single overhead camshaft, 2 valves per cylinder. Two Dellorto PHF 36 carburettors with pump. Fuel tank capacity: 22 litres. Maximum power: 65.3 hp at 7,250 rpm. Max. torque: 5.71 kgm at 7,250 rpm (measured). Bosch electronic ignition. 12V-200W electrical equipment with 12 volt 19 Ah battery. Wet sump forced lubrication, 3 litres oil. 5-speed gearbox. FRAME, FORKS AND RUNNING GEAR: Tubular Cr-Mo space frame. Marzocchi M1 front telescopic forks with 40 mm stanchions. Rear suspension: single Marzocchi PVS-4 cantilever hydraulic shock. 280 mm twin disc front brake. 260 mm disc rear brake. Tyres: 120/80-16" (front), 130/80-18" (rear). DIMENSIONS AND WEIGHT: Length: 2,110 mm. Width: 690 mm. Seat height: 750 mm. Wheelbase: 1,400 mm. Weight (dry): 168 kg. PERFORMANCE: Top speed (measured) 215 kph. 400 mt. standing start in 12.26 seconds.

FITTED IN A BEAUTIFUL CR-MO STEEL TUBULAR SPACE FRAME, THE F1 ENGINE HAS SOHC DESMO VALVE GEAR, CONTROLLED BY RUBBER TOOTHED BELTS. THE ANGLE BETWEEN THE VALVES IS 60°; THE DIAMETER OF THE INTAKE VALVE IS 41 MM; THAT OF THE EXHAUST VALVE IS 35 MM.

THE PRELOADING ON THE MARZOCCHI PVS 4 SHOCK, WHICH OPERATED ON A CANTILEVER SUSPENSION, CAN BE ADJUSTED USING A RING NUT.

RIGHT, THE F1 WAS DISTINGUISHED BY THE EXCELLENT BRAKING SYSTEM, TWIN 280 MM BREMBO FLOATING DISCS. THE FORK IS A MARZOCCHI

MODEL, WITH LIGHT ALLOY LEGS. THE REAR DISC (ABOVE RIGHT) WAS ALSO THE FLOATING TYPE. THE ALLOY WHEEL RIMS WERE MADE BY OSCAM, THE FRONT ONE MEASURING 16". HAPPIEST ON THE TRACK, WHERE IT BECAME EXTREMELY AGILE, THE F1 WAS A SUPERB RIDING EXPERIENCE FOR THE EXPERT RIDER.

THE F3 350 EMULATED THE STYLE OF THE F1 AND WAS A TRUE SPORT BIKE: WITH AN EXPERIENCED RIDER AT THE CONTROLS, WAS A THREAT TO EVEN THE MOST POWERFUL BIKES. IT WAS A GREAT SUCCESS IN JAPAN.

1985 From the F3 to the Montjuich

The F1 750 underwent significant development, like the works bikes used by the great racers: from Marco Lucchinelli to Benjamin Grau and Kenny Roberts. The Montjuich was designed to celebrate the victory on the track of the same name; the Seca commemorated the victory at Laguna Seca in the US and bears Lucchinelli's signature on the fuel tank. The Santamonica (a hybrid of the two) celebrated Marco's first place at Misano in the '86 World F1 Championship race. These twins developed a power of over 70 hp at the axle at 9,250 rpm and reached nearly 220 km/h. The semi-official versions (also prepared for private riders) developed 80 hp; the works bikes arrived at almost 90 hp and were fed by 2 carburettors with 41 mm choke. Experiments were made with a 90 plus hp engine, with two 43 mm carburettors, but the 851 had already arrived, and so they were set aside. The F3 (a "smaller" copy of the 750) deserves a separate mention. It was the "meanest" 350 of its time (31.6 hp at the axle at 9,500 rpm). The last version of this bike, the 400 F3, had a six-speed gearbox.

DERIVED FROM THE F1, THE MONTJUICH WAS CHARACTERISED BY CAMSHAFTS WITH A MORE SPORTY PROFILE, DELLORTO PHM 40 CARBURETTORS AND A STRAIGHT-THROUGH EXHAUST; THE SWINGING ARM WAS MADE OF ALUMINIUM RATHER THAN THE TUBULAR STEEL ON THE F1; IT ALSO HAD A BREMBO GOLD SEAL BRAKING SYSTEM: A FANTASTIC SPORT BIKE WHICH ARRIVED AT ALMOST 220 KM/H. BELOW, GIANFRANCO CASTIGLIONI ON THE WORKS F1, ABOUT TO BE TESTED BY KENNY ROBERTS. THIS BIKE IMPRESSED ROBERTS.

ABOVE, AT LAST THE INSTRUMENTS WERE SUITED TO THE SITUATION: HERE YOU CAN SEE THE VEGLIA BORLETTI F3 UNIT. LIKE A RACEBIKE, THE F3 SHOWN RIGHT WITHOUT ITS FAIRING - WAS DIFFICULT TO RIDE AND REQUIRED A DECISIVE RIDER. ITS 350 HP WAS MAINTAINED UP TO 10,000 RPM; THE RUNNING GEAR AND ENGINE WERE INSPIRED BY THE 750 CC VERSION, THE MAIN DIFFERENCE BEING THE WET CLUTCH RATHER THAN A DRY VERSION.

THE 750 SANTAMONICA (NAMED AFTER THE MISANO TRACK, WHERE LUCCHINELLI WON THE TT1 WORLD CHAMPIONSHIP RACE) WAS A POWERFUL DEVELOPMENT ON THE F1. IT REACHED CLOSE ON 220 KM/H AND DEVELOPED 73 HP AT 9,250 RPM.

"Spaghetti Western" setting for the Indiana 350, in a direct duel with the Morini Excalibur, with the same engine size.

1986

The Indianas

The advertising slogan went more or less like this: "A bike named horse", from the title of a famous film set in the West. The Indiana was an Italian custom bike which used the Pantah series engines, modified with a 180° rotation of the rear cylinder and with the carburettors placed at the centre of the V formed by the cylinders, like on the Cagiva Elefant. There was more chrome than on the street models, but the Ducati style remained. When talking of Italian custom bikes, we weren't mistaken: the Indiana had serious running gear, which allowed it to be ridden fast without taking a tumble, and the engines were powerful. The engines: the custom Ducati was made in the 350, 650 and 750 cc versions, with identical technical specifications. Perhaps they won't be remembered as "true" Ducatis, but they made an excellent impression on those who had the chance to ride them.

THE ALLOY WHEELS WITH FANCY STAR DESIGN WERE TYPICAL OF THE INDIANA SERIES (THE **350** IS SHOWN, LEFT). BELOW, THE **750**, FINAL DEVELOPMENT IN THE SERIES, WITH NEW PAINTWORK.

FROM AMERICAN DREAM TO ITALIAN REALITY: ABOVE, THE INDIANA TRANSFORMED FOR USE BY THE MUNICIPAL POLICE. THE INDIANA **650** WAS UNCOMFORTABLE ON LONG JOURNEYS, DUE TO THE ERECT RIDING POSITION WHICH CREATED "AERODYNAMIC" RESISTANCE. IT'S HARD TO GO SLOW ON A DUCATI...

TO "AMERICANISE" THE ENGINE, THERE WAS NOTHING BETTER THAN A GOOD LAYER OF CHROME ON THE BELT CASINGS.

INDIANA. UNA MOTO CHIAMATA CAVALLO.

DUCATI

DUCATI POLICE 350/650/750

ON THE COVER OF THE INDIANA BROCHURE, AN ITALIAN COWBOY RELAXES AFTER A LONG RIDE AND, ABOVE, THE CATALOGUE FOR THE "POLICE" VERSION INDIANA.

Paso 750

With the arrival of the new management, the Company needed a flag-ship bike, able to put Ducati back at the top, and not just in sporting terms. Hence the appearance on the scene of one of the most creative figures ever to frequent the motorcycle world, Massimo Tamburini, a designer transferred from Bimota. Tamburini was provided with the means to put his designs into production and, most importantly, a new Pantah 750 engine, with the rear cylinder turned through 180° and the carburettors housed in the V formed by the cylinders. Around this engine, he built a structure decidedly different to anything ever seen at Ducati: a box-section, bolted-cradle frame. But the real change was the delightful full fairing that hid all mechanical parts from view. The effect was incredible, and the Paso (dedicated to the unforgettable Renzo Pasolini) was beautiful; it became the world's most copied bike. Significant features were the twin-choke carburettor, obviously of automobile origin, and the rising rate rear suspension linkage. For a long time, the Paso, which on the road had a sport-touring character, was the favourite bike of British F1 engineers, who both rode it and greatly admired it.

Specification

ENGINE: Four-stroke 90° V-twin configuration. Aluminium alloy head and Si nickel carbide barrel liners. Air-cooled. Bore: 88 mm. Stroke: 61.5 mm. Capacity: 748.1 cc. Compression ratio: 10:1. Desmodromic single overhead camshaft, belt driven, 2 valves per cylinder. Weber 44 DCNF 107 twin-choke carburettor with 36 mm choke. Fuel tank capacity: 22 litres. Maximum power: 61.5 hp at 7,500 rpm. Max. torque: 6.38 kgm at 6,500 rpm (measured). Kokusan inductive discharge electronic ignition. 12V-300W electrical equipment with 12 volt 14 Ah battery. Wet sump forced lubrication, 3.5 litres oil. 5-speed gearbox. FRAME, FORKS AND RUNNING GEAR: Duplex, box section Cr-Mo steel cradle frame. Marzocchi M1R front telescopic forks with 42 mm stanchions. Rear suspension: single Ohlins Soft Damp hydraulic shock, rising rate linkage. Brembo 280 mm twin disc front brake. Brembo 270 mm disc rear brake. Tyres: 130/60-16" (front), 160/60-16" (rear). DIMENSIONS AND WEIGHT: Length: 2,000 mm. Width: 700 mm. Seat height: 780 mm. Wheelbase: 1,450 mm. Weight (dry): 204.5 kg. PERFORMANCE: Top speed 204.2 kph. 400 mt. standing start in 12.62 seconds.

THE FRAME, IN LINE WITH THE FASHION OF THE TIME, WAS MADE OF BOX-SECTION TUBING WHICH HUGGED THE ENGINE, DERIVED FROM THE PANTAH 750. THE REAR SWINGING ARM HAD RISING RATE LINKAGE.

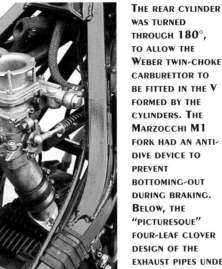

THE REAR CYLINDER WAS TURNED THROUGH 180°, TO ALLOW THE WEBER TWIN-CHOKE CARBURETTOR TO BE FITTED IN THE V FORMED BY THE CYLINDERS. THE MARZOCCHI M1 FORK HAD AN ANTI-DIVE DEVICE TO PREVENT BOTTOMING-OUT DURING BRAKING. BELOW, THE "PICTURESQUE" FOUR-LEAF CLOVER DESIGN OF THE EXHAUST PIPES UNDER THE ENGINE.

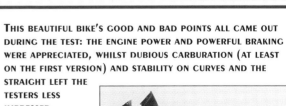

THIS BEAUTIFUL BIKE'S GOOD AND BAD POINTS ALL CAME OUT DURING THE TEST: THE ENGINE POWER AND POWERFUL BRAKING WERE APPRECIATED, WHILST DUBIOUS CARBURATION (AT LEAST ON THE FIRST VERSION) AND STABILITY ON CURVES AND THE STRAIGHT LEFT THE TESTERS LESS IMPRESSED. RIGHT, TAMBURINI'S DESIGN OF THE PARTS WHICH MOST INFLUENCE THE NON-EXPERT OBSERVER: THE SPLENDID BODYWORK.

750 PASO

MARCO LUCCHINELLI, NUMBER 618, LEADS TEAM-MATES STEFANO CARACCHI (SON OF RINO) AND JAMES ADAMO. THE FORMER WORLD CHAMPION IS SEEN HERE ON THE PROTOTYPE OF THE 750 CC LIQUID COOLED, 4-VALVE, DESMO DOHC. HE WENT ON TO WIN THE BATTLE OF THE TWINS.

1987/1988 The future starts at Daytona

It may read like a fairy-tale, but this incredible story is true: the exploits of a rider considered finished and two bikes that brought him to victory. The first was the ultimate development of the F1 Pantah, and it was with this bike that Marco Lucchinelli won the '86 Battle of the Twins. A year later, again at Daytona, Marco won again, this time on the prototype of the 851. Same rider, same race, but big differences: the latter bike represented the future of Ducati. The 4-valve DOHC twin design was developed with enthusiasm by designers Bordi and Mengoli. The first bike made its debut at the '86 Bol D'Or — in which it had no luck and ran practically unnoticed — with a 750 cc engine. In '87, redesigned and corrected, the bike, still with a 750 cc engine, was shipped across the Atlantic to run in the Daytona BOT, again with Lucky in the saddle. Although still in its teething stages, the bike demonstrated qualities that unsettled the Japanese. Its lap times and top speed matched those of the best four-cylinder bikes around. 1988 saw the start of the World Superbike Championship and Ducati already had a good deal of material to work on. The SBK '88 season went down in history thanks to Fred Merkel's victory, Davide Tardozzi's misfortune and the fifth place obtained by Ducati. With just a little more patience, the Company would soon be counting its numerous World Championship titles.

LUCCHINELLI-DUCATI VITTORIA A DAYTONA

La Casa bolognese ha bissato nella «Battle of the twins» il successo dello scorso anno. Wayne Rainey si è aggiudicato una opaca 200 miglia. Freddie Spencer messo fuori causa da una caduta durante le prove.

MARCO LUCCHINELLI HAD ALREADY WON THE BOT IN 1986 WITH ONE OF THE MOST BEAUTIFUL VERSIONS OF THE PANTAH F1.

THE RUNNING GEAR OF THE 4V (THE BIKE WAS NEVER GIVEN AN OFFICIAL NAME) CENTRED AROUND A TUBULAR STEEL SPACE FRAME, ALWAYS A DUCATI CHOICE. BELOW, THE ONE-PIECE IGNITION AND INJECTION BOX MADE BY WEBER IN COLLABORATION WITH MARELLI. THIS INNOVATION ALLOWED OPTIMUM ENGINE PERFORMANCE, MONITORING VARIOUS PARAMETERS (RPM, THROTTLE ANGLE, AIR AND WATER TEMPERATURE AND ATMOSPHERIC PRESSURE).

STILL TO BE REFINED, BUT TREMENDOUSLY EFFECTIVE, THE BIKE THAT MARCO LUCCHINELLI RACED AT DAYTONA ALREADY HAD THE BOSSES OF THE JAPANESE BIKE MAKERS SERIOUSLY WORRIED. THE FORMIDABLE ITALIAN TWIN HAD ARRIVED ON THE RACE TRACK.

TWO DETAILS OF THE 4V: THE LIQUID COOLED CYLINDER AND THE PISTON WITH CROWN POLISHED TO MIRROR-BRIGHTNESS, AS WERE THE CAMSHAFT AND CON-RODS.

163

851 Superbike Strada

Nineteen eighty six saw it debut at the Bol D'Or, and a year later, its victory at Daytona, but the most important year for the 851 was '88. After the first series, which went to collectors and racers (the 200 examples required for homologation), the 851 was introduced to the tracks of the newly-established Superbike World Superbike Championship (finishing fifth overall, with victories for Lucchinelli at Zeltweg and Donington, despite a shoestring budget). At last, the bike arrived at the dealerships. The 851 relaunched the Ducati image world-wide and immediately became a cult object in Japan. The Superbike Strada road version thrilled the testers, who didn't expect such a powerful, generous engine. The "road" 851 also revealed a few limitations caused by handling difficulties on the steering gear. This defect was eliminated on the SBK, which mounted 17" wheels in place of the standard 16" ones; but the major surprise was the discovery that a twin could leave 4-cylinder bikes standing. And to think that this bike was still just starting out.

Refinements made year after year, version after version, made it the indisputable number one 4-stroke bike. This demonstrated that Ducati was not just synonymous with sporting tradition, but also had an advanced technological laboratory.

LOW ON ITS 16" WHEELS, RED, WHITE AND GREEN COLOURS AND UNMISTAKABLE FRONT PROFILE: THE 851 SS WAS IMMEDIATELY A MUCH SOUGHT AFTER CULT OBJECT, DESPITE THE HIGH PRICE.

DUCATI 851
SUPERBIKE STRADA
BICILINDRICA TERRIBILE

Specification

ENGINE: Four-stroke 90° V-twin configuration. Aluminium alloy head and Si nickel carbide barrel liners. Liquid-cooled. Bore: 92 mm. Stroke: 64 mm. Capacity: 851 cc. Compression ratio: 10.4:1. Desmodromic twin overhead camshaft, toothed-belt driven, 4 valves per cylinder. Weber Marelli Alpha/n indirect electronic fuel injection with 2 injectors per cylinder. Fuel tank capacity: 22 litres. Maximum power: 88.03 hp at 8,700 rpm. Max. torque: 7.41 kgm at 8,400 rpm (measured). IAW inductive discharge electronic ignition. 12V-50W electrical equipment with 12 volt 16 Ah battery. Wet sump forced lubrication, 4 litres oil. 6-speed gearbox. FRAME, FORKS AND RUNNING GEAR: Tubular Cr-Mo steel space frame. Marzocchi M1 front telescopic forks with 41.7 mm stanchions and anti-dive system. Rear suspension: single Marzocchi Supermono shock, rising rate linkage. Brembo 280 mm twin floating-disc front brake. Brembo 270 mm floating-disc rear brake. Tyres: 130/60-16" (front), 160/60-16" (rear). DIMENSIONS AND WEIGHT: Wheelbase: 1,430 mm. Weight (dry): 204 kg. PERFORMANCE: Top speed 234 kph. 400 mt. standing start in 11.24 seconds.

THE "KNEE TO THE GROUND" ERA BEGAN DURING *MOTOCICLISMO*'S ROAD TESTS. THE **851** WAS ONE OF THE BIKES THAT MADE THIS TECHNIQUE POSSIBLE.

DETAIL LEFT, THE REAR SUSPENSION LINKAGE WITH UPPER CONNECTING ROD. THIS CONFIGURATION, LIKE MANY OTHER TECHNICAL FEATURES USED BY DUCATI, WAS THE RESULT OF RACING EXPERIENCE.

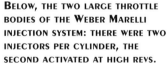

BELOW, THE TWO LARGE THROTTLE BODIES OF THE WEBER MARELLI INJECTION SYSTEM: THERE WERE TWO INJECTORS PER CYLINDER, THE SECOND ACTIVATED AT HIGH REVS.

THE **851** "KIT" PREPARED FOR HOMOLOGATION IN THE SBK CATEGORY WAS THE MOST SPORTY VERSION OF THE SS; FITTED WITH **17"** WHEELS, IT DID NOT HAVE REAR-VIEW MIRRORS INCORPORATED IN THE FAIRING AND MOUNTED SLICK TYRES. THE ENGINE USED DIFFERENT CAMSHAFTS AND THE IGNITION-INJECTION SYSTEM WAS CALIBRATED FOR RACING; THE MAXIMUM POWER DEVELOPED WAS **125** HP (AT THE CRANKSHAFT). DECIDEDLY AGAINST THE GRAIN WHEN COMPARED WITH THE BIKES PRODUCED IN OTHER COUNTRIES, THE SPACE FRAME WAS MADE OF STRONG, RIGID TUBULAR STEEL. THE SWINGING ARM PIVOTED ON THE CRANKCASE; THE SADDLE SUB-FRAME WAS BOLTED INTO PLACE.

A BIG JOB FOR *MOTOCICLISMO*'S TESTERS IN **1989**: THEY HAD TO TRY OUT THE **750 SS**, ABOVE, AND THE **851**, JUST BACK FROM THE WORLD SUPERBIKE CHAMPIONSHIP, LEFT.

1989 Chasing victory

This was a good year for those trying to follow the development of Ducati. As indicated by the February edition of *Motociclismo*, the Superbike proved a truly interesting race formula; a comparison of the bikes that competed in the first World Superbike Championship the previous year emphasised the greater competitiveness of the 851 twin engine as opposed to its four-cylinder rivals, namely the Bimota YB4, Yamaha FZ 750 and Honda RC30. In the '89 World Championship, the Ducati race team consisted of riders Raymond Roche and Baldassare Monti, with Lucchinelli as team manager (this passage from former champion to team manager was characteristic of Ducati). This proved to be a winning combination and the Frenchman was hindered only by electrical problems in his pursuit of victory. The engine capacity was 888 cc, whilst the fork used was made by Ohlins. For customers, there was the new 851 S, a superb bike which eradicated the few defects of the previous model and was one of the most popular bikes on the roads world-wide. For the nostalgic (or for those who couldn't afford the 851), there was the 750 Sport.

SUPERBIKE
LA VELOCITÀ IN QUATTRO TEMPI

THE GREAT AFRICAN RALLY SEASON CONTINUED AND CIRO DE PETRI'S CAGIVA-DUCATI TORE THROUGH THE AFRICAN DUNES WITH ITS POWERFUL ENGINE. RIGHT, SAME PERFORMANCE, BUT RADICAL RUNNING GEAR FOR THE **851 S** WHICH, WITH THE ARRIVAL OF **17"** WHEELS (USED IN COMPETITION SINCE THE PREVIOUS YEAR), DEMONSTRATED PRECISE, SATISFYING HANDLING.
THE BIKE FINALLY ADOPTED THE RED LIVERY THAT WAS TO BECOME CHARACTERISTIC OF DUCATI SPORT BIKES.

ABOVE, THE "OLD" PANTAH **750**, WITH REAR CYLINDER TURNED THROUGH **180°** AND FED BY A WEBER TWIN-CHOKE CARBURETTOR, WAS THE HEART OF THE **750** SPORT, AN AGILE BIKE WITH OPTIMUM POWER AND BRAKING. IT WAS EVEN REASONABLY PRICED!

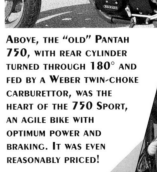

CHAMPION MARCO LUCCHINELLI BECAME THE FRONT-MAN FOR THE OFFICIAL **851** ADS.

Paso 906

At a glance, this bike may look like nothing more than a restyling of the Paso 750, but this is not the case. Especially from a development viewpoint, the 906 was a real milestone. But before describing the bike, it's necessary to take a step back in time to the period in which the 851 4V DOHC engine was designed. This engine was not the only design developed, but had a "sibling" with twin-valve SOHC valve gear, for touring bikes with a cylinder capacity that topped 750 cc. Development of the SOHC engine and the sporting commitment, amongst other considerations, held up its progress, but at last its moment arrived. The Paso 906 was fitted with this twin engine — finally put into production — with liquid cooling, six-speed gearbox and capacity of 904 cc. Thus, 906 meant "900 six-speed". The splendid bodywork of the Paso 750 remained ("bodywork" is an automobile term, but is acceptable in this case), as did the touring meets sport trim and a strong personality. The arrival of a more balanced running gear reduced the problems encountered in the first version, but the bike remained easy to handle and the steering had a good response both in fast curves and on the straight.

Specification

ENGINE: Four-stroke 90º V-twin configuration. Aluminium alloy head. Liquid cooled. Bore: 92 mm. Stroke: 68 mm. Capacity: 904 cc. Compression ratio: 9.2:1. Desmodromic single overhead camshaft, toothed rubber belt driven, 2 valves per cylinder. Weber 44 DCNF 107 twin-choke carburettor with 36 mm choke. Fuel tank capacity: 22 litres. Maximum power: 71.19 hp at 8,000 rpm. Max. torque: 6.98 kgm at 6,000 rpm (at axle). Marelli Digiplex inductive discharge electronic ignition. 12V-350W electrical equipment with 12 volt 19 Ah battery. Wet sump forced lubrication, 3.5 litres oil. 6-speed gearbox. FRAME, FORKS AND RUNNING GEAR: Modular, box-section steel duplex cradle frame. Marzocchi M1R front telescopic forks with 42 mm stanchions and anti-dive system. Rear suspension: Marzocchi Duoshock shock, 7-way adjustable. 280 mm twin disc front brake, 270 mm disc rear brake. Tyres: 130/60-16" (front), 160/60-16" (rear). DIMENSIONS AND WEIGHT: Length: 2,000 mm. Width: 700 mm. Seat height: 780 mm. Wheelbase: 1,450 mm. Weight (dry): 205 kg. PERFORMANCE: Top speed 218.5 kph (measured). 400 mt. standing start in 12.15 seconds.

These two photos speak volumes about the ability of designer MASSIMO TAMBURINI. The new engine had the same crankcases as the 851, but had twin-valve SOHC valve gear; the drawing shows the liquid cooling system. In action, this bike pleased many riders with its stability at high speeds; less impressive, was its unpredictability at low speeds.

The frame had bolted front down tubes, to allow quick engine release. Drawing, right: diagram of the rear suspension shows the SOFT DAMP single-shock model with rising rate linkage.

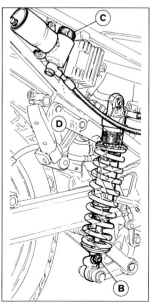

FALAPPA AHEAD OF ROCHE AT A CRUCIAL POINT IN THE RACE; THE FRENCHMAN WENT ON TO WIN THE WORLD SBK TITLE. LUCCHINELLI REMARKED: "OUT OF A HUNDRED CURVES, HE NEVER GOT ONE WRONG...".

1990 Year of triumph

Of all the years in which Ducati has been in business, 1990 was one of many victories, therefore, these pages are monopolised by sporting successes. Raymond Roche won the World Championship at the end of a thrilling year, whilst at the start of '90, Edi Orioli won the Paris-Dakar with the Cagiva Ducati Elefant 900. Thus, the two most important competitions reserved for bikes linked to mass production were won by Ducati twins. The bikes ridden by Roche and the brilliant, but unlucky, Falappa had a capacity of 888 cc and power of almost 134 hp. Moreover, during the season, the twin was continuously refined and compacted, until it weighed less than 150 kg. The official works team was led by Marco Lucchinelli.

FOR THE FIRST TIME, AN ITALIAN BIKE AND RIDER GAINED GROUND IN THE EXHAUSTING PARIS-DAKAR. MANY DETAILS DESTINED FOR STANDARD DUCATI BIKES WERE TESTED ON THE ELEFANT 900. LEFT, THE TRIUMPHANT EDI ORIOLI AND HIS BIKE HAILED BY FANS AT THE STADIUM IN UDINE DURING A LAP OF HONOUR BEFORE THE START OF THE UDINESE-MILAN MATCH ON 21 JANUARY 1990.

ABOVE, SERIOUS WORK AT THE DUCATI RACING DEPARTMENT: THE MAN IN THE WHITE SHIRT IS FRANCO FARNÉ, THE MAIN AUTHORITY ON ANYTHING BEARING THE DUCATI MARQUE. RIGHT, RAYMOND ROCHE TAKES A BREAK. ORIGINALLY A WORLD CHAMPIONSHIP 500 CC GRAND PRIX RIDER AND A MAN OF GREAT CLASS, HE KNEW HOW TO RELAX, EVEN AMID THE CONFUSION OF THE PITS.

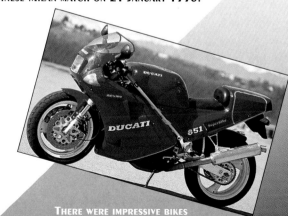

THERE WERE IMPRESSIVE BIKES EVEN FOR THE "NORMAL" RIDERS: THE 851 SP2 WITH 888 CC ENGINE AND MAXIMUM POWER OF 118 HP; THE SUSPENSION WAS MADE BY OHLINS, A REPLICA OF THE WORKS MODELS.

900 Supersport

THE 900 SUPERSPORT, WITHOUT NEEDING INCREDIBLE PERFORMANCE AND SOPHISTICATED RUNNING GEAR, WAS A FAVOURITE OF MANY BIKERS.

As often happens, there are bikes that start their career practically unnoticed, then assume a leading role and remain in production for years. The 900 Supersport was introduced in the 900 range in 1990 as "an economic alternative to the 851" and was mainly intended for foreign markets. It developed year after year, winning over the markets in numerous countries, but in particular in Italy. This long-lived wonder (the final limited edition version even appears in the '98 catalogue, whilst the new SS, designed by Terblanche, is one of the great innovations) can be explained by the sporty spartan nature of this bike and the reliability of an engine that uses the crankcases of the 851, the cooling system of the Elefant, the con-rod set of the Paso 906 and a Weber twin-choke carburettor. Even the running gear has some parts inherited from other bikes, especially the 851; the frame is a variation on the unit used on the Sport 750; this was followed by the arrival of 17" wheels which greatly improved stability compared with its predecessors. An article quite rightly pointed out that "it can't compete with the 4-cylinder bikes", but this simple, essential sport bike won the hearts of many riders thanks to the extraordinary power of its "twin valve" engine and its unmistakable personality.

Specification

ENGINE: Four-stroke 90° V-twin configuration. Oil- and air-cooled. Bore: 92 mm. Stroke: 68 mm. Capacity: 904 cc. Compression ratio: 9.2:1. Desmodromic single overhead camshaft, toothed rubber belt driven, 2 valves per cylinder. Two Mikuni vacuum carburettors with 38 mm choke. Fuel tank capacity: 17.5 litres. Maximum power: 73.49 hp at 7,500 rpm. Max. torque: 7.62 kgm at 6,750 rpm (at axle). Inductive discharge electronic ignition. 12V-300W electrical equipment with 12 volt 16 Ah battery. Wet sump forced lubrication, 3.5 litres oil. 6-speed gearbox. FRAME, FORKS AND RUNNING GEAR: Tubular steel space frame. Showa front telescopic forks with 41 mm reversed stanchions. Rear suspension: Showa Cantilever shock. Brembo 320 mm twin disc front brake with 4-piston caliper. 245 mm disc rear brake with twin-piston caliper. Tyres: 120/70-17" (front), 170/60-17" (rear). DIMENSIONS AND WEIGHT: Length: 2,030 mm. Width: 730 mm. Seat height: 780 mm. Wheelbase: 1,410 mm. Weight (dry): 186 kg. PERFORMANCE: Top speed 219 kph (measured). 400 mt. standing start in 11.82 seconds

TO LEAD THE PACK EVEN THROUGH CORNERS, YOU NEED OPTIMUM BRAKING: TOP LEFT, THE **320 MM** BREMBO TWIN FLOATING DISC AND FOUR-PISTON CALIPER FITTED ON THE FRONT WHEEL. RIGHT, AS ON MANY DUCATI SPORT BIKES, THE SADDLE CONFIGURATION IS EASILY CHANGED, BUT THE SINGLE-SEATER SOLUTION REMAINS THE BEST FOR THE BIKE'S LOOK.

LEFT, A "CROSS-SECTION" OF THE ENGINE SHOWS THE VALVE GEAR: SHIMS WERE USED TO ADJUST THE VALVE PLAY. ABOVE, THE HEAD HOUSES TWO VALVES: THE **43 MM** DIAMETER INTAKE VALVE AND THE **38 MM** EXHAUST VALVE. THE ESSENTIALITY OF THIS BIKE IS BEYOND DOUBT: THERE IS SIMPLY NO PLACE FOR SUPERFLUOUS ITEMS. THE SPACE FRAME DERIVES FROM THAT OF THE SPORT 750. THE TWIN-VALVE SOHC DESMO VALVE GEAR ENGINE WAS FED BY A WEBER TWIN-CHOKE CARBURETTOR ORIGINALLY DESIGNED FOR SPORTS CARS.

173

DOUG POLEN IN ACTION ON THE MUGELLO TRACK: THE AMERICAN RACER WON BOTH HEATS.

174

1991

The Polen phenomenon

The "master" arrived from the States and was called Doug Polen, an American rider who raced Japanese big bikes in the AMA Championship until '91. The turning point in his career was marked by Eraldo Ferracci, an Italian bike tuner who had worked in the US for some time, and who invited Polen to join his team. After encouraging tests, the pair decided to try their luck in the World Superbike category. At the start of the Championship, the official Ducati works team consisted of Roche and Falappa, but the company also decided to support Polen and Mertens with "satellite" teams. Doug's bikes were prepared by Nepoti and Caracchi. It soon became obvious that their rivals didn't stand a chance: The World Championship was won by Polen, with Roche in second place. Ducati also won in Europe, with Tardozzi and an impressive series of other races and national titles. The 888 was unbeatable!

SMILING WORLD CHAMPIONSHIP WINNER, DOUG POLEN LEFT HIS RIVALS STANDING. FOR SPORT BIKERS, THERE WAS THE 851 S (PHOTO UNDER THE HEADER), THAT IS TO SAY, THE "TOURING" VERSION OF THE "ROSSA"; IT WAS HOMOLOGATED FOR TWO, BUT THE PASSENGER IS NOT IN AN ENVIABLE POSITION! THE 900 SS, RIGHT, WAS ALSO RENEWED AND PRESENTED IN TWO VERSIONS: WITH FULL FAIRING AND WITH "HALF-FAIRING" THAT LEFT THE ENGINE AND FRAME IN VIEW.

THE 907 E (LEFT) WAS THE LAST OF THE PASO SERIES: ELECTRONIC INJECTION ARRIVED EVEN ON TWIN-VALVE TWINS AND THE WHEELS WERE 17" DURING TESTS, THE 907 REACHED A TOP SPEED OF 216 KM/H; THE POWER WAS 75.4 HP AT 8,500 RPM. LEFT, THE 750 SUPERSPORT (SCALED-DOWN 900) WAS AVAILABLE WITH TWO DIFFERENT TYPES OF FAIRING (IN THE PHOTO, REDUCED VERSION). ON THE STEERING GEAR, NOTICE THE SHOWA FORK WITH REVERSED STANCHIONS AND A SINGLE 320 MM FLOATING DISC. DESIGNED FOR SPORT RIDERS OR SPORT PRODUCTION RACES, THE 851 SP3 (LEFT) WAS CLOSELY RELATED TO THE WORLD CHAMPIONSHIP BIKE. THE CYLINDER CAPACITY WAS 888 CC, THE RUNNING REAR WAS HIGH QUALITY (OHLINS RACING FORK AND SHOCK, BREMBO CORSA BRAKES) AND THE ENGINE DEVELOPED NO LESS THAN 106.8 HP AT 10,250 RPM. THIS RATING WAS CONFIRMED DURING MOTOCICLISMO'S TESTS AND, NATURALLY, REFERS TO POWER AT THE AXLE.

ON THE PROFESSIONAL PLATE OF THE SP3 FORK THERE WAS A SMALL SILVER PLATE BEARING THE NUMBER OF THE BIKES PRODUCED AS PART OF THIS LIMITED EDITION (700 BIKES MADE IN 1991) AND THE TEXT COMMEMORATING THE TITLE WON THE PREVIOUS YEAR.

888 World Champion

Imagine sitting on the bike that currently dominates the SBK World Championship, on one of Europe's most demanding tracks, and with the engine and running gear adjusted by the reigning World Champion and his

MOTOCICLISMO'S TESTER TRIES OUT ROCHE'S BIKE ON THE ZELTWEG TRACK: GREAT COMMITMENT, GREAT SATISFACTION. SMALL PHOTO, THE CONTROLS AND SHORTENED FUEL TANK CUSTOMISED BY THE FRENCH RIDER.

team: this kind of experience is rare in the career of a rider-journalist and *Motociclismo* jumped at the chance to try the "rossa" "If you don't exaggerate with the throttle, the Ducati is easier to ride than the best 600 road bike... The braking is unbelievable, not far off that of a 500 GP... The acceleration seems contained, since the engine moves up through the rev range gradually and smoothly, but is impressive if you keep an eye on the panel that gives you the braking reference." It's easy to be enthusiastic about this kind of bike, given that this monster destroyed its 4-cylinder rivals thanks to its "general balance combined with the most powerful engine in the Championships."

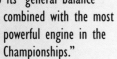

Specification

ENGINE: *Four-stroke 90° V-twin configuration. Liquid-cooled. Bore: 94 mm. Stroke: 64 mm. Capacity: 888 cc. Compression ratio: 12.5:1. Desmodromic twin overhead camshaft, toothed rubber belt driven, 4 valves per cylinder. Weber Marelli Alpha/n indirect electronic fuel injection with 2 injectors per cylinder. Kevlar fuel tank capacity: 20 litres. Maximum power: 133 hp at 11,500 rpm. Marelli IAW inductive discharge electronic ignition. Wet sump forced lubrication, 4 litres oil. 6-speed gearbox.* FRAME, FORKS AND RUNNING GEAR: *Tubular Cr-Mo steel space frame. Ohlins front telescopic forks with 43 mm reversed stanchions. Rear suspension: single Ohlins rising rate hydraulic shock. Brembo 320 mm twin disc front brake with 4-piston caliper. 210 mm disc rear brake with twin-piston caliper. Tyres: 120/60-17" (front), 180/50-17" (rear).* DIMENSIONS AND WEIGHT: *Length: 2,030 mm. Seat height: 780 mm (Roche bike). Wheelbase: 1,430 mm. Weight (dry): 143 kg (racing trim).*

THE REAR SECTION IS DOMINATED BY THE PRONOUNCED BODYWORK AND TWO TERMIGNONI CARBON FIBRE EXHAUST PIPES, THREATENINGLY ANGLED UPWARDS SO THAT THEY DON'T TOUCH THE TRACK IN THE TURNS. BELOW, DETAILS OF THE REAR SUSPENSION SHOWING THE LINKAGE POSITION AND THE FULLY ADJUSTABLE OHLINS SHOCK.

THE FRAME IS IDENTICAL TO THAT OF THE STANDARD BIKES WITH 1,430 MM WHEELBASE. THE RAKE IS 94 MM, WHILST THE ANGLE OF THE STEERING HEAD IS 24.5°. THE OHLINS FORK HAS 43 MM REVERSED STANCHIONS AND A 120 MM TRAVEL. CONTINUOUS DEVELOPMENT OF THIS WORLD CHAMPIONSHIP BIKE BROUGHT THE MAXIMUM POWER TO 133 HP AT THE AXLE AND THE WEIGHT TO 143 KG. THE MOST WORTHY RIVALS (FOUR-CYLINDERS) HAD A SIMILAR POWER, BUT WEIGHED-IN AT 165 KG AS PER THE REGULATIONS. ROCHE'S 888 WAS FITTED WITH MICHELIN TYRES, WHILST POLEN PREFERRED DUNLOP. APART FROM THAT, THE TWO BIKES WERE PRACTICALLY IDENTICAL.

MUCH CARBON FIBRE WAS USED IN ORDER TO REDUCE THE WEIGHT OF THIS BIKE. THE AERODYNAMICS OF ALL COMPONENTS, EVEN THOSE OF SECONDARY IMPORTANCE, WERE CAREFULLY STUDIED - A WORLD CHAMPIONSHIP IS SOMETIMES WON ON DETAILS!

GIANCARLO FALAPPA, A GREAT RACER AND LIKEABLE MAN IN ACTION ON HIS DUCATI.

1992 King without a crown

This chapter has to be dedicated to one of the greatest Italian riders of recent years, Giancarlo Falappa. Loved by the public for his limitless generosity and sheer likeable character, this rider from the Marche province has never won a World Championship, but his victories on Ducati bikes during the seasons from '91 to '94 (the year of a serious accident that left him fighting for his life) have left a lasting mark. Giancarlo is the Ducati spirit personified. The fans know this, as is demonstrated by their affection for him and their interest in his activities even though, unfortunately, he no longer races. His is the story of a king without a crown. The '92 SBK title went to Polen who, whenever possible, also competed successfully in the AMA Championship in the United States. Polen was Falappa's team-mate in the team managed by Franco Uncini (another name which reappears in Ducati's history). Roche had his own team. Other works bikes were prepared for Mertens, Amatriain and Tardozzi. The 888 from '92 was practically identical to the '91 model, but carbon fibre discs appeared for the first time on Polen's bike.

A VIEW OF POLEN FAMILIAR TO HIS COMPETITORS DURING THE '92 SEASON. MANY HAD THE CHANCE TO READ HIS NAME ON THE BACK OF HIS LEATHERS! RIGHT, A MOMENT FROM THE 1992 SUPERBIKE WORLD CHAMPIONSHIP RACE SHOWS POLEN CLOSE ON THE HEELS OF FALAPPA.

AT THE END OF THE YEAR THE RENEWED ROAD VERSIONS CAME OUT. THE 888 SUPERBIKE STRADA WAS THE "MOST SUBDUED" VERSION IN THE SERIES AND HAD A TWO-SEATER SADDLE. THE NEW CYLINDER CAPACITY WAS DETERMINED BY THE BORE, WHICH PASSED FROM THE 92 MM USED ON THE 851 TO 94 MM. THE POWER WAS 100 HP AND THE BIKE REACHED A TOP SPEED OF 250 KM/H.

THE SP5, DESIGNED FOR THE SPORT PRODUCTION CATEGORY, HAD MANY CARBON FIBRE PARTS AND A POWER OF 120 HP.

350 Supersport Junior

Ducati's commitment in the 350 class (the company once led the track races and even won the World Championship) has always been impressive, from the times of the singles with helical gear engines to the Pantah series twins. It also mass-produced many excellent versions of the 350, and it would have been a crime not to present a bike of this capacity in the Nineties. Enter the Pantah 350 SS, an interesting product, even from the point of view of development of twin-cylinder bikes. The "old" Pantah 350 was updated with adjustments to the cooling system, and the fitting of 38 mm Mikuni carburettors, a 2 in 1 exhaust, six-speed gearbox and wet multi-plate clutch, unlike the other SSs (750 and 900) which had a dry clutch. Light, stable and agile, the 350 had the same frame and form as its predecessor. The high-revving engine guaranteed optimum performance and the bike reached 180 km/h during tests by Motociclismo in '92.

COMPACT AND ECONOMIC, BUT TOUGH WITH IT, THE **350 SS JUNIOR** WAS AN EXCELLENT CHOICE FOR YOUNG SPORT RIDERS.

Specification

ENGINE: Four-stroke 90° V-twin configuration. Air-cooled. Bore: 66 mm. Stroke: 51 mm. Capacity: 341 cc. Compression ratio: 10.7:1. Desmodromic single overhead camshaft, toothed rubber belt driven, 2 valves per cylinder. Two Mikuni carburettors with 38 mm choke. Fuel tank capacity: 17.5 litres. Maximum power: 37.31 hp at 10,250 rpm. Max. torque: 2.69 kgm at 7,500 rpm (at axle). Inductive discharge electronic ignition. 12V-300W electrical equipment with 12 volt 16 Ah battery. Wet sump forced lubrication, 3 litres oil. Wet, multi-plate clutch. 6-speed gearbox. FRAME, FORKS AND RUNNING GEAR: Tubular Cr-Mo steel space frame. Showa front telescopic forks with 41 mm reversed stanchions. Rear suspension: Showa rising rate shock. 320 mm twin floating-disc front brake with 4-piston caliper. 245 mm floating-disc rear brake with twin-piston caliper. Tyres: 120/60-17" (front), 160/60-17" (rear). DIMENSIONS AND WEIGHT: Length: 2,020 mm. Width: 730 mm. Seat height: 770 mm. Weight (dry): 177.6 kg. PERFORMANCE: Top speed 180.3 kph (measured). 400 mt. standing start in 14 seconds.

THE LINE OF THE **SS** FAMILY WAS BORROWED FROM THE SMALLER **350**. UNCOMFORTABLE AND WITH A STIFF REAR SUSPENSION, THE **SS** WAS NOT THE BEST OF BIKES FOR THE CITY STREETS. IT WAS MOST AT HOME WITH A MIXTURE OF FAST CURVES AND THE STRAIGHT AND THE **38** HP DEVELOPED AT **10,250** RPM GUARANTEED GOOD PERFORMANCE. AN INTERESTING FEATURE OF THE INSTRUMENTS (INSET, LEFT) WAS THE REV COUNTER WITH A RED LINE AT **11,000** RPM. THE SUSPENSION WAS A LIGHT ALLOY SWINGING ARM WITH SHOWA CANTILEVER SHOCK.

A HAND FROM THE JAPANESE, FOR THE ENGINE WAS FED BY MIKUNI **38** CARBURETTORS. THE VALVE GEAR WAS A SOHC DESMO WITH TWO VALVES PER CYLINDER. BELOW, THE **350** WAS DEVELOPED TO CREATE THE IDENTICAL **400** CC VERSION, RESERVED FOR THE JAPANESE MARKET.

THE HIGH-TECH, QUALITY STEERING GEAR CONSISTED OF A SHOWA FORK WITH **41** MM REVERSED STANCHIONS AND A **320** MM BREMBO FLOATING DISC AND **4**-PISTON CALIPER.

RED RACING LIVERY, SILVER PLATE BEARING LIMITED EDITION NUMBER AND CARBON FIBRE FRONT MUDGUARD: THESE WERE THE INSTANTLY RECOGNISABLE FEATURES OF THE SUPERLIGHT.

1992 Light as a feather

Horsepower is not everything when defining a sport bike; in fact, a great deal of power is practically useless if the weight is all wrong. Thus, in order to make the 900 SS more competitive and attractive, the Ducati people decided that it would be a good idea to reduce the weight to a minimum. To do this, they used carbon fibre parts, special lightweight components (such as the clutch covers) and good running gear from the 851. Made as a limited edition (500 examples), the Superlight weighed 180 kg; at the end of the season the two-metal composite wheels were substituted with others made completely of alloy. Its reduced weight and responsive engine (curiously, it was a unit with Japanese-made ignition and carburettors) gave the bike optimum performance. During tests its top speed was 220 km/h and it took just 11.86 seconds to cover 400 m from a standing start, with a final speed of 184.2 km/h.

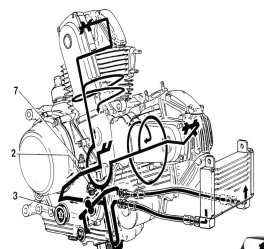

THE **904** CC WAS AIR- AND OIL-COOLED. NOTICE THE WELL-CRAFTED ALUMINIUM OIL COOLER (THE DIAGRAM SHOWS THE LUBRICATION CIRCUIT), AND THE DRILLED DRY CLUTCH COVER.
THE SHOWA FORK HAD **41** MM REVERSED STANCHIONS, THE TWIN DISC WAS A **320** MM BREMBO GOLD SEAL; THE WHEELS WERE BEAUTIFUL MODULAR ALUMINIUM AND MAGNESIUM MARVIC UNITS.

AT THE END OF THE YEAR THE NEW VERSION OF THE SUPERLIGHT ARRIVED ALSO, CHARACTERISED BY WHEELS IN LIGHT ALLOY AND A "SERIE ORO" CALIPER AT THE REAR.

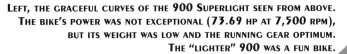
LEFT, THE GRACEFUL CURVES OF THE **900** SUPERLIGHT SEEN FROM ABOVE. THE BIKE'S POWER WAS NOT EXCEPTIONAL (**73.69** HP AT **7,500** RPM), BUT ITS WEIGHT WAS LOW AND THE RUNNING GEAR OPTIMUM. THE "LIGHTER" **900** WAS A FUN BIKE.

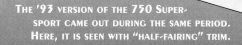
THE '**93** VERSION OF THE **750** SUPER-SPORT CAME OUT DURING THE SAME PERIOD. HERE, IT IS SEEN WITH "HALF-FAIRING" TRIM.

THE M900 WAS NOT ONLY ONE OF THE BEST LOOKING BIKES OF THE NINETIES, IT WAS ALSO A PLEASURE TO RIDE, THANKS TO ITS POWERFUL ENGINE AND SOLID RUNNING GEAR.

1993 Watch out for the Monster!

Officially dubbed the M900, this bike rapidly became known to all and sundry as the Monster. It upset the consolidated market rhythms and balances, but above all revolutionised the many "niche" categories invented by marketing experts (who are not always bike experts). Designed by Miguel Galluzzi, the M900 was an immediate best-seller, thanks to a magnificent line (Miguel is obviously familiar with and loves motorcycles) and its highly successful technical content. Its knock-out good looks come partly from an array of Ducati components: the frame is that of the 888 with some minor adjustments, it has a Showa fork and Boge shock. The engine is the 904 air/oil cooled version from the 900 SS, with six-speed gearbox, shorter gear ratio and "flatter" power curve. A thrill to ride, the M900 is an individual with character.

A SPARTAN BIKE WHERE TECHNICAL FEATURES PREDOMINATE. ACCORDING TO ITS CREATOR, THE MOST INTERESTING PARTS OF THE M900 ARE THE ENGINE AND THE RUNNING GEAR. AT LAST, A DESIGNER ON THE SAME WAVELENGTH AS THE BIKERS! BELOW, THE BREMBO GOLD SEAL CALIPER ON THE 245 MM SMALL REAR DISC.

THE MONSTER'S CHARACTER IS SUCH THAT YOU DON'T EVEN NEED TO READ THE DUCATI NAME TO KNOW WHERE IT COMES FROM. THE MERIT FOR THE DISTINCTIVE, UNMISTAKABLE LINE AND ATTENTION TO EVERY DETAIL ON THE M900 GOES TO DESIGNER MIGUEL GALLUZZI, WHO HAD ALREADY RESTYLED THE SUPERSPORT SERIES AND, WITH THE "MOSTRO" PROVED YET AGAIN THAT HE IS ONE OF THE MOST GIFTED DESIGNERS IN THE MOTORCYCLING WORLD.

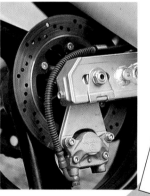

DURING THE SPORTING SEASON, DUCATI WON THE MANUFACTURER'S TITLE IN THE SBK WORLD CHAMPIONSHIP; BRITISH RIDER FOGARTY, IN THE PHOTO, BECAME THE NUMBER ONE RACER. MEANWHILE, DOUG POLEN HAD RETURNED TO THE AMA SUPERBIKE CHAMPIONSHIP, WINNING AGAIN ON HIS DUCATIS.

Supermono 550

The Sound of Singles (known as the Supermono Championship in Italy), reserved for 4-stroke singles, is one of the most interesting insights into modern motorcycle technical features available to us. The bikes used in the Championship have impressive, sophisticated engines (of unlimited capacity), characterised by technical choices which allow scope for the designers' imagination and maximum freedom in the choice of running gear; in a word, it's just the opposite of the World Championship! Since the end of the Forties, Bordi considered a special engine, basically a "slice" of his 4V desmo twin. Later, Claudio Domenicali brought the Supermono to life with the aid of designer Terblanche, who defined the splendid look. The hi-tech technical features (twin con-rods, electronic injection, liquid cooling) made this single the most competitive bike in its category.

DESPITE HAVING AN ENGINE MUCH SMALLER THAN THAT OF ITS RIVALS, ON THE TRACK THE **500** CC SUPERMONO DUCATI "THRASHED" ITS RIVALS.

Specification

ENGINE: Four-stroke single cylinder. Liquid-cooled. Bore: 100 mm. Stroke: 70 mm. Capacity: 550 cc. Compression ratio: 11.8:1. Desmodromic twin overhead camshaft, toothed belt driven, 4 valves per cylinder. Weber indirect electronic fuel injection with 2 injectors. Fuel tank capacity: 15 litres. Maximum power: 175 hp at 10,000 rpm. Max torque: 5.8 kgm at 8,000 rpm. IAW inductive discharge electronic ignition. Wet sump forced lubrication, 4 litres oil. Wet, multi-plate clutch. 6-speed gearbox. FRAME, FORKS AND RUNNING GEAR: Tubular Cr-Mo steel space frame. Ohlins front telescopic forks with 42 mm reversed stanchions. Rear suspension: single Ohlins rising rate hydraulic shock. Brembo 280 mm twin floating-disc front brake with 4-piston caliper. 220 mm disc rear brake with twin-piston caliper. Tyres: 310/480-17" (front), 155/60-17" Michelin slick (rear). DIMENSIONS AND WEIGHT: Length: 1,960 mm. Width: 670 mm. Seat height: 760 mm. Wheelbase: 1,360 mm. Weight (dry): 118 kg (racing trim). PERFORMANCE: Top speed: not available. 400 mt. standing start in 11.28 seconds.

THE REFINED SPACE FRAME WAS MADE OF CR-MO STEEL TUBING AND THE BIKE WAS EXTREMELY COMPACT: MAXIMUM LENGTH 1,960 MM, WHEELBASE 1,360 MM AND DRY WEIGHT 118 KG. THESE WERE VALUES COMPARABLE TO THOSE OF A 125! THE ENGINE FEATURED A SAND-CAST CRANKCASE AND INDIRECT ELECTRONIC FUEL INJECTION WITH TWO INJECTORS. IT BORROWED PRACTICALLY ALL OF THE FEATURES OF THE 851-888 SERIES. ATTRACTIVE AND REFINED, IN ACTION THE SUPERMONO WENT WILD. THE ENGINE DEVELOPED 75 HP AT 10,000 RPM AND ITS TIME IN 400 M FROM A STANDING START (11.2 SECONDS WITH A FINAL SPEED OF 197.8 KM/H) WAS COMPARABLE TO THAT OF A BIG SPORT BIKE.

THESE TWO VIEWS EMPHASISE THE COMPACTNESS AND EXCELLENT AERODYNAMICS. ALTHOUGH IT WAS DESIGNED AS A RACEBIKE - AND SO REQUIRED GOOD SOLID COMPONENTS - THE SUPERMONO WAS VERY ATTRACTIVE.

LEFT, THE AUXILIARY CON-ROD, DESIGNED TO LIMIT VIBRATIONS. LEGEND HAS IT THAT THIS WAS AN IDEA THAT CAME TO BORDI ONE SUMMER'S DAY AS HE DROVE ALONG IN A CAR WITHOUT AIR CONDITIONING.

187

1994 A legend is born

In an historical promotional piece published in January '94, *Motociclismo* revealed the secrets of the 916, just after its triumphant presentation at the Autumn shows. Bordi described the design guidelines: "An intake manifold that is as straight as possible, fuel injection, careful study of the exhaust system." Many aspects of this engine originated in Formula One technology, as Bordi confirmed when asked why the head was fitted with only one, central spark plug: "BMW designed a head for its F1 4-cylinder turbo in which you could fit one, two, or even three spark plugs... It seems that the three different solutions didn't show a marked improvement." The designer was convinced that the engine would arrive at 12,500 rpm: mission accomplished! The running gear included the famous tubular space frame, the lower section hugging the swinging arm pivot so as to strengthen the splendid single-arm structure.

DETAILS OF THE FIXING OF THE FRONT WHEEL WITH A **25** MM AXLE PIN BY MEANS OF A SPLIT PIN. A PRACTICAL CHOICE FOR EVERYDAY USE, BUT ESSENTIAL AND FAST FOR RACES; AN ADDITIONAL ADVANTAGE IS THAT THIS SET IS ALSO VERY ATTRACTIVE. LEFT, THE SHOWA FORK WITH **43** MM REVERSED STANCHIONS. THE CARBON FIBRE MUDGUARD AND BREMBO RACING DISCS REVEAL THAT THIS IS THE PROTOTYPE OF THE RACEBIKE. BELOW, A COMPARISON BETWEEN THE CON-RODS USED ON THE ROAD MODEL AND THOSE FOR SBK RACES: THOSE ON THE RIGHT, FOR COMPETITION USE, ARE MADE OF TITANIUM. ABOVE, THE STEERING HEAD HAS A PATENTED SYSTEM FOR QUICK ANGLE VARIATION: THIS ALSO ALTERS THE RAKE.

PERHAPS THE RIDERS WHO ENJOY THE PERFORMANCE OF THE **916** ON THE TRACK DON'T REALLY APPRECIATE ALL THE WORK THAT WENT INTO ITS CREATION... THE DIAGRAM SHOWS THE 4-VALVE DOHC DESMO VALVE GEAR. THE COMPUTER ERA HAD ARRIVED, AND AT DUCATI COMPUTER AIDED DESIGN WAS USED TO HELP DESIGN THE FRAMES. RIGHT, A PROTOTYPE STUDIED AT THAT TIME.

THE SPORTING HISTORY OF THE **916** BEGAN WITH THIS PROTOTYPE: IT HAD MARCHESINI ALUMINIUM AND MAGNESIUM WHEEL RIMS, OHLINS SHOCK AND SLICK TYRES.

1994

The motorcycles that made history

916

Suddenly the 888 seemed outdated: this was the brutal comment of an expert when the new 916 appeared. A phenomenon such as the 916 was the only thing that could put a bike that had won three SBK titles into retirement. *Motociclismo* tried out the first version on the track at Monza. This was the road version, still a long way from its current perfection, but whose potential emerged in a decisive fashion. This bike, with its graceful curves, is not only good to look at, but is extremely fast into bends and is an innovative Ducati bike in that it is very responsive when changing direction. It goes without saying that the engine is extremely powerful, from the moment you open the throttle, its power reminding the testers of a good wine: in fact, they described it as "full-bodied". The rated power is 114 hp at 9,000 rpm, but you can tell instinctively that the twin-cylinder engine is capable of much more. The 916 is not only more powerful than the 888, it is also 15 kg lighter. This first version, designed by Tamburini and whose lines are still splendid, was followed by other 916s and, of course, the SBK World Championship bikes.

A BREATHTAKING LINE COMBINED WITH TOP-LEVEL TECHNICAL FEATURES AND POWER: THE 916 WAS "STATE OF THE ART" FOR ITS CATEGORY.

L'evoluzione del motore

Specification

ENGINE: Four-stroke 90° V-twin configuration. Liquid-cooled. Bore: 94 mm. Stroke: 66 mm. Capacity: 916 cc. Compression ratio: 11:1. Desmodromic twin overhead camshaft, toothed rubber belt driven, 4 valves per cylinder. Weber-Marelli Multipoint indirect electronic fuel injection. Fuel tank capacity: 17 litres. Maximum power: 114 hp at crank (rated). Max. torque: not available. IAW inductive discharge electronic ignition. 12V-350W electrical equipment with 12 volt 16 Ah battery. Wet sump forced lubrication, 4 litres oil. Wet, multi-plate clutch. 6-speed gearbox. FRAME, FORKS AND RUNNING GEAR: Tubular Cr-Mo steel space frame with removable rear sub-frame. Showa front telescopic forks with 41 mm reversed stanchions. Rear suspension: Showa adjustable rising rate shock. 320 mm twin floating-disc front brake with 4-piston caliper. 220 mm floating-disc rear brake with twin-piston caliper. Tyres: 120/70-17" (front), 190/50-17" (rear). DIMENSIONS AND WEIGHT: Length: 2,050 mm. Width: 685 mm. Seat height: 790 mm. Wheelbase: 1,410 mm. Weight (dry): 195 kg. PERFORMANCE: Top speed 260 kph (approx. rated). 400 mt. standing start in 11.19 seconds.

THE DISTINCTIVE FRONT OF THE **916**. RIGHT, THE REFINED STRUCTURE THAT SUPPORTS THE FRONT OF THE FAIRING, THE INSTRUMENTS AND FRONT LIGHTS. BELOW, THE AIRBOX WITH THE TRUMPETS OF THE ELECTRONIC INJECTION SYSTEM CHOKES.

ABOVE, SIDE BY SIDE, THE MOST ATTRACTIVE SPORT BIKE OF THE SEVENTIES AND THE WINNER OF THE NINETIES: THE **SS 750** AND THE **916**. LEFT, THE INSTRUMENT PANEL WITH TWO ANALOG DIALS. THE REV COUNTER HAD NO OVER-REV RED LINE: NO PROBLEM, THERE WAS A REV LIMITER. THE **916** WAS EXCELLENT ON CURVES AND THE STRAIGHT. IT WAS NO COINCIDENCE THAT IT MADE ITS DEBUT IN THE **SBK** WORLD CHAMPIONSHIP.

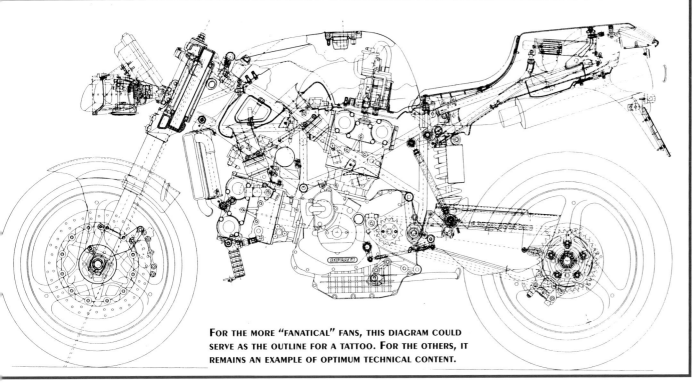

FOR THE MORE "FANATICAL" FANS, THIS DIAGRAM COULD SERVE AS THE OUTLINE FOR A TATTOO. FOR THE OTHERS, IT REMAINS AN EXAMPLE OF OPTIMUM TECHNICAL CONTENT.

191

FOGARTY'S FAVOURITE RACE TACTICS: START FAST AND LEAD ALL THE WAY. IT WORKED OFTEN FOR HIM DURING THIS YEAR. THE DUCATI TEAM MANAGER WAS ANOTHER FORMER CHAMPION, VIRGINIO FERRARI. HE TOO STARTED HIS CAREER ON THE BOLOGNESE TWINS.

1994 Fogarty and the 600s

A wild look, an aggressive front that masked great shyness, and an unusual amount of determination, combined with top-level riding skills: this sums up Carl Fogarty, an English rider, son of another famous motorcyclist (his father, George, raced Ducatis in the TT). He was undisputed leader of the '94 season, during which he won the riders' and manufacturers' titles in the Superbike World Championship with the new 916. In this configuration, the engine capacity was bigger (955 cc). Meanwhile, Orioli won the Paris-Dakar again on the Cagiva Ducati 900s which, during that period, were the best desert bikes, along with the Yamaha SuperTénéré. But the innovations also included an increasingly popular cylinder capacity: the 600. The M600 arrived on the scene, painted bright yellow, as did the Supersport 600 which completed the "SS" family that extended from 350 to 900 cc.

THE SUPERSPORT RANGE WAS ENHANCED BY THE ADDITION OF THE 600, WHICH USED THE GLORIOUS PANTAH ENGINE WITH BORE AND STROKE MEASURING 80 x 58 MM, AND WITH 583 CC CAPACITY. THE GEARBOX HAD 5 SPEEDS AND THE RUNNING GEAR BORROWED FROM THE LINES SEEN ON THE OTHER SSs.

THE FAMILY OF "MONSTERS" GREW. RIGHT, THE YELLOW M600, WHICH EMPLOYED THE SAME ENGINE AS THE SUPERSPORT, WITH IDENTICAL CAPACITY. IN CONTRAST TO THE 900, IT HAD ONLY ONE FRONT DISC AND THE SWINGING ARM WAS MADE OF STEEL RATHER THAN ALUMINIUM. THERE WAS NO OIL COOLER, AND THE GEARBOX HAD ONLY FIVE SPEEDS.

FOGARTY'S BIKE WAS THE NEW 916, SEEN HERE AT THE MILAN SHOWROOM THE PREVIOUS YEAR, AND WAS AN IMMEDIATE WINNER. THE ENGINE WAS DESIGNED BY TAMBURINI. UP FRONT,

NOTICE THE CARBON FIBRE DISCS WITH BREMBO CALIPERS AND THE OHLINS FORK WITH 46 MM REVERSED STANCHIONS. RIGHT, ANOTHER MOMENT OF GLORY FOR THE

MOTOCICLISMO TEST CENTRE, TESTING THE WORLD CHAMPION BIKE. THE RIDER WAS NOT INTIMIDATED BY THE 150 HP DEVELOPED AT 11,000 RPM.

THE CAGIVA "PROTOS" (WITH RED BODYWORK) AND THE MARATHON, PREPARED FOR THE PARIS-DAKAR RACE HAD THE 900 CC ENGINES OF THE SS AND M900 AND EXPERIMENTED WITH NEW DEVELOPMENTS FOR THE DIFFICULT AFRICAN LONG-DISTANCE RACES.

MAGNIFICENT WHEN STATIONARY, BUT CERTAINLY MORE AT HOME ON THE TRACK, THE **748** AGAIN PRESENTED THE SAME VALID FEATURES AS THE **916**.

1995 The 748

"Unrivalled" was the title of a thorough test by *Motociclismo*, dedicated to the Supersport Ducati. The new class, with the same name as the glorious 750 and 900 made by the Italian company, with a formula similar to that of the Superbikes, pitted against one another the 4-cylinder 600s and the twins with a capacity up to 750 cc. The result was a series of spectacular, important races between bikes derived from the standard models. The 748 was created as a scaled-down version of the 916, with an identical frame and the possibility of adjusting the angle of the steering head (from 23° 30' to 24° 30'), similar running gear (wheels and brakes) and engine, the only differences being the bore and stroke (88 x 61.5 mm). A swift look at the Ducati history reveals that these were the measurements of the first 4V to run at the Bol D'Or! The 748 became the number one road bike, and the SP version was immediately competitive on the race tracks. Its differs from the two-seater in that it has carbon fibre exhaust mufflers, a reprogrammed Eprom, an Ohlins single-shock (in place of the Showa), cast iron brake discs, and many other small details which noticeably improved its lap times. The power was increased to 100 hp, around 8 more than on the standard model.

THE 748 ALLOWED FOR A PASSENGER. NOTICE THE SPECIAL PASSENGER FOOT RESTS: A GREAT DEAL OF AGILITY WAS NEEDED TO HOP ON THE BACK!

FOGARTY AND THE 916 DOMINATED THE '95 SBK CHAMPIONSHIP, TAKING BOTH THE RIDERS' AND MANUFACTURERS' TITLES. THE SEASON'S DUCATI RIDERS ALSO INCLUDED LUCCHIARI, CORSER, MEKLAU, PIROVANO AND CHILI; IN THE STATES, FREDDIE SPENCER RACED WITH FERRACCI'S BIKE. THE CAPACITY OF THE WORKS BIKES WAS 955 CC, WITH MAXIMUM POWER 140-145 HP AT 12,000 RPM.

THE FRAME AND ENGINE WERE THE SAME AS ON THE 916; THE ENGINE BORE AND STROKE MEASUREMENTS WERE THE SAME AS THOSE USED ON THE FIRST, LIQUID-COOLED 4V DESMO THAT RAN IN THE BOL D'OR. THE BATTERY WAS MOVED FORWARD SO AS TO CONCENTRATE THE WEIGHT AT THE CENTRE OF GRAVITY.

THE SP VERSION - DESIGNED FOR SPORT PRODUCTION RACES AND, LATER, FOR THE SUPERSPORT CHAMPIONSHIP - WAS DEVELOPED ALONGSIDE THE MORE "SUBDUED" MODEL AND WAS ALREADY READY FOR THE TRACK.

M900

Press the "rewind" button and take the imaginary tape of this history back to the 1992 Cologne Show, when the Monster, or M900, was unveiled for the first time. This was, without a shadow of a doubt, the most original bike of our times. Just a few years have gone by, yet the "M series", which grew with the arrival of the 600 and 750, has conquered the world. It remains a unique, highly individual bike that is also fun to ride, thanks to its powerful twin-cylinder engine. The M900 developed with a slowness justified by the limited need to "up" the performance; this was compensated by the refined look, partly owed to the tuners, who went to work on a myriad of variations. The "M series" created a completely new attitude to bikes. "Monster" apparel was designed, accessories were created, with entire lines dedicated to this twin, which failed to convince many experts when it first appeared, this entire phenomenon even upsetting sociology experts. This is perhaps the first Ducati after the Scrambler to have attracted the interest of those who know little or nothing at all about technical features and sport.

MAGNIFICENT FROM ITS VERY FIRST APPEARANCE, IN THE NOW DISTANT 1992, THE M900 (ABOVE, THE FIRST VERSION) HAS CONQUERED (AND RECONQUERED) THOUSANDS OF PEOPLE, WITH ITS SPARTAN YET FUN STYLE.

Specification

ENGINE: Four-stroke 90° V-twin configuration. Liquid- and air-cooled. Bore: 92 mm. Stroke: 68 mm. Capacity: 904 cc. Compression ratio: 9.2:1. Desmodromic single overhead camshaft, toothed rubber belt driven, 2 valves per cylinder. Two Mikuni BDST 38 carburettors. Fuel tank capacity: 18 litres. Maximum power: 73 hp at axle. Max. torque: not available. Inductive discharge electronic ignition. 12V-350W electrical equipment with 12 volt 16 Ah battery. Wet sump forced lubrication, 3.5 litres oil. Wet, multi-plate clutch. 6-speed gearbox. FRAME, FORKS AND RUNNING GEAR: Tubular Cr-Mo steel space frame with removable rear sub-frame. Showa front telescopic forks with 41 mm reversed stanchions. Rear suspension: Boge rising rate shock. 320 mm twin floating-disc front brake with 4-piston caliper. 245 mm floating-disc rear brake with twin-piston caliper. Tyres: 120/70-17" (front), 170/60-17" (rear). DIMENSIONS AND WEIGHT: Length: 2,090 mm. Width: 770 mm. Seat height: 770 mm. Wheelbase: 1,430 mm. Weight (dry): 184 kg. PERFORMANCE: Top speed 190 kph plus (rated). 400 mt. standing start in 14.28 seconds.

THE M900 IS BEAUTIFUL, BUT ALSO HIGHLY EFFICIENT ON THE ROAD, ESPECIALLY ON CURVES AND THE STRAIGHT, WHERE THE POSITIVE CHARACTERISTICS OF ITS ENGINE ARE REVEALED. BELOW, WITH THE ARRIVAL OF THE M750, AN INTERMEDIATE MODEL THAT MOUNTED THE SAME ENGINE AS THE SS 750, THE RANGE WAS COMPLETE. THE SEVEN-FIFTY MAKES ACROBATICS POSSIBLE, BUT THE 600 (LEFT) ALSO HOLDS ITS OWN! THE M900 ALSO RACED IN A FUN MONO-MARQUE TROPHY CUP ORGANISED IN COLLABORATION WITH TECHNA RACING.

FOR THE '97 SEASON, THE M900 WAS FITTED WITH A LOW HANDLEBAR FAIRING WHOSE LINE EVOKES THAT OF THE 98 SPORT SEEN FORTY YEARS EARLIER. IT WAS NOT A DELIBERATE PLOY: THE SIMILARITY WAS NOTICED BY BORDI DURING THE DRAFTING OF THIS BOOK...

HERE, THE FINE TUBULAR SPACE FRAME, A THROWBACK TO THE 888 SERIES, IS COMBINED WITH THE SUPERSPORT SERIES AIR/OIL-COOLED ENGINE WHICH, ON THE TEST BENCH, DEVELOPED 71.13 HP AT 7,250 RPM.

197

THIS M900, ON WHICH ATTENTION HAS BEEN PAID TO EVERY DETAIL, BY CH RACING, HAS ALL THE INTRICATE REFINEMENT OF A RENAISSANCE JEWEL.

1995 Special fever

Ducatimania is contagious and its engines have made us dream since the times of the Cucciolo. From the old Scramblers, transformed into Spaggiari-replicas, to the M900s with numerous carbon fibre components not even seen in the SBK: the creativity of the designers just grew and grew. Special running gear, improvement kits and anodised fittings that look like jewels are the striking features of a phenomenon unrivalled anywhere in the world. The Specials based on Ducatis are as attractive and well-made as an American custom bike, but remain one step ahead, since every detail is designed to improve the bike. It should be remembered that the tuners' passion for Ducati engines dates back to the Fifties. It is as difficult to grasp as the blue smoke that curled from Taglioni's cigarettes, perhaps has the face of Farné as, fully at ease, he describes the difference between two bikes built forty years ago, as if he's telling you his phone number, and the inspiration of Bordi as he solves a technical problem.

RIGHT, THE DESIGN ENGINEER TIRELLI FITTED A **900 SS** WITH A SINGLE-PIECE SWINGING ARM IDENTICAL TO THAT USED ON THE **916.**

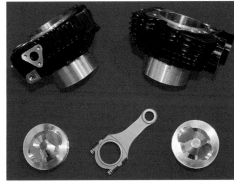

MANY SPECIAL COMPONENTS FOR ALL DUCATIS ARRIVE FROM GIO.CA.MOTO: FROM **1998** THE CATALOGUE FOR THESE COMPONENTS WILL BE DISTRIBUTED BY DUCATI, WHICH HAS ALWAYS WORKED CLOSELY WITH BOTH SPECIALISTS AND FANS.

LEFT, ANOTHER OF GOLINELLI'S CREATIONS. HERE, HE HAS RADICALLY TRANSFORMED A **748.** THE BATTERY CASING BEARS THE INSCRIPTION "GOD BLESS ME 748 TIMES". THE M900, LEFT, HAS BEEN FITTED WITH A LIQUID-COOLED **888** ENGINE: THOSE WHO HAD THE CHANCE TO RIDE IT WERE LITERALLY LEFT SPEECHLESS.

ABOVE, BLACK AS NIGHT, PREPARED AS A RACEBIKE: THIS MONSTER MEETS THE DEMANDS OF EVEN THE MOST EXPERT RIDER. RIGHT, THE SPECIALIST ENGINEER GOLINELLI PREPARED THIS ALUMINIUM RUNNING GEAR FOR A **900 SS** USING RACE COMPONENTS.

INSPIRATION AND GOOD TASTE COMBINED WITH SOLID TECHNICAL KNOW-HOW ARE THE ESSENTIAL CHARACTERISTICS OF A GOOD DUCATI "SPECIALIST": ABOVE, A TRULY SPECIAL **900 SS** PREPARED BY LIGURIAN MARCO MOZZONE.

1996 Corser and the Japanese frenzy

A big change marked the start of the World Superbike World Championship: Fogarty had passed over to the Honda team and Ducati, to save the situation, secured John Kocinski, ace of the 500 World Championship. Although the rules brought the weight of the twins to 162 kg in order to stem the power of the Italian engines, Ducati still won the riders' and manufacturers' titles. The winner was the less well-known, but brilliant Troy Corser. The works bike had a capacity of 966 cc, thanks to its 98 mm bore. But the "Ducatista" of the year was Kazushige Usui, a Japanese mechanic who loved Italian engines. "Kazu" began by purchasing the separate components of a "customer" TT2 600, which he restored and made road-worthy as soon as he returned to Japan. Then, without demanding a fee, he decided to make a scaled-down replica. He took a 4-stroke Honda 50 engine and fitted in one of the "pantograph" frames designed by Verlicchi during the Eighties. To make it all more realistic, Usui-san added a second (fake) vertical cylinder with carburettor and exhaust to the Honda engine. The "bonsai" built by Usui was extremely compact and was a hit with the local fans. His next project: a replica of a 900 SS. Best of luck!

THE DUCATI BOOM IN JAPAN MADE ALL OF THE BORGO PANIGALE WORKERS PROUD. BELOW, THE REAL PANTAH TT2 WITH THE "SCALED DOWN" REPLICA BY KAZUSHIGE USUI. THE MINI TT2 HAS A TUBULAR STEEL FRAME VERY SIMILAR TO THAT OF THE ORIGINAL, A WHEELBASE OF JUST 1,220 MM AND WEIGHS 76 KG. THE ENGINE IS A 50 CC 4-STROKE HONDA MONKEY WITH HORIZONTAL CYLINDER; THE UPPER CYLINDER WITH EXHAUST AND CARBURETTOR IS FALSE. BELOW, USUI ON HIS SPECIAL: NOTICE THE "SELVIZIO ITALIA" STICKER (WHICH SHOULD READ "SERVIZIO ITALIA"): THE JAPANESE NEITHER SAY, NOR READ THE LETTER "R"!

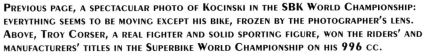
PREVIOUS PAGE, A SPECTACULAR PHOTO OF KOCINSKI IN THE SBK WORLD CHAMPIONSHIP: EVERYTHING SEEMS TO BE MOVING EXCEPT HIS BIKE, FROZEN BY THE PHOTOGRAPHER'S LENS. ABOVE, TROY CORSER, A REAL FIGHTER AND SOLID SPORTING FIGURE, WON THE RIDERS' AND MANUFACTURERS' TITLES IN THE SUPERBIKE WORLD CHAMPIONSHIP ON HIS 996 CC.

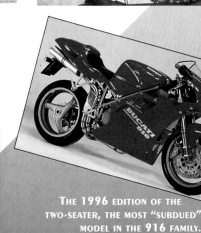
THE 1996 EDITION OF THE TWO-SEATER, THE MOST "SUBDUED" MODEL IN THE 916 FAMILY.

Works 916

TREMENDOUS AND CONSTANT: THIS IS HOW THE POWER OF THE '96 WORKS VERSION OF THE 996 CC BIKE MAY BE DESCRIBED. CORSER WON THE CHAMPIONSHIP WITH AN IDENTICAL ENGINE.

"The 'rossa' is so responsive that it may, initially, take the rider unawares; but afterwards the only reaction can be enthusiasm". These words of wisdom were written by Roberto Ungaro, the *Motociclismo* tester who had the honour of trying out the Ferrari team works bike, Kocinski's "tool of the trade" in the '96 World Championship, on the track at Monza. Ungaro perfectly describes the emotions provoked by such a bike... "The silencers, two 54 mm diameter outlets, give out a roar like thunder. It's a tone that almost intimidates the rider. The sound appears and fills your ears, vision and mind... It's like riding a 250 with a high saddle and low handlebars... You have to flatten yourself against the fuel tank to mould yourself to its profile. The mechanic helped us in the test from a standing start, to prevent damage to the clutch. But starting on a Ducati is easier than you would think... You understand what it means to be sitting on a potential 160 hp. The strength required to resist the acceleration practically takes your breath away." It isn't easy to drive a racebike, even when you haven't got time limits to beat, but riding a 1000 adjusted for the American ace is even more of a challenge!

COMPARED WITH THE DUCATIS OF PREVIOUS YEARS, MANY THINGS HAVE CHANGED DUE TO THE RACE REGULATIONS WHICH SET THE SAME MINIMUM WEIGHT OF **162** KG FOR BOTH TWINS AND FOUR-CYLINDER BIKES. THE ENGINE HAS BEEN MODIFIED TO PROVIDE MORE POWER: WITH THE **98** MM BORE, THE CYLINDER CAPACITY HAS BECOME **996** CC.

A MAGNIFICENT HAND-MADE TRIPLE CLAMP, ADJUSTABLE FORK, STEERING DAMPER AND DIGITAL INSTRUMENTS: THESE WERE ALL SPECIAL COMPONENTS WHICH FUELLED THE IMAGINATION OF ENTHUSIASTS! THE TWO EXHAUST OUTLETS HAVE A **54** MM DIAMETER; THE SILENCERS ARE MADE OF CARBON FIBRE, WHILST THE ENTIRE EXHAUST PIPE IS TITANIUM.

CHANGES IN RACE REGULATIONS ALSO OUTLAWED CARBON FIBRE DISCS, THEREFORE, THE **916** MOUNTS CAST IRON BREMBO DISCS WITH CALIPERS THAT HAVE PISTONS OF TWO DIFFERENT SIZES. THE SPECIAL OHLINS FORK IS ALMOST COMPLETELY HAND-MADE, WITH SOME ONE-OFF PARTS. BELOW, THE EXTREMELY COMPACT FRONTAL AREA: THE RIDER HAS TO TUCK RIGHT DOWN AT HIGH SPEEDS IN ORDER TO BENEFIT FROM THE PROTECTION OF THE FAIRING.

1997 At the TT with the ST2

The Tourist Trophy is one of those unshakeable institutions in the motorcycle world. The charm of one of the world's oldest races, but above all, the prospect of a week of full-immersion in the creative world of the British bikers, attracts enthusiasts from other countries. For a whole week, the sleepy Isle of Man becomes the destination of a picturesque pilgrimage on two wheels that transforms it into an encampment where all the languages of the "Old Continent" are to be heard. *Motociclismo* went on assignment there, on the new ST2, a twin that combines sport and touring features in a charming mixture. This bike is perhaps a radical addition to the Ducati range, against the grain, but undoubtedly widens the company's production horizons. You'll find details of our journey (Europe from South to North and back) on the next pages. But now, the ST2.

THE MOTORCYCLE IS PERFECT: IT'S FAST, COMPACT, BUT HAS ONE PROBLEM - IT WON'T FLOAT. THUS, THE ST2 HAD TO WAIT FOR A FERRY TO CROSS THE CHANNEL AND THE STRAIGHT WHICH SEPARATES THE ISLE OF MAN FROM THE MAINLAND.

PREVIOUS PAGE, CRUISING THE ISLE OF MAN STREETS ON THE ST2: IT SEEMS STRANGE TO SEE A DUCATI WITH SADDLE-BAGS... HOWEVER, THE SETTING IS VERY SPORTY, AS CONFIRMED BY THE STAGE (ABOVE) FOR THE TOURIST TROPHY PRIZE PRESENTATIONS.

LEFT, COMPARING TWINS: A GLORIOUS BSA WITH RIDER TRADITIONALLY DRESSED STYLE AND THE NEW DUCATI TOURING MODEL. ABOVE, A PARKING ZONE RESERVED FOR MOTORCYCLES, THE REAL STARS OF THIS "HOLY WEEK" ON THE ISLE OF MAN.

THIS BOOK COULD NOT BE PUBLISHED WITHOUT A PHOTO OF PIERFRANCESCO CHILI, ONE OF THE RIDERS MOST POPULAR WITH THE PUBLIC. WE'D LIKE TO EXPRESS OUR ADMIRATION FOR THIS TRUE CHAMPION!

1997 Sport-Touring, the ST2

The history of Ducati touring bikes is by no means glorious and perhaps enthusiasts couldn't be faulted for preferring to remember the "SSs" before the "GTs". The time has come to set this situation right; enter the ST2, an optimum finishing touch to the range. A touring bike must have protective fairings and saddle-bags which, on this bike, are fitted with the sporting flair typical of Ducati. It has a fine 916-style tubular space frame, the suspension is worthy of a sport bike, whilst the major innovations are in the engine. This is a liquid-cooled twin-valve SOHC desmo with 944 cc capacity (bore and stroke measuring 94 x 68 mm) with a sophisticated electronically controlled ignition and injection system. The maximum power is 83 hp at 8,500 rpm, giving it a top speed of around 225 km/h. The ST2 is a bike which eats up the kilometres, even with saddle-bags and a passenger, but when necessary, also handles like a sport bike.

THE STEERING GEAR HAS A SHOWA FORK WITH REVERSED STANCHIONS AND AN ADJUSTABLE 320 MM TWIN DISC WITH FOUR-PISTON CALIPER.

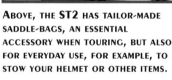

TWO ANALOG INSTRUMENTS (SPEEDO AND REV COUNTER) AND A DIGITAL DISPLAY WITH CLOCK, FUEL GAUGE AND COOLANT TEMPERATURE.

ABOVE, THE ST2 HAS TAILOR-MADE SADDLE-BAGS, AN ESSENTIAL ACCESSORY WHEN TOURING, BUT ALSO FOR EVERYDAY USE, FOR EXAMPLE, TO STOW YOUR HELMET OR OTHER ITEMS.

ROAD, TRAVEL, FREEDOM: MOTORCYCLE TOURING IS THIS TOO. WHY NOT TOUR ON A DUCATI? THE SPORTY CHARACTER OF THE ST2 IS ENHANCED IN THE ALL-RED VERSION. ABOVE, THE FRAME IS BORROWED FROM THE 916 SERIES; THE WHEELBASE IS 20 MM LONGER THAN THAT OF THE SPORT VERSION DUE TO THE USE OF AN EXTENDED SWINGING ARM.

IT MAY HAVE BEEN DESIGNED FOR TOURING AND WITH A PASSENGER IN MIND, BUT THE ST2 HAS NEVER FORGOTTEN ITS ROOTS AND CAN CORNER WITH AN IMPRESSIVE LEAN.

916 SPS

FOLLOWING THE ESTABLISHED TRADITION ON SPECIALS, THE SPS HAD A SILVER PLATE OF AUTHENTICITY, NUMBERED FROM 1 TO 800.

Want somewhere safe to put your savings? Look no further. Invest in one of the very rare SPS high performance and, if you'll pardon the expression, "exotic" versions of the 916. Very few road bikes come this close in features and performance to their race versions. If you have followed the race history of Ducati this far you will have noticed that the works race department has chosen to compensate for weight regulations by increasing engine capacity, in some cases nearly reaching the regulation limit of 1,000 cc. The SPS registered and road taxed tops 996 cc. It was necessary to change the casings (the same operations done the previous year on the Championship bikes) moving the stud bolts to the outside to leave room for the barrel liners. Two injectors per cylinder were added together with generously proportioned 50 mm throttle bodies. Fuel injection was sequential. One of the injectors operated all the time while the other operated in response to mapping commands to enrich the mixture when required. 800 examples were built and were sold out immediately. A kit was available with special exhausts and a remapped Eprom to increase power by 3 hp. *Motociclismo* clocked a top speed of 275.4 kph on the SPS.

Specification

ENGINE: Four-stroke 90° V-twin configuration. Liquid-cooled. Bore: 98 mm. Stroke: 66 mm. Capacity: 996 cc. Compression ratio: 11.5:1. Desmodromic twin overhead camshaft, toothed rubber belt driven, 4 valves per cylinder. Weber-Marelli electronic fuel injection with 2 injectors per cylinder. Fuel tank capacity: 17 litres. Maximum power: 111.8 hp at 9,500 rpm (measured). Max. torque: 9.26 kgm at 6,750 rpm (measured). Inductive discharge electronic ignition. 12V-350W electrical equipment with 12 volt 16 Ah battery. Wet sump forced lubrication, 4 litres oil. Wet, multi-plate clutch. 6-speed gearbox. FRAME, FORKS AND RUNNING GEAR: Tubular Cr-Mo steel space frame with removable rear sub-frame. Showa front telescopic forks with 41 mm reversed stanchions. Rear suspension: Showa shock with rising rate linkage. 320 mm twin floating-disc front brake with 4-piston caliper. 220 mm disc rear brake with twin-piston caliper. Tyres: 120/70-17" (front), 190/50-17" (rear). DIMENSIONS AND WEIGHT: Length: 2,050 mm. Width: 685 mm. Seat height: 790 mm. Wheelbase: 1,410 mm. Weight (dry): 195 kg. PERFORMANCE: Top speed 270.1 kph (measured). 400 mt. standing start in 10.84 seconds with final speed of 220.6 kph.

PHOTOS CLEARLY SHOWING THE MODIFICATIONS TO THE CRANKCASE. THE LEFT CASING OF A STANDARD 916 HAS BEEN JOINED TO THE RIGHT CASING OF AN SPS. NOTE THE STEP BETWEEN THE TWO PARTS AND THE DIFFERENT CENTRE-TO-CENTRE BETWEEN THE STUD BOLTS. PLEASE NOTE: IN ORDER TO AVOID UNPLEASANT SURPRISES, DO NOT ATTEMPT TO FIT SPS CYLINDERS ONTO STANDARD 916s. THE FOUR-VALVE DESMO-HEAD HAS A SINGLE SPARK PLUG IN THE CENTRE. THE INSIDE OF THE COMBUSTION CHAMBER HAS BEEN MILLED AT THE SIDES (SEE THE TWO FINGER-NAIL SHAPES) TO LOWER THE COMPRESSION RATIO, IMPROVE GAS TURBULENCE AND PROVIDE A BETTER FLAME PATH. THE INLET VALVES ARE 30 MM; THE EXHAUST VALVES ARE 36 MM. VALVE CONTROL IS, OF COURSE, BY DESMO DOHC.

THE SINGLE-PIECE, SOLID CRANKSHAFT HAS LIGHTENED AND CUT-DOWN BLADES AND FIVE TUNGSTEN INSERTS FOR BALANCING. THE AUSTRIAN PANKL CON-RODS ARE PAINTED IN BLUE TO INDICATE THAT THEY HAVE PASSED THIS MANUFACTURER'S QUALITY CONTROLS. IN BRIEF, THE CENTRE-PIECE OF THE SPS IS WITHOUT DOUBT THE ENGINE. TO INCREASE ENGINE CAPACITY TO 996 CC NEEDED ALL DUCATI'S RACE EXPERIENCE AND A LOT OF MODIFICATIONS. MAXIMUM RATED POWER AT THE REAR WHEEL WAS 118.8 HP AT 9,500 RPM. ANOTHER 2 HP COULD BE SQUEEZED OUT OF THE ENGINE USING A DUCATI KIT.

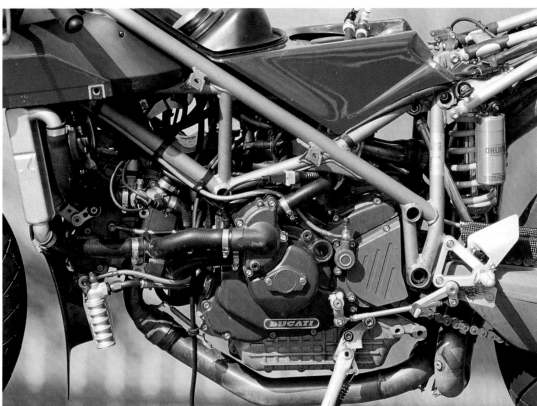

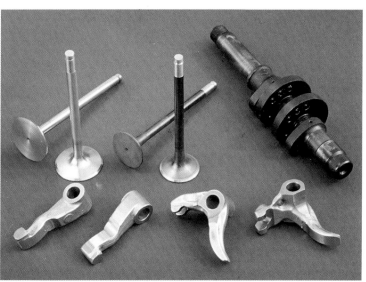

1997 Taking the beast out for a spin

Motociclismo tested the SPS. Good points in the test report were: exclusive image, aerodynamic design, precise gear change, powerful engine, stable, good roadholding and track handling and good riding position. Under bad points there is a single (but very important) item: high price. Nobody's perfect. A power kit designed for this bike included Termignoni stainless steel exhaust pipes (in 0.8 mm thick steel) and an Eprom with high-performance programming. The running gear featured new Brembo cast-iron discs, a tubular space frame, Showa top-of-the-range forks and an Ohlins shock. Up to 9 kg weight could be saved by fitting carbon fibre parts. During the test, the machine reached a top speed of 270 kph at 9,900 rpm (275.4 on the kit version). Despite a very long first gear ratio the bike clocked a blazing 10.8 seconds over the standing start 400 metres with a final speed of 220.6 kph. On the race track it was difficult to get the riders to return to the pits!

BREMBO AGAIN WITH A CAST-IRON FRONT DISC BRAKED BY A 4-PISTON CALIPER. THE REAR SHOCK IS A MULTI-ADJUSTABLE OHLINS. THE SINGLE SWINGING ARM IS ANOTHER BREMBO CREATION.

A SUPERB FRONT VIEW, ONE OF THE MOST ATTRACTIVE FEATURES OF THIS STYLISH SPORT BIKE.

RIGHT, THE SPS TAKES A PERFECT LINE THROUGH A LONG BEND. THE EXCELLENT RUNNING GEAR ENABLED SOME SUSTAINED HIGH SPEEDS ON THE TRACK BUT PROVED TO BE A LITTLE MORE DIFFICULT TO HANDLE IN NORMAL TRAFFIC. BUT THERE AGAIN, WHO WOULD USE THIS BIKE TO GO TO WORK IN THE MORNING?

THE ELECTRONIC ENGINE CONTROL UNIT (CONTROLLING FUEL INJECTION AND IGNITION) AND THE TWO SILENCERS UNDER THE TAIL SECTION.

ON YOUR MARKS..! THE ROAR OF OLD ENGINES (AND A WHIFF OF CASTROL R40) FILL THE AIR.

1997 The roar of history

Races for the bikes of yesteryear are very popular world-wide, and Ducati is always present at such events. There are two types of race for oldies. Highly valuable vintage machinery parade sedately past in memorial events. And then there are the real races for less rare but truly competitive machines, the work of engineers who took these machines to victory in the Sixties. These machines turn in some truly incredible performances. Just think, a Ducati 450 racing in Group 5, 500 class turns in faster times than Agostini's MV racing on the same track in the past. These times are largely the result of today's modern Avon tyres. A good starting point if you want to go classic racing is a Ducati Scrambler with a modified frame (or a replica chrome-moly steel frame), special con-rods (there are those who win with perfectly standard items), straight-tooth primary drive and dry clutch. Specially crafted replica brakes are used; Fontana and Oldani copies made today are much safer. Today, a 250 Ducati develops 30 hp, while a 500 can easily top 50 hp. In the Seventies Augusto Brettoni had 10 hp less.

OLD BIKE, MODERN LEAN. BELOW, ALBERTO PERUZZI (A LEADING ITALIAN SPECIALIST) WITH A 450. ABOVE RIGHT, ZACCARELLI RACING AT MISANO.

SPECIALISTS AT WORK. TOP RIGHT, DEL BIONDO PUSHES AN INCREDIBLE DRY-CLUTCH DESMO DOHC ONTO THE STARTING GRID. ABOVE, MARCELLO PERUZZI TRIES TOUGH TACTICS TO RESTART LISERANI'S BIKE.

A MIX OF THE NEW AND THE OLD ON GROUP 5 MACHINES RACED IN ITALY. THE PHOTOS SHOW STEERING DAMPERS, MODERN CARBURETTORS, ANODISED BOLTS AND REINFORCED FRAMES - PLUS THE OLD TANK BADGES - ON THESE TWO DUCATIS.

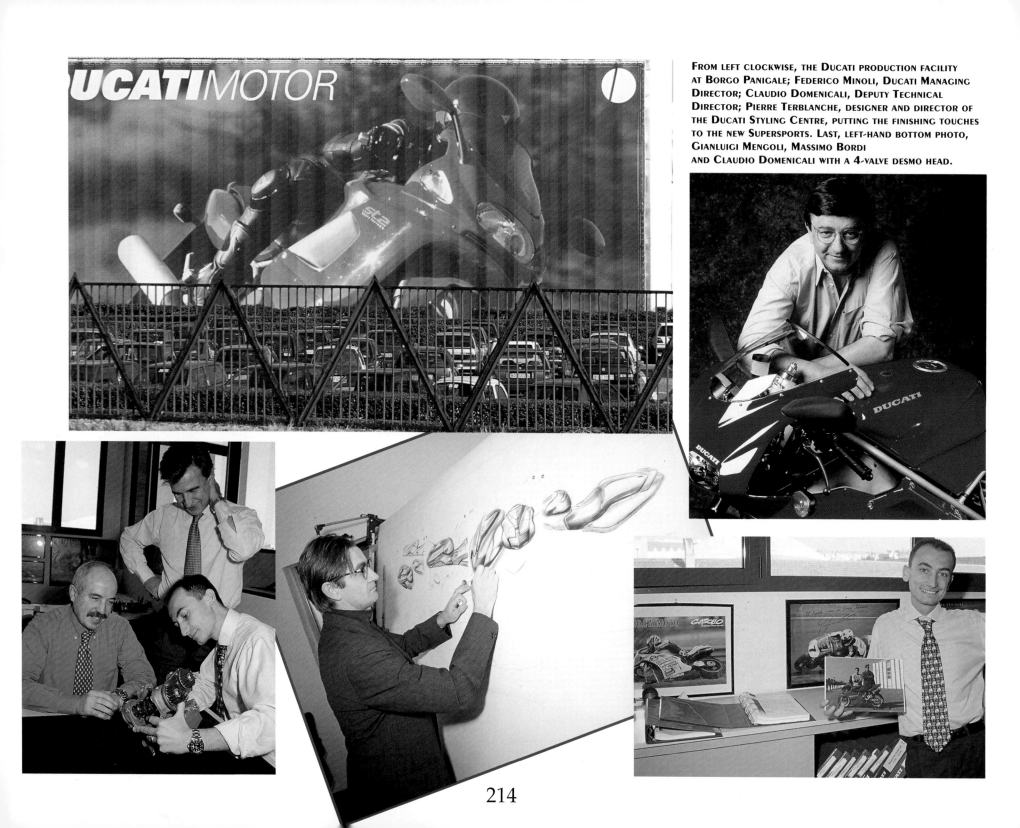

FROM LEFT CLOCKWISE, THE DUCATI PRODUCTION FACILITY AT BORGO PANIGALE; FEDERICO MINOLI, DUCATI MANAGING DIRECTOR; CLAUDIO DOMENICALI, DEPUTY TECHNICAL DIRECTOR; PIERRE TERBLANCHE, DESIGNER AND DIRECTOR OF THE DUCATI STYLING CENTRE, PUTTING THE FINISHING TOUCHES TO THE NEW SUPERSPORTS. LAST, LEFT-HAND BOTTOM PHOTO, GIANLUIGI MENGOLI, MASSIMO BORDI AND CLAUDIO DOMENICALI WITH A 4-VALVE DESMO HEAD.

2000

Past, present ...

Interview with Massimo Bordi

On the previous pages we talked about the past and the history of Ducati. Now let us move forward to talk about the present and the future in an interview with Massimo Bordi, Ducati General Manager and creator of Ducati's top-of-the-range 4-valve double overhead camshaft desmo engine.

Why has the Ducati Marque always been identified with the name of an engine designer, first Taglioni and then yourself?

"Yes, it's true. There has always been this link. This is something which happens frequently when you work in a high-technology area like motorcycle engineering. The product is identified with the person who designed and perfected it. Today, however, innovation is never the work of one person alone. It is the result of team work, a team of highly skilled specialists".

Since you joined Ducati in 1978 the Company has been run by four different managements. What have been the differences?

"Under the

management of a State holding Company EFIM we produced outboard motors, motorcycles and diesel engines in the belief that we could compete in these very different and difficult markets. This approach was narrow and superficial and we had to compete on many fronts with limited means. We tried to do too many things at once and ended up doing only a few of them well. After that we passed under another state-run holding, Finmeccanica. It was decided that we should concentrate on the "useful" sectors of our production and therefore we concentrated on diesel engines. We made great leaps forward in quality, production was heavily rationalised and this was one of those moments when Ducati came close to stopping motorcycle production altogether. Ducati then entered the Cagiva Group. (The mediator in this operation was Romano Prodi, then president of the state holding IRI and now Italian Prime Minister). The Company mission changed once again. We were now part of a motorcycle manufacturing group. We could exploit the economies between the various Marques inside the group, a group dedicated to revival and growth, a group with a very strong distribution network. Ducati grew in this period thanks also to the enthusiasm and commitment of the new owners. The limitations of a group operating on many competitive fronts in a difficult.

ABOVE, MASSIMO BORDI, DUCATI GENERAL MANAGER AND WORLD FAMOUS ENGINE DESIGNER WITH ONE OF HIS CREATIONS, THE SUPERMONO ENGINE. RIGHT, DUCATI SETS A STYLING TREND. IF YOU WANT TO TEST RIDE A DUCATI, TRY THIS "MONSTER", MADE FAR AWAY FROM BOLOGNA...

2000
...and future

financial environment soon became evident. Today, 49% of Ducati belongs to Cagiva and 51% to an American investment fund, the Texas Pacific Group. The conditions now exist for us to reap the benefits of past improvements and take the Company forward towards the objectives that it merits. Ducati must become an international, global company, strong on technological innovation and marketing. Even though we are opening up to the outside world with a positive integration between the local and international management teams, the company must nevertheless retain its uniquely Italian and local Bolognese character".

Well, that covers the Company side of things. But what about the bikes and engines. What does the future hold?

"The twin-valve, air-cooled engine has a great history behind it and is destined for a great future with continuous developments and innovations. Thanks to electronic injection, port line and twin ignition, this engine will continue to be the powerhouse for our big bikes; simple, light and easy to maintain. To date the four-valve engine has also given a good account of itself. There are many development projects for this engine which has been our major player both on and off the track. We are also working on a completely new engine, a desmo 90° V-twin. At the same time we have other projects underway for all the product families, for the frame, running gear and other vehicle components. In brief, we have got a lot of great ideas to develop".

Will Ducati continue on the race track, its traditional testing ground?

"We've always raced. Out of enthusiasm. To promote and test our products. Today, all components can be tested without racing, but we still need racing triumphs to promote our company image. And then there is still our passion for racing. We will always race".

A MONSTER TO SUIT ALL TASTES. ABOVE, A **900** WITH A SPLENDID CHROME TANK. BELOW, THE **M600** DARK, STARK, LIGHT, ECONOMICAL AND RIPE FOR CUSTOMISING. BOTTOM LEFT, THE SUPER SPORT FINAL EDITION FITTED WITH PRESTIGE COMPONENTS, A COLLECTOR'S BIKE WHICH MARKS THE END OF AN ERA. TOP RIGHT, TRACES OF THE OLD SUPERSPORT CAN STILL BE SEEN IN THIS AGGRESSIVE FRONT VIEW OF THE NEW **900** SUPERSPORT. BOTTOM RIGHT, THE **916 SPS '98**, MEAN AND POWERFUL AS ALWAYS.

THE MODERN LINES OF THE **900** SUPERSPORT RESTYLED BY TERBLANCHE. THE ENGINE HAS ELECTRONIC IGNITION AND HAS UNDERGONE A THOROUGH-GOING REDESIGN. RIGHT, THE **916** SENNA, FOR THOSE LOOKING FOR A REFINED BIKE. MANAGEMENT AND EMPLOYEES POSE FOR A GROUP PHOTO IN FRONT OF THE CRATES WHICH TAKE DUCATIS ALL OVER THE WORLD.

Ducati Hall of Fame

GRAND PRIX

1958 125cc GPs
Isle of Man TT, 6/6
2nd Romolo Ferri
3rd Dave Chadwick

Dutch TT, Assen, 6/28
2nd Luigi Taveri

Belgian GP, Spa-Francorchamps, 7/6
1st Alberto Gandossi
2nd Romolo Ferri

Swedish GP, Hedemora, 7/27
1st Alberto Gandossi
2nd Luigi Taveri

Ulster GP, Dundrod, 8/9
2nd Luigi Taveri
3rd Dave Chadwick

GP des Nations, Monza 9/14
1st Bruno Spaggiari
2nd Alberto Gandossi
3rd Dave Chadwick

1959 125cc GP
Isle of Man TT, 6/6
3rd Mike Hailwood

West German GP, Hockenheim, 6/14
3rd Mike Hailwood

Dutch TT, Assen, 6/27
2nd Bruno Spaggiari
3rd Mike Hailwood

Belgian GP, Spa-Francorchamps, 7/5
3rd Luigi Taveri

Ulster GP, Dundrod, 8/8
1st Mike Hailwood

GP des Nations, Monza, 9/6
3rd Luigi Taveri

1972 500cc GP
GP des Nations, Imola, 5/21
3rd Bruno Spaggiari

WORLD SUPERBIKE CHAMPIONS
1990 Raymond Roche
1991 Doug Polen
1992 Doug Polen
1994 Carl Fogarty
1995 Carl Fogarty
1996 Troy Corser
1998 Carl Fogarty

WORLD SUPERBIKE RACE WINS
1988
Round 1, GB, Donington Park
Marco Lucchinelli

Round 4, Austria, Osterreichring
Race 1 Marco Lucchinelli

1989
Round 4, USA, Brainerd
Races 1 & 2 Raymond Roche

Round 8, Germany, Hockenheim
Races 1 & 2 Raymond Roche

Round 9, Italy, Pergusa
Race 2 Raymond Roche

1990
Round 1, Spain, Jerez
Races 1 & 2 Raymond Roche

Round 2, GB, Donington Park
Race 2 Giancarlo Falappa

Round 3, Hungary, Hungaroring
Race 2 Raymond Roche

Round 5, Canada, Mosport
Races 1 & 2 Raymond Roche

Round 8, Japan, Sugo
Race 1 Raymond Roche

Round 9, France, Le Mans
Races 1 & 2 Raymond Roche

1991
Round 1, GB, Donington Park
Race 1 Doug Polen
Race 2 Stephane Mertens

Round 2, Spain, Jarama
Races 1 & 2 Doug Polen

Round 4, USA, Brainerd
Races 1 & 2 Doug Polen

Round 5, Austria, Osterreichring
Race 1 Stephane Mertens
Race 2 Doug Polen

Round 6, San Marino, Misano
Races 1 & 2 Doug Polen

Round 7, Sweden, Anderstorp
Races 1 & 2 Doug Polen

Round 8, Japan, Sugo
Races 1 & 2 Doug Polen

Round 9, Malaysia, Shah Alam
Races 1 & 2 Raymond Roche

Round 10, Germany, Hockenheim
Race 1 Doug Polen
Race 2 Raymond Roche

Round 11, France, Magny-Cours
Races 1 & 2 Doug Polen

Round 12, Italy, Mugello
Race 1 Doug Polen
Race 2 Raymond Roche

Round 13, Australia, Phillip Island
Race 2 Doug Polen

1992
Round 1, Spain, Albacete
Race 2 Raymond Roche

Round 2, GB, Donington Park
Race 1 Raymond Roche
Race 2 Carl Fogarty

Round 3, Germany, Hockenheim
Races 1 & 2 Doug Polen

Round 4, Belgium, Spa-Francorchamps
Race 2 Doug Polen

Round 5, Andorra, Jerez
Race 2 Doug Polen

Round 6, Austria, Osterreichring
Races 1 & 2 Giancarlo Falappa

Round 7, San Marino, Mugello
Races 1 & 2 Raymond Roche

Round 8, Malaysia, Johor
Race 1 Raymond Roche
Race 2 Doug Polen

Round 9, Japan, Sugo
Races 1 & 2 Doug Polen

Round 10, Holland, Assen
Race 1 Doug Polen
Race 2 Giancarlo Falappa

Round 12, Australia, Phillip Island
Race 2 Raymond Roche

Round 13, New Zealand, Manfeild
Race 1 Doug Polen
Race 2 Giancarlo Falappa

1993
Round 1, Ireland, Brands Hatch
Races 1 & 2 Giancarlo Falappa

Round 2, Germany, Hockenheim
Race 1 Giancarlo Falappa

Round 3, Spain, Albacete
Races 1 & 2 Carl Fogarty

Round 4, San Marino, Misano
Races 1 & 2 Giancarlo Falappa

Round 5, Austria, Osterreichring
Race 1 Andreas Meklau
Race 2 Giancarlo Falappa

Round 6, Czech Republic, Brno
Race 1 Carl Fogarty

Round 7, Sweden, Anderstorp
Races 1 & 2 Carl Fogarty

Round 8, Malaysia, Jahor
Races 1 & 2 Carl Fogarty

Round 9, Japan, Sugo
Race 1 Carl Fogarty

Round 10, Holland, Assen
Races 1 & 2 Carl Fogarty

Round 11, Italy, Monza
Race 2 Giancarlo Falappa

Round 13, Portugal, Estoril
Race 2 Carl Fogarty

1994
Round 1, GB, Donington Park
Race 1 Carl Fogarty

Round 3, Italy, Misano
Race 2 Giancarlo Falappa

Round 4, Spain, Albacete
Races 1 & 2 Carl Fogarty

Round 5, Austria, Osterreichring
Races 1 & 2 Carl Fogarty

Round 6, Indonesia, Sentul
Race 1 James Whitham
Race 2 Carl Fogarty

Round 8, Holland, Assen
Races 1 & 2 Carl Fogarty

Round 9, San Marino, Mugello
Race 2 Carl Fogarty

Round 11, Australia, Phillip Island
Race 1 Carl Fogarty

1995
Round 1, Germany, Hockenheim
Races 1 & 2 Carl Fogarty

Round 2, Italy, Misano
Races 1 & 2 Mauro Lucchiari

Round 3, GB, Donington Park
Races 1 & 2 Carl Fogarty

Round 4, San Marino, Monza
Race 1 Carl Fogarty
Race 2 Pierfrancesco Chili

Round 5, Spain, Albacete
Race 2 Carl Fogarty

Round 6, Austria, Salzburgring
Race 1 Carl Fogarty
Race 2 Troy Corser

Round 7, USA, Laguna Seca
Race 2 Troy Corser

Round 8, Europe, Brands Hatch
Races 1 & 2 Carl Fogarty

Round 9, Japan, Sugo
Race 1 Troy Corser
Race 2 Carl Fogarty

Round 10, Holland, Assen
Races 1 & 2 Carl Fogarty

Round 11, Indonesia, Sentul
Race 1 Carl Fogarty

Round 12, Australia, Phillip Island
Race 1 Troy Corser

1996
Round 1, San Marino, Misano
Races 1 & 2 John Kocinski

Round 2, GB, Donington Park
Races 1 & 2 Troy Corser

Round 4, Italy, Monza
Race 2 Pierfrancesco Chili

Round 5, Czech Republic, Brno
Races 1 & 2 Troy Corser

Round 6, USA, Laguna Seca
Race 1 John Kocinski

Round 7, Europe, Brands Hatch
Race 1 Pierfrancesco Chili
Race 2 Troy Corser

Round 8, Indonesia, Sentul
Races 1 & 2 John Kocinski

Round 11, Spain, Albacete
Races 1 & 2 Troy Corser

1997
Round 2, San Marino, Misano
Race 1 Pierfrancesco Chili

Round 3, GB, Donington Park
Race 2 Carl Fogarty

Round 4, Germany, Hockenheim
Race 2 Carl Fogarty

Round 5, Italy, Monza
Race 2 Pierfrancesco Chili

Round 7, Europe, Brands Hatch
Race 1 Pierfrancesco Chili
Race 2 Carl Fogarty

Round 8, Austria, Osterreichring
Race 1 Carl Fogarty

Round 9, Holland, Assen
Race 2 Carl Fogarty

Round 12, Indonesia, Sentul
Race 2 Carl Fogarty

1998
Round 1, Australia, Phillip Island
Race 1 Carl Fogarty

Round 4, Spain, Albacete
Race 1 Pierfrancesco Chili
Race 2 Carl Fogarty

Round 5, Germany, Nurburgring
Race 2 Pierfrancesco Chili

Round 7, South Africa, Kyalami
Races 1 & 2 Pierfrancesco Chili

Round 8, USA, Laguna Seca
Race 1 Troy Corser

Round 9, Europe, Brands Hatch
Race 2 Troy Corser

Round 11, Holland, Assen
Race 1 Pierfrancesco Chili
Race 2 Carl Fogarty

OTHER SIGNIFICANT DUCATI VICTORIES

TT F2 World Champion
1978 Mike Hailwood

TT F2 World Champion
1981, 1982, 1983 & 1984
Tony Rutter

World Superbike Manufacturers'
Champions
1991, 1992, 1993, 1994, 1995, 1996
& 1998

Daytona Superbike race winners
1977 Cook Neilson

American Superbike Champions
1993 Doug Polen
1994 Troy Corser

German Pro-Superbike Champions
1992 & 1993 Edwin Weibel
1994 Udo Mark
1996 Christer Lindholm

(KEL EDGE)

The DUCATI story through the pages of MOTOCICLISMO

This is a list of all the articles about Ducati motorcycles which appeared in Motociclismo between 1949 and the present day. The list shows (from left to right) the title of the article, the issue number and year of publication, and the number of the page on which the article appeared.

MOTOCICLISMO D'EPOCA

Bibliography

Many books have been written about Ducati over the years. One of the problems frequently faced by the authors has been the lack of original material. Unfortunately, systematic records were not kept by either Ducati or motorcycling publications until the nineteen sixties and hence the lack of material. The one happy exception to this has been the Motociclismo archives which have provided the material for this book. This book is the first document covering the complete fifty-year history of Ducati. The bibliography below lists the most readily available books about Ducati and is required reading for any Ducati enthusiast.

IN ENGLISH:
— Cycle World on Ducati 1962/80, Vari, Ed. Brooklands Books
— Cycle World on Ducati 1982/91, Vari, Ed. Brookland Books
— Ducati Desmo, Walker, Osprey Publishing
— Ducati 1960-1973 Gold Portfolio, Vari, Ed. Brooklands
— Ducati 1974-1978 Gold Portfolio, Vari, Ed. Brooklands
— Ducati 1978-1982 Gold Portfolio, Clarke, Ed. Brooklands
— Ducati 600, 750, & 900 2 valve twins 1991-96, Vari, Ed. Haynes
— Ducati Superbikes, Conti, Giorgio Nada Editore
— Ducati Tuning V-twin with bevel drive camshafts, Eke, Ed. Lodgemark Press
— Ducati Twins Restoration, Walker, Osprey Publishing
— Ducati Twins, Walker, Osprey Publishing
— Ducati Singles Restoration, Walker, Osprey Publishing
— Ducati Twins, Walker, Osprey Publishing
— Ducati V-Twins 1971-1986, Motorcycle Monographs No 19, Bacon, Ed. Niton Publ.
— Illustrated Ducati Buyer's Guide, Walker, Ed. Motorbooks
— The Ducati Story, Falloon, Ed. PSL-Haynes
— Ducati Super Sport, Falloon, Haynes

IN ITALIAN:
— Ducati 916, AA.VV., FBA Edizioni
— Ducati Power, B. De Prato, FBA Edizioni
— Ducati Scrambler Desmo e Mark 3, M. Clarke, Giorgio Nada Editore
— Ducati Superbikes, Conti, Giorgio Nada Editore
— Storia della Ducati, Bruno Cavalieri Ducati, Editografica
— AAVE Ducati 250, 350, 450 catalogo ricambi, I° parte, motore, Vari, Ed. Ducati- AAVE Ducati 750cc manuale d'officina e catalogo ricambi, 2° parte, ciclistica, Vari, Ed. Ducati
— AAVE Ducati: i monocilindrici 1946-1977, dal Cucciolo ai desmo, Vari., Ed. AAVE
— AAVE Ducati: istruzioni per l'uso e la manutenzione 250/350/450, Mark 3 250/350/450 Desmo, 250/350/450 Scrambler, Vari, Ed. Ducati
— AAVE Ducati Motoleggere monoalbero, istruzioni per le stazioni di servizio, Vari, Ed. Ducati

IN GERMAN:
— Ducati, Tons, Ed. Art Motor Verlag
— Ducati Calender, Vari, Ed. Art Motor Verlag
— Ducati Desmoquattro 748, 851, 888, 916, Zeyen, Ed. MBV
— Ducati, die Konigswellen-Twins, Motorrader die geschichte Machten, Shafer, Ed. MBV
— Ducati Exklusiv, Cathcart, Ed. MBV
— Ducati Motorrader, Cathcart, Ed. MBV
— Ducati Technothek, Walker, Ed. Heel

IN FRENCH:
— Ducati Forza Italia 1946-93: l'histoire des grandes marques moto, Vari, Editions Freeway
— Motoscopie n° 5: Ducati, les V-Twins à couples coniques, Guislain, Editions Gallett
— Ducati Paso 750, Paso 906, Revue Moto Téchnique hors série n° 7, Vari, Ed. ETAI

Ducati Motor Spa was founded on 26th September 1996 as a joint venture between Claudio and Gianfranco Castiglioni, owners of the Cagiva Group, and Texas Pacific Group, an American investment fund. In 1998 Texas Pacific acquired the entire company.

The Ducati strategic plan put forward by the new management proposes a reorganisation of the company and an increase in capital funding to develop new projects.

The objectives proposed by the new management are as follows: to increase motorcycle production in 1998 to 28,000 units (up from 21,000 in 1995); to create new business opportunities including in exclusive brand clothing and shops; to increase Company employees (the number of employees has increased by 164 over the last year to the current total of 714); to increase quality through a commitment to quality control, assurance and constant improvement.

Quality has been improved through the implementation of the following measures:

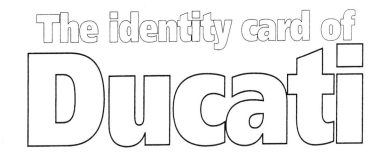

— February 1997, 40 CAD workstations were installed in the Engineering Department;

— production has been further automated and computerised, with the introduction of a new production process and hi-tech robot technology;

— a wide ranging quality control program has been implemented on all assembly lines and finishing stations to ensure top quality assembly and finishing standards;

— the sales network is being reorganised and is being strengthened on leading overseas markets. Joint ventures are being set up with official importers; the first two, Ducati France and Ducati Japan, are already operating.

On the Italian market, the Company has set up a high-quality, customer-oriented dealership network. Other broad-ranging projects implemented by the Company include a Ducati museum at its Borgo Panigale production facility. This houses all the Company's most famous models, from the Cucciolo through to the legendary 916.

OTHER BOOKS OF INTEREST

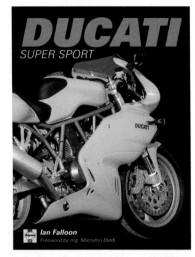

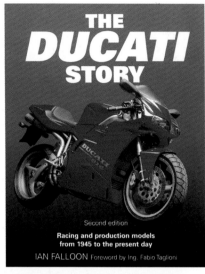

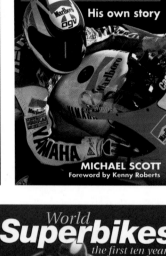

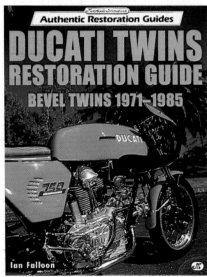

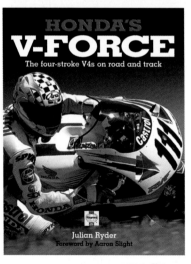

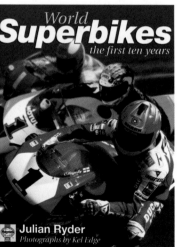

For more information please contact:
Customer Services Department, Haynes Publishing, Sparkford, Nr Yeovil, Somerset BA22 7JJ
Tel. 01963 440635 Fax: 01963 440001 Int. tel: +44 1963 440635 Fax: +44 1963 440001
E-mail: sales@haynes-manuals.co.uk Web site: http://www.haynes.com

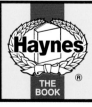

Haynes
THE BOOK